THE
RETARDED
CHILD

THE
RETARDED
CHILD

by

Nancy W. Faber

CROWN PUBLISHERS, INC., NEW YORK

To the selfless dedicated workers
throughout the world
who struggled in an age of darkness
to bring their less fortunate brethren
into the light

Part of the proceeds of this book will be donated to the International League of Societies for the Mentally Handicapped, 12, rue Forestière, Bruxelles 5, Belgium.

Table of Contents

Foreword

MENTAL RETARDATION RESPECTS NO CLASS, NO CREED, NO PERSON. IT COULD happen without warning to any one of us. While we have found some answers and solutions, and are hearteningly close to others, there remain great unknown areas and wide gaps in our knowledge.

The causes of mental retardation cover a broad, complex, multi-faceted spectrum of medical, physiological, psychological, and social factors. And while we are constantly embarked on a world of discovery, parents with a retarded child cannot wait for the ultimate breakthrough. They need all of the help that the community can assemble —now.

We cannot be proud of much of the history of mental retardation throughout the world. We are finally, however, at that period of time when the mentally retarded can no longer be shunned, ignored, or inhumanely treated.

The past few years, especially, have seen momentous strides in public and governmental concern and aid. The battle has only begun.

When Mrs. Faber began her research in mental retardation, I was glad to open for observation the facilities of the Flower and Fifth Avenue Hospitals, the oldest and most inclusive center of its kind in the world.

This book speaks not only to parents and professionals but to the general public as well. Written with poignancy, understanding, and acute perception, it offers a uniquely useful and practical approach to a highly complex field. The style is clear, concise, and alive.

Mrs. Faber has managed to avoid a sense of hopelessness or morbidity. Through the use of human interest case illustrations, she has stressed the positive values and potentials inherent in even the most damaged child. The reader, and even the parent, will come away with a new sense of hope.

The author is to be thanked for her years of exhaustive and devoted research in the interest of advancing knowledge and public concern for improved care for the retarded.

MARGARET J. GIANNINI, M.D.
Director of Mental
Retardation Center
Flower and Fifth Avenue Hospitals
Professor of Pediatrics
New York Medical College

January 1, 1968
New York City

Preface

A WORTHY GENTLEMAN STEEPED IN THE FIELD OF RETARDATION ONCE said that if you live to a hundred you will never finish reading all the books written on mental retardation.

My answer was that I wouldn't want to.

This was not due to a lack of desire to learn but because most of the books, however erudite in content, were simply unreadable for me. Surely retardation could be presented in such a way as to interest the reader and still make a practical contribution. How?

Curiosity is a human foible. Say what we may, most of us are interested in other people's affairs. What better way to enlist sympathy, understanding, and cooperation than by taking the reader into other people's homes and letting him see at first hand what happens to families affected by retardation.

It is traumatic enough to be told your child is retarded, confusing enough to be given conflicting opinions and advice. Not to know where to begin or how to help your child must be a slow crucifixion. The lack of coordination of services in mental retardation is one of its greatest problems the world over. There must be a centralization of information so that the family can receive a definite diagnosis, prognosis, and a program of training.

Much has been done for the retarded but much remains to be done. There is a growing supply of public and private funds but it still falls far short of the need. And concentration on institutionalization is not the answer.

Lifetime institutionalization currently costs billions of dollars. It has been proven beyond any doubt that better than half the retarded population can be trained to work in the community. The one- to three-year training period costs but a fraction of lifetime care. For the small percentage of retardates with whom there can be no possible communication, an institution seems to be an answer. When families cannot cope with training the retardate, institutions can and should be utilized. Other than that, the child and his family are usually best served when he can remain at home. The emotional security of a loving and understanding family serves to stimulate the retarded child to his maximum potential.

This book has tried by the use of everyday drama, taken from case histories in twelve different countries around the world, to point up the similarities of problems from Japan and Hong Kong to Switzerland and England despite the differing cultures. The second half of the book concentrates on the United States and, besides describing the emotional impact on the American family, tries to collate the existing resources for diagnosis, prognosis, training, and job possibilities. Therefore this book is a plea to parents, professionals, and the general public for an opportunity to be offered to the retardate to return to his community, to work, to earn his own way, and to accomplish the miracle of self-realization.

It is a book filled with hope for the retarded.

1

The Challenge

I READ THE GENERAL DELIVERY POSTCARD IN THE DUSTY SUNBEAMED POST office and laughed aloud. My son hated writing but had a talent for it nevertheless. My husband and I were on a September trip through the Midwest. Returning to the car, I handed the card to him and he chuckled with me.

Just before starting on this trip we had given my son a birthday party. Grandma, who adored him, had given him a sizable sum to add to his bank account, and we had laughed because he had written that at compounded interest, he would have his first Cadillac at the age of sixty-five.

Last year, at the age of twelve, my son had graduated from his New York City school and entered the seventh grade or first form of an out-of-town school. The idea of commuting daily had appealed to him. I remembered the important air with which he had checked out train schedules and bus connections. Almost before my eyes, the boy had become a man. I had worried about him and suffered with him as all mothers do for their children, and now I felt entitled to enjoy his growth and his normal, healthy eagerness for new experiences.

I had distant relatives living in this Midwestern town, and they had invited us to tea. I knew that they had a son, a retarded boy who was now about twelve, but I had never seen him. I wasn't particularly troubled, though I had written a book about an emotionally disturbed child who had functioned as a retardate, and the subject of mentally retarded children continued to hang stubbornly on the periphery of my consciousness.

My cousin greeted us and led us through an arched white wooden gate. We walked into a garden where white asters, purple dahlias, and small pompoms still bloomed. A tall bronze-skinned boy limped from the house. At the sight of us, he jumped into the air, pointed, and sent an almost inhuman screech ripping through the soft September air. My heart dived in terror. I remained rigid and rooted.

"Be quiet, Seth," the boy's mother told him firmly, "be quiet!" But he continued to jump up and down, screaming all the while.

His grandmother came toward us, saying, "Don't be frightened. He is happy to see you. He loves people but we don't have many visitors."

Finally the boy stopped screaming. His mother said, "These are your cousins, Seth," but his eyes kept looking first this way, then that, as if searching for something he had lost. His mouth was slack, and he held his arm in the manner of a spastic. His grandmother led him away.

Later, I went inside to help my cousin with the tea. Seth was seated at an oilcloth-covered table, with a towel around his neck in lieu of a bib. He used his spoon so awkwardly that most of his mashed food plopped back onto his plate. Suddenly he got up, went to the refrigerator, opened the door, and pointed to a rich dessert inside. His grandmother shook her head. The boy began to jump up and down and utter short guttural cries. His mother took him by the hand and sat him down again. "When you have finished your supper, Seth," she said, "you will have dessert. Not until then."

He sat staring vacantly at his plate. The grandmother began feeding him. He opened and closed his mouth obediently, automatically. Then he finished and limped from the room. Soon came strains of music. I glanced up questioningly.

"It's Seth. He's playing the hi-fi," his mother explained. "He knows how to work the machine, and he picks out the records he likes." There was a pause. "He has little else to do."

I asked about that "little else," and hesitatingly they led me into the basement. The floor was covered, to a depth of one foot, with tiny scraps of torn-up newspapers.

"The butcher saves the papers for us," the grandmother explained. "He knows how Seth likes to tear them up."

I stood there stunned. All I could think of was the hundreds of wasted hours that Seth must have spent tearing up all that paper.

"Doesn't he go out on walks?" I asked.

"Never alone anymore. One day he was almost run over. George, the boy next door, saved him. You know, his mother was furious. She screamed at George, 'You might have been killed yourself saving the life of a dummy who would be better off dead!'"

"How about a school?"

"No school will take him," his mother answered, adding in a quote, "'Education for subnormal children is not mandatory in this state.' The private ones are prohibitively expensive and too far away."

"How about a state training school?"

The mother and grandmother shook their heads simultaneously.

"Some state schools—"

The mother interrupted me: "We wouldn't put an animal in ours, much less a human being." Her voice was bitter as she added, "A human being who is regarded as an animal because he can't express himself. No one knows what it is like and no one cares to know."

I care, I cried inwardly. I was appalled and filled with compassion. Heretofore, the mentally retarded were far removed from any experience I had ever had. I had read and felt sorry but my feeling had lacked passion. Seth was my first personal contact with that reality. My mind kept protesting that things like this don't happen to people like us.

But it did. And it might have been *my son*. Or *your daughter*.

That episode translated a general idea, something I had known theoretically, into a compelling concern. I had to understand what retardation really was. I began to visit the public libraries and the library at the American Academy of Medicine. I read everything I could find, even a technical book lent to me by an editor friend. Then someone suggested I visit the Sheltered Workshop on 22nd Street and Second Avenue.

Dr. Max Dubrow, the director, and Dr. Jack Tobias, the psychologist, spent hours with me. I was moved by what I observed and deeply impressed with their habilitation and rehabilitation program, but I came away feeling that I was approaching retardation from the wrong end. I wanted to start at the beginning.

I decided to call the National Association for Retarded Children and made an appointment to see the then executive director, Dr. Gunnar Dybwad, and his wife, Rosemary. Dr. Dybwad listened to me and suggested that if I really wanted to familiarize myself with the problem, I should read all the back copies of *Children Limited,* the newspaper published by the National Association for Retarded Children since 1952.

It is a large job, he warned, most people don't want to take the time. I asked if they could be put in the library for me, and for two weeks I pored through ten years of back newspapers.

I read of twelve-year-old Jennie tied to a pigpen; of a six-year-old boy lost in California, unable to communicate with anyone; of a mother in Wisconsin who kept three subnormal children in an unheated attic, summer and winter, subjecting them to sick, excessive punishment. I read of these and many more, delaying visiting a school or institution, for I wanted to know what I was dealing with.

I encountered varied views on retardation. It was a curse—a blessing —a punishment—insanity—a disease. Actually it is none of these things.

How had these notions been built up? What constructive contributions had been made, if any?

The Albert Einstein Medical Center granted me permission to use their library, and I settled in their archives to try to find out.

Superstition and fear cause many of the misconceptions about retardation.

In 400 B.C., Hippocrates was the first to combat superstition scientifically. He guessed that successive seizures of the epileptic caused retardation rather than supernatural communication from the gods. The frequency and duration of the seizures, he found, affected the degree of brain damage. He cracked open an epileptic cadaver's skull and looked inside of it. His famous essay, "The Sacred Disease," was the first step in separating medicine from superstition.

Aristotle (384–322 B.C.) recognized mental deficiency and defined it, but the term "mental retardation" was not known for centuries.

In the latter half of the second century, Aretaeus stumbled on the endocrine system, whose malfunction was later proved to cause mental retardation. The pituitary gland, which lies at the base of the brain, and the thyroid gland, which consists of two lobes on either side of the trachea, are the ones most involved.

Glandular disturbances, either because of oversecretion or undersecretion of their specific hormonal substances, may lead to diminished mental function. Babies born without a thyroid gland or with a thyroid that does not function properly frequently are cretins who, unless treated, will generally show some degree of retarded mental development. Happily, however, if the correct diagnosis is made and substitution therapy commenced before the infant reaches the age of six months, there is good reason to hope for proper intellectual development.

For centuries after Aretaeus, despite sporadic medical contributions, superstition and cruelty far overshadowed any further scientific interest. If the mentally deficient survived at all, they were relegated to the status of society's lepers.

In the thirteenth century, the Church was forced to provide sanctuary, "asylums" for the retarded, but no attempt was ever made to treat or educate them, and society continued to look upon them as freaks or worse. They were locked up, hidden away, or put into cages like animals in a zoo to be displayed for public amusement.

Handicapped people have always been feared, and most people thought they were "possessed of the devil," and therefore the common treatment was to take them out and beat the devil out of them. This was particularly true during the Protestant Reformation.

Despite all this, over 700 years ago a feeble light cast its beam on man's efforts for his unfortunate brethren. The people in the village of Gheel, Belgium, began a plan, which is continued to the present day, of "family care" for the mentally retarded, epileptic, and psychotic: generation after generation of the normal inhabitants of Gheel have taken the mentally ill and retarded into their private homes, treated them as members of their family entitled to love and respect, and, when rehabilitated, returned them to their own families. If one of them is unwanted, he remains with his foster family. This plan has only recently been rediscovered and has begun to be adopted by our twentieth-century institutions.

In 1620, Dr. Juan Pablo Bonet's lone voice cried out in Madrid on the possibilities of rehabilitation. Over a hundred years went by again before a small stream of men began to contribute ideas on mental deficiency. Among these was the great humanist Jean-Jacques Rousseau, who believed all persons could develop the ability to learn if given the adequate stimulation he set forth in his famous *Emile*.

It was not until Jean Marc Gaspard Itard (1774–1838) that the story of mental retardation began to be told. Itard, the first realist, the first educator to practice the "observation" of the pupil in the way the sick are observed in the hospitals, was a French physician famous for his experiment with the wild boy captured in the forest of Aveyron, and diagnosed by the great physician Philippe Pinel as severely retarded. Itard worked with the boy for years on the premise that only in the heart of society can man achieve his ultimate destiny. His efforts marked great changes in the captured boy's behavior and understanding, but he was unable to teach him to talk or live independently in society. After five years, he considered his experiment a failure, but we know it was not. Students in the field of mental retardation regard it as the first scientific attempt at training a retarded child. Itard was the trailblazer. The residential school program in the United States can be traced directly to him.

No matter how briefly, one feels impelled to mention Johann Jacob Guggenbühl (1816–1863), who started the important trend toward specialized residential care at his establishment at Abendberg near Interlaken, Switzerland, in 1840.

Edouard Seguin (1812–1880), one of Itard's most brilliant students, wrote a remarkable series of papers which have been referred to as "The Magna Carta of Mental Emancipation for the Imbecile Class." Seguin came to this country in 1850. He was briefly head of a school in Pennsylvania, and began a day school in New York City, but his greatest contribution in this country was as a consultant to people who were establishing residential schools. He became the president of what is known today as the American Association on Mental Deficiency. Yet according to Maria Montessori, the famous educator, his theories were never properly understood. She based her belief on the fact that she could never locate a copy of his works in any English-speaking library.

The twentieth century has brought forth innumerable physicians, psychologists, therapists, and educators of the retarded. A partial listing of their work has been supplied in the Bibliography.

The greatest progress has undoubtedly been made in the last hundred years, but as recently as twelve years ago, 150 retarded women squatted, played, defecated, and urinated on a cement floor of a Midwestern institution. When the stench became unbearable, water hoses were brought, and the hosing left the floor and the inmates perpetually damp.

This institution has been demolished, but much brutality remains.

How much is graphically illustrated in the recently published book *Christmas in Purgatory*.

Many mentally retarded are thrown into institutions with the insane. While there is a high correlation between retardation and emotional disturbance, retardation is a far cry from insanity, and only further deterioration can result from such commitment.

What then is mental retardation?

The National Association for Retarded Children states it is a condition in which intelligence is prevented from attaining full development, limiting the victim's ability to learn and put learning to use. It ranges from the profound to the mild—from individuals handicapped to the point of total helplessness to those who cannot keep up with a regular school program but can learn sufficiently to become self-supporting and achieve a considerable degree of social independence.

With mandatory programs of education and rehabilitation, at least half to three-quarters of the mentally retarded could be returned to the community.

What causes mental retardation?

Lack of oxygen to the brain, with subsequent carbon dioxide accumulation can critically damage the intellect. To offset this possibility, Virginia Apgar, M.D., a renowned anesthesiologist, has devised a unique scoring system which nicely relates to brain oxygenation. To be useful, the scoring must be done during the first fifty seconds after a baby is born. It consists in checking heart rate, color, muscular tone, respiratory rate, and the irritability reflexes. (See table on page 8.)

In this manner, the doctor is immediately alerted to the presence of hypoxia and neonatal distress. Air passages are cleared immediately, and oxygen is rushed to the brain. The Apgar score has been adopted in major hospitals all over the country.

Some metabolic disorders causing retardation are determined by heredity and include such conditions as galactosemia and PKU whose formidable nomenclature is phenylketonuria. Phenylketonuria is an intolerance of a certain type of protein. A synthetic diet provides protein necessary for growth and must be maintained during the first six years of life. Diagnosis in early infancy can prevent extensive brain damage. Most states have adopted a law which makes mandatory a blood test to determine the presence of this condition in the newborn.

SIGN	0	1	2
HEART RATE	NONE DETECTABLE	SLOW (BELOW 100)	OVER 100
RESPIRATORY RATE	ABSENT	SLOW IRREGULAR	OVER 100
MUSCLE TONE	FLACCID	SOME FLEXION OF EXTREMITIES	ACTIVE MOTION
REFLEX IRRITABILITY	NO RESPONSE	GRIMACE	CRY
COLOR	PALE BLUE	BODY PINK EXTREMITIES BLUE	COMPLETE PINK

Galactosemia relates to a body error in metabolism of lactose or carbohydrate found in milk. Infants with this abnormality frequently cannot tolerate milk. Galactosemia may eventuate in blindness, jaundice, severe mental retardation, or death, if the milk sugar is not dietarily eliminated very soon after birth.

Until recently, Mongolism (Down's syndrome) had various and unknown causes postulated. Mongolism is now thought to result from abnormal chromosomal groupings in body cells from the time of the fertilization of the ovum.

There are over two hundred known causes of mental retardation. In addition to those already cited, others include jaundice of the newborn due to the Rh factor, infectious diseases of childhood such as meningitis, encephalitis, and measles, diseases due to physical or traumatic agents, including injuries incurred in difficult deliveries, as well as social, economic, cultural, and psychological factors.

However, experience in this country has fortunately shown that for the majority of those affected no gross brain abnormality can be demonstrated; most cases fall within the range of mild retardation of intellectual development.

This formidable array of factors leading to mental retardation made me stop and want to find out the frequency with which this occurred.

Here are the cold facts. Three percent of our total population is considered to be retarded.

Statistically, one mentally retarded child is born every five minutes; 126,000 are born every year; 4,200 (1 out of every 30) will be profoundly retarded and unable to care for themselves. Approximately 12,000 (4 out of 30) will remain, intellectually, below the seven-year level. And 110,000 (the remaining 25 out of 30) are those with mild retardation and represent those who can, with special training and assistance, acquire limited job skills and achieve a high measure of independence.*

In 1960, out of a population of 179 million in the United States, 5.4 million were classified as having some degree of mental retardation. If this remains true, then in 1970, due to the constancy of the population explosion, out of an estimated 214 million population, 6.4 million will fall below the average intelligence level.

Mental retardates and the families they affect add up to 15 to 20 million people, about 10 percent of our whole population.†

As I was searching for information in this country, an unhoped-for opportunity came to see how it was in other countries. My husband had to go on a business trip around the world and invited me to go with him. The journey would not take me to all the places I wanted to go but the proverbial half a loaf would be better than none. But whom would I contact? Where could I go?

At the suggestion of my husband, who is the most human of all encyclopedias, I contacted the United States Information Service in Washington, D.C. But the month of December brings a general exodus, and offices limp along toward the holidays on skeleton crews. My letter was finally discovered and rescued by Mr. Alex Fanelli of the State Department. He sent an aerogram to all the cities I proposed to visit, alerting them to help me on my arrival.

On January 2, 1963, I set out on my journey around the world.

---

* "President's Panel on Mental Retardation," p. 7.
† *Ibid.*

2

Hawaii

MY FIRST STOP WAS HAWAII. IN WAIMANO, A STATE INSTITUTION HIGH ON a volcanic mountain not far from Pearl Harbor, came a terrifying moment for me—my first sight of a severe hydrocephalic.*

Outside, the scent of white oleanders hung on the air. Inside, the fumes of formaldehyde were stifling. We passed from floor to floor and found children sitting listlessly around, starved for a soothing sound or the reassuring pat of a gentle hand; † rows of high cheekbones and aimless straight black hair; rows of heads like small coconuts with a fringe on top; of crippled figures with the frightened and bewildered look of children who have been deliberately lost; rows of particular wheelchair cases—the broad-shouldered boy with undersized arms and legs, a bulbous nose, a mask of pimples, and anonymous eyes that traveled without focus; a girl with a narrow head and face who resembled a lightless lantern. . . .

Suddenly, cold fright plunged through me, leaving me speechless and rigid before the misshapen monstrosity that lay in a bed, blue-black in the last dark throes of dying. It looked like a huge bloated kidney until my eyes found the tiny face of a human being at the lower end. The rest of that foot and a half bean was head! A minute body was attached to this shockingly swollen head, its bones with little or no musculature lay in a heap, with no movement possible.

---

* Hydrocephalic children will vary in degree of retardation. Some may function on a reasonably good level. Others are so severely affected as to be unable to function at all. The size of the enlargement does not necessarily bear any relation to the degree of impairment or to the size of the brain.

† The lack of staff for individualized attention, I later discovered, was a universal problem.

"Hydro" means water, "cephalic," brain. That is literally what the condition is: "water on the brain." The interior of the brain contains symmetrical spaces which are called ventricles. The various parts of this ventricular system are continuous with one another. Normally, cerebral-spinal fluid is derived from the choroidal vessels and fills the ventricles. This liquid freely passes through these ventricles into the spinal canal. Excess fluid is absorbed by the same choroidal plexus. Obstruction of any part of this ventricular system can cause an abnormal accumulation of this fluid, resulting in a localized internal hydrocephalus. The fluid continues to be manufactured despite the fact that it is not being passed on in the normal anatomic pathway.

As the collection of fluid mounts, the pressure on the brain increases until the child dies.

Neurosurgeons have tried valiantly for years to relieve this pressure by creating a tubular shunt between the ventricles and any other vessel of the circulatory system controlled by an anatomic valve.

The tube usually is a polyethelene one and frequently is guided under the skin of the scalp, face, and neck into its newly created outlet. This permits the fluid to pass into the bloodstream and thus relieves the cerebrospinal pressure.

The difficulty that this surgical treatment presented was that any time the blood pressure in the receptacle vessel exceeded the cerebrospinal pressure, a reversal of the flow would ensue.

That would be very unwise.

What then was the answer?

A tiny valve was needed which would prevent the blood from going back to the brain, but permit the cerebrospinal fluid to come out. It had to consist of material that the body would tolerate. It had to be able to withstand tremendous pressure on very little surface.

A neurosurgeon and his group tried and failed and tried again and again.

No salutation could suffice to repay the struggle of scientists in the interest of mankind, but history has shown what human desperation can sometimes do for the scientist. One morning John Holter appeared carrying his little son, Casey.

Casey was a very, very severe hydrocephalic.

The prognosis: Casey would soon die.

But Mr. Holter refused to accept the verdict. "There must be a way out. There must be something we can do!"

And the doctor said, almost to himself, "What we need is a tiny valve but we'll never make it."

Mr. Holter said, "I'm a valve engineer. How much time do we have?"

The answer was a couple of weeks.

So Mr. Holter came into the operating room while the neurosurgeon explained the problem, went home to his garage in central Philadelphia, and in one week he had designed such a valve. Then rose the problem of finding the proper material.

The physician and his staff wired all over the world and finally located the material they needed in another garage just a couple of miles away from Philadelphia.

And so the VJ (ventricular-jugular) shunt was born.

It is claimed that there are now 25,000 children alive in the world with VJ shunts who would be dead if it were not for this.*

The shunts may be obtained from the John Holter Company in Philadelphia.

But obviously no valve had been perfected soon enough for the creature who lay before us now (1963).

Our guide smoothed the bed sheet, then ever so gently stroked that misshapen head.

We walked down a corridor and as the guide sorted his keys to open the locked iron door,† I began to stiffen. I had not as yet recovered from the dying hydrocephalic. What further tragedies were housed at Waimano?

The door swung slowly open.

It was a baby—a small, dear baby who had been abandoned by her parents because she was a Mongoloid. The crib was immaculate, and she was beautifully clean. She lifted herself on her hands and looked at us.

---

* While the operation has had tremendous success, it does not always work. At the Institute Psicopedagógico in San Juan, I saw a child who had been operated on without success. There is no hope for her.

† According to my last communication from Waimano, on December 26, 1967, all doors are now open. None are ever locked.

Clothes are scarce at the institution, and the baby wore mismated socks, but each had a tiny perky bow. The baby had been adopted by a group of nurses who took turns caring for it. They handled the baby as often as possible and the child had a contented, well-cared-for look.

Outside, among gardens of bougainvillae and red poinsettias, adults in dun-colored housedress-type uniforms milled around the well-kept grounds. One large colored woman stood out from the group. The guide told us she was an aggressive homosexual.

Sex drives, so far as planning and carrying out an attack go, have shown themselves to be very low among retardates, but Dr. Satoru Izutsu told me that masturbation in the severely and moderately retarded and homosexuality present problems for Waimano. Professional opinion indicates that since the retardates' judgment is low or nonexistent, the problems would be greatly reduced if there were more ongoing programs or constructive physical occupation.

For the most part, the residents seemed talkative and lively. This group tested in the 50–80 IQ range and had been trained to help not only with the laundry and kitchen work but with the less fortunate as well.

The annual report of the Department of Health in Hawaii states that emphasis has been shifted from custodial to rehabilitation at Waimano, so now the job is twice as hard.

In this changing picture, one aspect remains essentially the same— the major part of the residents' daily care comes from the attendants and hospital nurses, who comprise the majority of employees.

The remainder of the staff consists of physicians, social workers, psychologists, occupational and physical therapists, rehabilitation specialists, laboratory technicians, and clerical, business, and maintenance employees when any or all of these can be obtained.

Volunteers from the community help to provide many of the religious, recreational, and entertainment activities and greatly assist in the overall institution program.

Brave new attempts have been made and new staff has been added, but, with the new policy of returning retardates to the community wherever possible, and as Waimano's fame spreads, educables or mildly retarded are being replaced by an ever-increasing number of moderate, severe, and profound retardates. This further complicates the institution's problems by reducing the help previously available from the mildly retarded residents. Here as elsewhere, seriously handicapped are unable to help themselves, much less others.

People from all over bring their children here, deposit them permanently, and disappear. Few return, even for a visit.*

The dearth of visiting parents is not peculiar to Waimano. It is a common affliction of retardates.

Hawaii has long been associated with the National Association for Retarded Children on the mainland. The state has established an Evaluation Service for more than 400 people. Adults are handled individually, and children at 33 child development clinics at Oahu and 14 itinerant clinics on neighboring islands. Legislation, passed here long before it was in many of our other states, has resulted in 92 classes for retardates in the elementary schools. The educable or mildly retarded are limited to 15 in a class; the more severe, to 10.

Even the most handicapped are now being given an opportunity to learn self-care and to live with others.

The Educational Department will not take retarded children until the age of eight. Cognizant of the needs of the children as well as of their parents, the state set up 5 special schools to care for retardates from the ages of four to eight. One of these schools was allocated to hyperactive children.

As yet there is no nursery school or group for the mentally handicapped under the age of four. Except for private schools or some public state institutions, this is generally true all over the world.

A school for parents of brain-damaged as well as of normal children has been formed. Classes are held for them quarterly. Approaches to training are discussed and the parents are given the opportunity to "tell someone." They talk over their problems, laugh at their mistakes and anxieties, and share their experiences with one another. The school has been so successful that classes have been limited in number, and there is a large waiting list of parents waiting to be admitted.

We had a brief visit with John O'Brien, an ex-newspaperman who is now Executive Director of the Association for Help to Retarded Children. He believes the community is probably one of the most active and

* The superintendent states this is no longer true in the majority of cases. The families do maintain some type of contact.

enlightened in the world. A scout program, 4-H Club, teen canteen every Friday night, and dances are part of the yearly program. There are a summer camp, a summer recreation playtime program, and a weekend recreation program that includes beach parties, visits to the zoo, the aquarium, and a pineapple factory, and attendance at prep and college football and professional baseball games.

A series of nondenominational and denominational Sunday school classes has been formed. Every avenue is being explored to help the retardate develop to his maximum potential.

We learned that work (or vocational) training centers have been established on four of Hawaii's islands—Oahu, Kauai, Maui, and Hawaii itself.

We asked to make a visit to a workshop. Mr. O'Brien suggested Lanakilla, at 1700 Lanakilla Avenue. We found it to be a private non-profit organization which is entirely self-supporting. It is a shop for the physically as well as the mentally handicapped. Only 25 percent of their 125 trainees are mentally retarded. Their IQ's range from 30 to 75.

Mrs. Kam, the bright-eyed lady in charge, told us that some IQ's of 30 perform as well as those with IQ's of 70.

Unless the applicant is already able to function and earn money in the shop, the family pays a $50 fee for the training period. An evaluation is made. Sometimes a retardate may measure zero but Mrs. Kam said that when tried on a real job for thirty days, some amazing abilities may develop.

The categories of work are office work, janitorial, packaging and stapling, clothing, weaving, and bookbinding.

Each work area is broken down into separate skills.

In the clothing unit, for example, the individual is taught to cut, thread a needle, sew, and work a simple hand machine, then an electric one.

Lanakilla takes in old things and remakes them. They also make Hawaiian piggy banks, doll banks, Chubby Hula, muumuu and holoku dolls; drums, coconut hats, hula skirts, artificial flowers and leis, a large collection of toys, hand-screened wrapping paper, and some jewelry. How deeply the Hawaiians have delved into the island's resources to create a reservoir of potential revenue! Mrs. Kam said they are all constantly on the alert to exploit new ideas.

3

Japan

THE HEART OF TOKYO IS A CITY OF COILING STREETS, THIN ALLEYS, LITTLE houses jostling each other, small strong people hurrying about, of statistics and a certain impersonality. Mothers still carry their babies on their backs, but the custom, like the wearing of kimonos, seems to be gradually disappearing.

On the ride from the airport, my greatest shock was the sight of so many people wearing gauze masks over their noses and mouths. I had immediate visions of dying from a contagious disease far from home and children. But I soon learned that TB had been a relentless enemy of the Japanese for many years, and though it had been brought under control, the people were still afraid. They wore these masks to prevent breathing in any germs.

When I saw a gloved uniformed girl at the foot of the escalator in the department store wiping the hand belt as it came down, I felt that Japan should be awarded the International Medal for Most Antisepticized Nation of the Year.

The next morning, without so much as a "so sorry," a bevy of white locusts swarmed in all over the hotel room, leaving my mouth and the door wide open. Fortunately I had a robe on. Two girls made my bed, one flew into the bathroom, another disturbed the dust as little as possible, and the fifth ran in to see that nothing was done thoroughly and, in their antiseptic white uniforms, they departed, leaving the door and my mouth still wide open.

I thought this light cleaning at odd variance with their germ-consciousness.

The USIS had made arrangements for me to visit the Seicho school. The principal, Dr. Yamato Komiyama, would make inquiries as to whether any parents of the retarded children would be able to receive me.

The doorman of the hotel wrote out the directions to the school and gave it to a taxi driver with verbal instructions, and I was off alone in the city of no street signs.*

The ride to that part of the city was flat and uninteresting. I wondered why so many homes had walls around them, even rather poor homes. I discovered later that they are built to keep out the evil spirits.

The street we finally turned into was wide and muddy. A long, barracks-like building lay on the left. Some boys were hammering and sawing in the yard. As I came in the door, someone led me to the principal's office. It was furnished with old Western-style rattan summer furniture and was freezingly cold. Everyone wore thick padded clothing and drank rivers of tea. I was immediately handed a cup.

A few teachers stood around smiling, and I had the feeling that they were very anxious to be of assistance, but they spoke no English and I no Japanese. I beamed back at them and spoke to them in English, hoping that they would at least understand that my attempt at friendliness meant I also wished to be of some help.

Dr. Komiyama came to my rescue—in English. He translated what I hoped were some bons mots for his staff and then we went on a tour of the building. As in many other countries of the world, he said, the first provisions for the education of the mentally retarded were made about half a century ago.

The upper corridor looked like a European train, with compartments on one side which turned out to be classrooms. I saw academic, sewing, weaving, box-making, and ceramic classes in progress. In one area there was a large damp room of urinals. The odor was potent. There were no doors, and it was flagrantly open for contemplation.

No one walks into any room in Japan without taking off his shoes. The cement toilet floors had a cold, wet look. When I saw the boys in their stockinged feet, I wondered how it would feel if one removed one's shoes to enter an outhouse.

Dr. Komiyama glanced at his watch and suggested we leave since the

---

* As a result of preparations for the Olympic Games many streets are now named.

family visits would take considerable time. He promised to brief me on the program of the Seicho school before I left.

We went out and secured a taxi for our first home visit. Dr. Komiyama told me three parents of retarded children had agreed to have me visit their homes. I was delighted.

I asked him how much of a potential he thought some retardates might have. He shook his head and shrugged. Who could know?

Children Limited of February, 1957, told the story of Yamashita,* referred to as the Van Gogh of the Orient.

Yamashita was slow-witted and childish, and could not do ordinary work or be economically independent without someone's supervision. He did nothing but make pictures and took his entire solace from life from this.

Except for long periods of roaming the countryside, he had lived, since the age of twelve, at the Yawata Home for Retarded Children.

He had a talent for "hari-e," an art form that consists of tearing up colored papers and pasting bits onto canvas.

In 1949, at the age of twenty-six, he began experimenting with oils by daubing paints directly from the tube onto the canvases, and he then progressed to brushes.

In Kobe, 200,000 people attended his display in a single day.

Japan's top magazines vie for his work. A theatre in Osaka used one of his paintings as a design for a curtain. A portfolio of full color reproductions is a best seller in Japan.

At the request of his mother, 10 percent of the profits from his sales go to a fund for the education of the mentally retarded in Japan.

I related the story to a friend of mine, an artist and caricaturist for *The New York Times.*

"Art," he said, "is an expression of inner feeling, not of an inner IQ."

Dr. Ryuzaburo Shikiba, a leading psychiatrist and the guardian of Yamashita, calls him an "idiot savant"—a riddle and challenge to science.

The taxi leaped and bounced into a narrow street before it exploded

---

* A film entitled *The Naked General,* based on the life of Yamashita, was reviewed in *The New York Times* in December, 1964.

to a stop. The Matzuzawa home was small like those of its neighbors, all pushing against one another to retain their sparse space. We entered a tiny dim vestibule and there was a display of slippers. I had seen enough movies to know what that meant and I immediately removed my shoes. We climbed a narrow, steep flight of stairs, so highly polished that with the unsteady grip of the slippers I was sure I was going to break my neck. But I finally made it to the next landing.

The floor was of as highly polished grain as the stairs; the hall was again reminiscent of a European train with compartments along one side. Mrs. M. slid a shoji screen along by inserting her fingers in small black holes in the wooden frame. These sliding doors have paper inserts which are finished in gray, giving the appearance of opaque glass. As I started to enter, Mrs. M. let out a small scream of distress. The Japanese are less given to emotional outbursts than anyone in the world, and I was startled. I glanced down and remembered that you have to take your slippers off when you enter sleeping and living quarters. I discovered long afterward that that was only half the reason. The other was that I was stepping on the threshold. Apparently there is the superstition that great evil will befall you if you step on the threshold itself.

A bare bulb hung from a wire in the ceiling. In the center of the room was a low mahogany table with a hand-crocheted cover, two rattan chairs on either side. Eight straw mats covered the floor. I learned that a room is designated a four-, eight- or twelve-mat room according to size. One end of the room held a pile of cushions. The only discordant notes were an inexpensive modern desk, a Western chair, and a cheap alarm clock that ticked noisily. They seemed like strange intruders in this fastidious room with its otherwise simple decoration.

A Japanese calendar complete with snow-topped mountains adorned one of the bare walls. Dr. K. explained that this stark black and white room, reminiscent of a Van Gogh, was really the bedroom. The sleeping mats were rolled up during the day and lay behind the shoji screens along one side of the room.

I felt myself grow hot with embarrassment. What a fool Dr. Komiyama must have thought me back at the school with my idiotic pressing of why they didn't teach the girls bed-making at Seicho. He had merely shrugged his shoulders politely to indicate he did not know the answer. It was really quite simple. There were no beds to make.

Mrs. M. excused herself. As she left the room I wondered. Was it humility, submissiveness, obedience, or deference that made her walk that way. And then I felt the pressure of sadness and knew it was her child whom she still carried on her shoulders. In a few minutes she returned and brought us tea in the handleless cups of the East. I drank it slowly. It was my fifth that morning.

Mrs. M. began to speak. Dr. Komiyama translated softly, and the story ran on like the gentle murmur of a brook.

Mrs. M. was a college graduate. Her husband was in charge of a large factory which makes communications equipment for public utilities. I watched Mrs. M. as she spoke. She had the typical demeanor, the reserve and bowed head, of the Japanese. Her face was broad as a dahlia, but the dark eyes were deep with intelligence.

She had had a long and difficult labor. No instruments were used, but the child's brain was damaged during the delivery. The boy's cry was very weak at birth. He had very poor eating habits. At fifteen months, he could barely walk, and he started to say only very simple words at the age of three. He moved constantly and jerkily, very much in the manner of a palsied child. His right leg was affected and he still drags it.

At the age of three there was great unhappiness in the house. The father was desperately despondent at the boy's slowness of thought and action, his poor coordination which caused him to drop and break things. The boy's lack of perception and conception made the father decide he was deaf.

Mrs. Matzuzawa resolved to check every possibility.

Japan is divided into 46 prefectures. For community care, they have 820 public health centers, 133 child guidance centers, 55 mental health clinics attached to public health centers, and 46 centers for mentally deficient persons. Residence institutions and 60 day care centers for the mentally deficient charge for a whole or part of the actual expense of the retardate based on the income of the person responsible for his support or on his own income if he has one.*

Testing is very inexpensive in Japan and the diagnostic clinics have

---

* This is similar in policy to that of many places in the United States.

no waiting lists.* Child welfare officers obtain the history of the child's development. The Japanese child welfare officers are similar to our social workers. One welfare officer is assigned to every 100,000 to 130,000 people in Japan. The population of Japan is about 100 million.

Mrs. M. took her boy for every conceivable type of testing—hearing, speech, sight, etc.—in order to get the best possible diagnosis and most accurate prognosis.

The family of the Matzuzawas felt great sympathy for the boy and were very kind. The neighbors pretended not to notice but since Mrs. Matzuzawa had always been very sensitive, the boy widened the gap between her and society. When she met her neighbors in the street, she nodded briefly and hurried past.

There was no history of mental retardation on either side of the family. This boy was the first.

At great personal sacrifice, Mrs. M. sent him to a private nursery. From there, he went to a public school and entered one of the 3,793† classes for educables or mildly retarded in Japan.

There were few children in the Matzuzawa neighborhood, so the child was spared cruelty and had very little teasing. No one bothered him and he bothered no one. He could not go out to play with anyone but he seemed quite content to stay with his younger brother who is not only a brilliant student but has great kindness and sympathy for his damaged sibling.

Mrs. Matzuzawa said they were fortunate for he finally won admittance to the Seicho school. He has been placed in a factory job and will earn about $30 a month.

On the way out we met the younger brother in his cadet-type uniform. He had the round rosy face of a Japanese boy doll and his black eyes were bright with curiosity. In that moment he seemed to have summed me up so thoroughly that I was certain he probably even knew the number of pearls in my necklace.

As we bade Mrs. Matzuzawa good-bye, I asked her if in all these

---

* In answer to my questionnaire, while the clinics did extensive testing, they did not have physiotherapists, art, play, or speech therapists assigned to the clinic.

† It was planned to establish 7,000 special classes by 1965, and 10,000 by 1968.

difficult years she had ever thought of placing him in a residential institution.

She slid her hands into the sleeves of her Western dress and with folded arms bowed her head. She remained in deep thought. Then she lifted her head and looked directly into my eyes. "Not for a moment. I felt that if my child could be helped even a fraction, I would do everything in my power to keep him where he belonged—at home and with his family."

The Izawa house was narrower and darker than the Mazuzawas'. As we entered there were two broad steps in the vestibule with a staggering display of slippers.

"They are either on sale or the owners are octopuses!"

Dr. Komiyama smiled. "Neither. Both father and son are dentists. These are for their patients."

A slim Japanese woman in a kimono parted the curtains and bowed. At a gentle nudge from the good Dr. Komiyama I went ahead through a small dark room where I half expected to see a dental chair, but there was only a table piled high with sewing. Mrs. Izawa managed to get in front and back of me with great adroitness until we reached the back room which was apparently the living room. This time I remembered to take off the slippers, and I could see from the fleeting smile on the face of my hostess that she was pleased.

The floor was covered with the traditional tatami mats. In the center of the room was a green formica table no higher than ten inches from the floor. As if that were not curious enough, a beige challis tablecloth, instead of being on top of the table, was between the tabletop and the floor so that it looked like a slip that was much too long and showed out from beneath a dress. I thought that an extremely odd way to put on a tablecloth, but I adopted the Japanese method of remaining impassive.

Four pillows were placed around the table. The house was cold like the first one, and I hugged my coat to me as I sat down and curled my legs underneath me. Our hostess and Dr. Komiyama slid their legs under the table. I was fascinated. Where on earth had they gone? After several urgent signs from my hostess, I gingerly slid my legs under the table. I was startled to have them drop into a well at the bottom of which was a warm hibachi stove. I relaxed and enjoyed it.

The grandmother, on her knees, placed a collation plus the inevitable cups of tea on the table and retired.

I sensed a deep philosophy among these people and a delicate awareness of beauty. But one way in which we diverge sharply from the Far East is in the sense of color. Their greens, blues, and pinks are completely violent.

One of the delicacies on the table was called a cherry blossom. It was made up of some brown mashed substance, covered with what looked like rash-pink absorbent cotton and gracefully wrapped in a green leaf. I discovered that the brown substance was mashed soybeans. I never did discover what the pink cover was made of. I tasted a little of it to see if I could guess its identity and must sadly admit that it did taste like pink absorbent cotton. But the gracious hospitality with which it was offered left a fine taste in my mouth.

There were five children in this family. None of them was at home. The oldest was twenty-two years old, and he was the child whose brain had been damaged.

He had been born normal and healthy in Tokyo before the bombing of Pearl Harbor. The parents were proud and happy. Try as he would, the mother murmured, the father's delight in his firstborn escaped through his mantle of modesty and deprecation.

Mrs. Izawa, almost musically translated by Dr. Komiyama, went on. He was such a good child . . . so bright. There were so many things he could do. . . . We were too proud. . . .

There was a silence and then she continued. When he was one year and ten months old, he became ill with a high fever. We were in the country then. Living in Tokyo had become unwise. I became alarmed and sent my husband to fetch a doctor. But it was wartime, a time for death, not for life. The doctors were scarce and overworked. Ours was a long time coming. By then the convulsions had started—the wild, racking, spasmodic movements that seemed to take him farther and farther away from us.

Mrs. Izawa's doelike face and body became very still. It was as if the slightest movement might bring back the pain of that night.

The boy was sick a long time. When he got well, it was as if everything within him had stopped. He could barely stand up. When he did begin to walk again, it was on his toes, dragging his left leg. There was a heaviness to his speech, and it seemed to take him forever to say something.

The affection his father had for him became lost in exasperation. He would ask the boy to bring something and become impatient with his confusion and slowness in following directions. Then the boy would become rattled and drop what he was trying to carry. It would result in a bewildered boy, confused and unable to form a correct concept of what his father wanted and the mother in tears.

The father had slipped silently in a few moments before. He was a large man, his face heavy and marked like a cauliflower. When he spoke, it remained impassive but his voice was surprisingly light and gentle. "My wife was lucky, she could cry. I would come home and find her asleep with the child in her arms, the tears having made a pattern on her face. Those she could wipe off, but"—he pointed to his breast—"the marks in here one cannot wash off. I did not cry . . ."

The wife interrupted. "But he was always so kind, always . . ."

Her husband continued as if she had not spoken. "The more apparent the helplessness became, the more tightly did my wife wind her arms around the boy and the farther away I traveled." The sigh seemed to rend him as he said slowly, "I began to detest the sight of my own son! When I heard the approaching of the hippety-hop, hippety-hop, it seemed as if I could not bear it. I did not want to see him, to remember he belonged to me. I buried myself in my work. As a father, I was a failure—a complete coward. I wanted only to run away."

His wife put out her hand as if in protest, then withdrew it. She turned back to us. "We sent the boy to a country school. It was so small the teacher could teach them one by one. The teacher was very polite. He never gave my son a name. Neither did my family. They were very kind."

"Has that been true of other people?"

Mrs. Iazawa frowned. "Other people?" She shrugged. "Confucius says, 'Look upon your own shortcomings before you attack someone else's.'"

One up for Confucius, thought I.

"Had no one suggested an intelligence test?" *

"Japan was fighting a war. The bombing made such a venture impossible. It was anyone's guess as to who would survive."

"And after the war?"

"I learned of clinics for diagnosis and testing. I visited many places.†
After the boy was tested they told me of the protective institute. I hesitated to speak of it. One evening I began, and my husband interrupted me almost violently.

"We will not send him away!"

"My heart filled, and for a moment I thought it would break. The tears rolled down my face, but for joy, not sorrow. For in my husband's unthinking rejection I knew that he truly loved the boy; that I was not alone in knowing of our boy's goodness, his willingness to share. I hastened to explain to my husband that it was a day center, that if he could learn enough, he could one day apply to the Seicho school where he might learn a trade and be somewhat as others. My husband was silent a long time. Finally he spoke. 'So be it.' We were fortunate. Out of many hundreds of applicants our boy was chosen."

"And so the story had a happy ending."

"Not quite. My son failed to qualify for his job. He had to return to Seicho for another six months. The day I was summoned to the school for the second time was very bad. If he failed this time, it would have meant institutionalization."

"And would you have complied with the decision of the state?"

Mrs. Izawa slipped her hands into the wide sleeves of her kimono and gave me an enigmatic reply. "The state does its best to decide what is right for the people of Japan."

History has molded the Japanese people's position in relation to the state. Up until little over a hundred years ago there was barely a crack in that mold. If scientific theories concerning retardation did not flourish, if attempts at rehabilitation were late starting, the past of the Japanese people partially explains it.

---

* Japan was the only country in all of Asia that had a standardized I.Q. test.

† Japan, a little more than half the size of Texas, had 136 diagnostic and testing clinics in 1967.

For centuries Japan was a feudal state, its people serfs. It was not unusual in the old days for crowds to stand silently by as a man, whose only crime had been to appeal to the Shogunate for justice, was marched to a large vat of boiling oil and thrown in. The state had its standards for justice and none could challenge them.

People were born into fixed classes of society and there they had to remain. Below the Imperial family and court nobles were four Japanese castes ranked in hierarchal order—warriors (samurai), farmers, artisans, and merchants. Below them were the outcasts or untouchables.

The head of a family had to post on his doorway his class position and required facts about his hereditary status. The clothes he could wear, the foods he could buy, the amount he could spend on a wedding or a funeral, the kind of house he could legally live in were regulated according to this inherited rank.

International trade was unknown. Domestic trade was severely restricted by setting up required customs barriers with strict rules about letting goods through. Capital punishment resulted if a boat was built or operated over a certain size. The closed-door policy remained rigidly in force until Commodore Perry exerted counterforce on it in 1855. Then the door opened, but slowly.

In Japan decisions are a result of top-level policy. When the State stakes out its own official field in the area of local concern also, its jurisdiction is accepted with deference.*

Buddhism and Shintoism are the principal religions in Japan. Neither requires regular temple attendance except for certain days when worshippers visit their shrines. There is no one central, dominating, powerful religious group. In Japan, the State comes nearer, in the people's eyes, to being the supreme good, and that is why so many Japanese will still so readily accept the decisions of the government.

The day had winged breathlessly by. There was no time left to visit the third family, and Dr. Komiyama had to return to the school.

Mrs. Izawa and the grandmother accompanied us to the street, anxiously helping us to get a taxi quickly. They remained there bowing and gracefully waving us on our way.

---

* Ruth Benedict, *The Chrysanthemum and the Sword*. (Boston: Houghton Mifflin Co., 1946).

Dr. Komiyama settled back in the seat and gave me a summary of the status and goals of the Seicho school.

The Seicho school is under the jurisdiction of the Institute of Education. It was founded after World War II. It enrolls educables or the mildly retarded between the ages of thirteen to eighteen years of age. On the primary school level, educables, known also as moderate, independent, or marginally independent (IQ 50–75), are assigned to special classes. Trainables, designated also as severe and semidependent (IQ 25–49), are assigned to special schools. The very severe, custodial, or dependent retardates (IQ 0–25) are assigned to institutions.

The course at Seicho is divided into junior and senior. Those of thirteen to fifteen years old are in the junior course; those sixteen to eighteen in the senior. Unfortunately Seicho has room for only 30 new students a year. Approximately 300 apply for enrollment. They are carefully screened and the most promising are taken. If the pupil has many difficult problems, the school will not take him because they feel they cannot handle him. If the problems are slight, they are admitted.

Seicho will take children of 80–100 IQ with more difficult problems for they have found that under their tutelage they rarely have trouble with them once they are admitted.

Everything at Seicho is divided into three parts, including the school year. The first term is from April through June, the second from September to December, and the third is from January to March.

Dr. Komiyama told me that the program is a mixture of academic training and those manual arts which best train the children for job placement.

The junior course at the school is divided into three parts in an attempt to fit training to the individual differences and the ability to learn. There are the fast group, the slower, and the slowest. There is an average of 10 boys to a class, with two classes for boys and one for girls in each grade.

Seicho uses the summer vacation as the trial placement period for senior course students. The student is placed on a job when the school thinks he is ready. If he can function in it, he remains there and does not return to Seicho. If he fails, he is permitted to come back for another six months, or two terms. He is then given a second job opportunity. If he is still unable to function adequately the parents are notified of his failure and asked to place him in an institution. There are 340 such housing institutions with a capacity of 23,967 as of 1967. This individual placement is requested in one to two cases out of every thirty.

I asked Dr. Komiyama how he felt the parents reacted to this verdict. He said naturally they were unhappy but they accepted the decision of the state for they felt it knew best, just as they accepted the Eugenic Protection Law: "It is legal for retardates to marry, but according to the Eugenic Protection Law, a foeticide or eugenic operation must be performed."

Up until 1959, the Seicho school was the only one of its kind, but a law was passed that all the mentally retarded must be cared for, and as of 1967, 70 other schools like Seicho have come into existence.

As a result of the law requiring education for all retardates, Japan's trainables had to be taken into account, children of below 45 or 50 IQ. In order to provide for them, day centers in addition to the old-style institutions were formed. As of 1963 there were 41 of them. These day centers are governed by the Minister of Welfare.

As of 1967, there are 71 day centers in Japan, of which 12 are in Tokyo. Children are permitted to enter them at the age of four, which coincides with many educators' and psychologists' belief that retardates should enter school earlier and remain later than the so-called normal child.

There is only one private nursery school in Tokyo, which is prohibitively expensive. The mothers have been organizing makeshift nurseries themselves much as they are doing in this country. They are guided by their own national association for retarded children, the "Parents Hand in Hand Association for the Mentally Retarded,"* which also teaches them how to run the new schools.

For a nation that suffered serfdom for so many centuries, their amazing strides, knowledgeableness, and increasing provisions for the mentally retarded are a tribute to their industriousness and ability to adapt other people's achievements to their own needs and purposes.

---

* Address: Dai 7, Mori Building, 2 Shiba Nishikubo Tomoe-cho, Minoto-ku, Tokyo.

4

Taiwan

In Taipei, capital of Taiwan (formerly known as Formosa), I visited an orphanage and saw a Chinese father in a ragged army overcoat speaking importunately with one of the directors. She shook her head, and he bent down and played with his small daughter. I was told the mother had deserted them and the father wanted the orphanage, a refuge for mentally retarded, to take the child from him so that he could try to get work and support himself.

The orphanage had no place for the child, but the father made it clear he would not leave until the little girl was taken from him. All the while he continued to play with her with endless patience and tender lovingness.

The Chinese adore children. They believe that children bring good luck, and the parents are devoted to them. Even when a desperate parent is forced to abandon a child, he slips into the shadows nearby, hides, and will wait for hours if necessary until he sees that the baby is picked up and cared for.

It has not been at all unusual for three generations and several related families to live in the same household. The whole clan group accepts the responsibility for the well-being of every member. If the parents, brothers, or sisters reject a retardate, there is always a grandmother, aunt, or uncle to care for him. Family pride normally prevents them from appealing to outsiders for help.

Family unity has been found to be so strong that National Taiwan Hospital asks the mother or some family member to act as a nursing aide for the patient during hospitalization.

Why, then, abandon the children at all?

Perhaps because up until now nothing had ever been done for the mentally retarded. Over the years, there were a few scattered efforts by individual teachers, social workers, or community leaders who attempted to get retardates together for custodial care, took them into their homes, or put them on farms, but no movement ever amounted to much. There was absolutely no help available anywhere.

In the past retardation was considerably less of a problem in China, because the Chinese were accustomed to caring for their own retardates within the family. In poor and ill-fed families, the less hardy children and the retarded died off at an early age.

Taiwan is largely agricultural. There is little industry. People work seven days a week in order to survive. One night we passed one of the tallest buildings in Taipei, a brightly lit night school. Here the people came after twelve to fifteen hours of work, seven days a week.

Learning is costly, and school buildings have been commandeered for the children who are likely to compete in society easily rather than those who are not.

Education is compulsory in Taiwan from the ages of six to twelve, but a retarded child who cannot keep up in his studies may either remain at home or be requested to do so.

At the USIS, Mr. P. L. Chen efficiently arranged an appointment for me with Dr. Tsung-yi Lin, the eminent psychiatrist pioneer and director of programs for the mentally retarded and their families. As we drove along, we passed fruit carts filled with mountains of glistening oranges, and why I never could get a glass of fresh orange juice in all the time I was there, I will never know.

We drove past several blocks of buildings that had recently been erected and that are referred to as bazaars. Like stage sets, the fronts of the buildings are wide open. Each tradesman shuts his place at night with iron fences, but during the day all the stock is available for everyone to see. At least the problem of window display is eliminated.

Dr. Lin, who I later discovered has a worldwide reputation, said it was the people at the Medical Health Center who were the pioneering group in retardation. They talked and researched the problem for fifteen years before any program became a reality. They felt the work had to go slowly and soundly in order to be of any lasting value. They wanted no government interference. Once caught up in red tape, the necessary processes might have been drastically slowed and unimportant ones emphasized.

However, as Dr. Lin wryly explained, there had been no great difficulty with the government, for it had been too busy with other things. Before Taiwan became the seat of the Nationalist Government, the population was a little over 5,000,000. It has since swelled to over twice that—10,661,000. The Taiwan government was mainly interested in sending superior children on to a higher education. As a matter of fact, there are ten colleges in Taiwan, five of which are public. There is an insignificant attendance fee. This is not a bad beginning for the percentage at present able to attend college.

Once Dr. Lin outlined his project, the government provided the funds to get it started.

Dr. Lin interviewed principals all over the island and finally chose the head of the Chungsan school for normal children as the person who had the most empathy with the project. The schools generally are very crowded, each averaging about 8,000 students, with 60 to 80 to a class. Arrangements were made to take over a couple of rooms with special teachers for a small group of the mentally handicapped.

Two pilot classes and a control group were set up for a three-year period, to teach them work from the first through the third grade. When the project became known, there were 150 applicants. Dr. Lin wanted 25 educables whose chronological age did not exceed ten and whose IQ's ranged from 50 to 75. He selected those who did not suffer from too much physical disability and whose parents would be most cooperative.

Actually Dr. Lin ended up with 27 children whose IQ's ranged from 38 to 75.

A group of 15 children in the same IQ range was assigned to a regular class in the public school with normal children as the control group. At the end of three years, a comparison will be made as to what has been accomplished in the two groups.

The pilot class of educables, the mildly retarded, will emphasize self-care, daily chores, self-expression, behavior, attentiveness, and study habits. They will then go on to a vocational training program. Up until this time there has been no workshop or vocational training center of any kind in Taiwan.

The more advanced of this educable group has a full-time teacher and an assistant. A small group of lower IQ's was put into another room with a single teacher in charge.

Dr. Lin suggested that, since it was too late in the day to observe at the school, I might like to visit the Yi-Kuang orphanage where, it turned out, I was to see the father trying to give away his child.

I was greeted at the door by Miss Tsai yi-Lin who, like most Chinese women, wore slacks to protect her from the winter cold. Her black hair was worn in a long bob with a band around it. She moved with efficiency.

While Chinese women were always encouraged to be obedient and submissive, some of them quietly took the initiative and built family fortunes whereas others remained parasites. However, they had one thing in common: they did not participate in community problems.

The Chinese have traditionally always cared for their own. There was little need for social workers in their society. Today, along with compulsory education, there have been many changes in that society. There is now a social urgency to think of others. Miss Tsai yi-Lin is one of the new crop learning to respond to that need.

The orphanage was founded by American and English women, including two wives of AID officials, Mrs. Abbott and Mrs. Harrison. These kind women prevailed upon the International Women's Club to acquire the present building and donate it for the care of mentally and physically handicapped orphans. It has been in existence for two years. Dr. Lin's team of workers* visits there regularly. In addition, the government pays for a full-time psychologist, nurse, and social worker to strengthen the team.

There were two tiny rooms with 20 trainable, rather severely retarded children sitting and doing nothing. One small boy of eight was tied to the wooden bars of an improvised stockade. He was a hyperactive retardate and there was no medicine available to quiet him. Miss Tsai yi-Lin said that if he were not tied hand and foot he would destroy everything around him, including himself.

A small five-year-old Mongoloid sat apart. Miss Tsai yi-Lin gently urged her to join the children who were able to move about. The child looked up with a lost look but did not stir. Then she dropped her head and sank back into apathy.

There were 40 children in the orphanage, 20 of whom were re-

---

* Dr. Lin's nuclear team consists of Dr. Hsu, who is another psychiatrist, Mr. Ko, a psychologist, and Miss Lee, a psychiatric caseworker.

tarded. Every six months they are given a mental test and divided into two groups. Those who appear ready to profit from academic training are given the opportunity to learn. The other children have only group activity outside, such as ball playing and singing.

One of the large problems is toilet training. It took almost nine years to train one child. Another child of eleven with an IQ of under 20 has yet to be trained.

In a long dormitory-type room with a regiment of beds, cerebral-palsy children lie limply and never stir. They have no speech and have to be fed.

Each child gets three meals a day plus mashed fruit in the evening. The cerebral-palsy children have more milk and richer food when it is available. The meals consist of a mixture of egg, rice, meat, and vegetables. Milk is given once a day.

Children in orphanages, schools, or training centers were better fed than many children who lived at home. In fact, in some day centers the hot meal they got there was the only one of the day. I found that to be especially true when I got to Hong Kong where the refugees' problem was most accute. I asked if Taiwan had many refugees from the mainland.

Miss Tsai yi-Lin said very few. The distance from the Chinese mainland to Taiwan is too great and the journey too expensive.

There are only 7 people to run this place on 24-hour duty for 40 handicapped children, and Miss Tsai yi-Lin added wistfully, "It is difficult to run such a place with so small a staff."

Before I departed, I saw the room where the very young babies were lined up in their cribs, some of them crying. Other little ones were standing around on the floor waiting patiently for a chance to sit in one of the three tiny rockers which were in constant use.

After I left, I sent them some rockers.

The next day I went to the Chungsan Primary School where the pilot classes for the retarded were being held. Dr. Lin's psychiatric social worker, Miss Sophia Lee, acted as my guide and interpreter. We visited the educable or mildly retarded group of 60 IQ or over. They had just finished a period of writing. The letters were still on the board, and the papers were being collected.

Miss Lee said the teachers had been working to lengthen the attention span of these children. At first the children were able to concentrate on a subject for only 10 minutes, then 20. The extreme limit for any constructive span of learning was 30 minutes. I think this has been found to be generally true all over the world.

The first order of the day at school in the morning is to clean the classroom. The children are given brooms, pails, water, and cloths. They also wash the cups for their allotment of milk. There is a mild amount of breakage, but it is not serious. Thus the first 50 minutes of the school day passes in practical activity.

After the letter writing, which had just been completed as we arrived, the teacher wrote a simple song on the blackboard. She went over the words with the class, then they all sang them together. There is an organ which the senior teacher plays. One boy, Liang, kept jumping out of his seat and disrupting the procedure. The assistant teacher spoke with him gently. He quieted down for a few minutes, then jumped up again. I was told he was the worst behavior problem in the whole class.

The teacher continued to play the organ, and the children were taught to step in time to the music. Music is frequently used during the day, as it is in many other countries. The teachers explained that it has a very quieting effect on the children.

After the children returned to their seats, the teacher put a large picture on the board. The children were asked to raise their hands and volunteer to talk about the picture. Several of them did, despite constant interruption by Liang. Finally the teacher gave Liang some papers to distribute, which he did with good coordination. When he finished, he sat down and remained quiet.

We then went next door to what they called the "trainable or moderately retarded" group.

The floor was of the same rough, cold, uneven cement. The walls were painted in blue and white by the teachers whose working day often does not end until eight o'clock at night. Fish were painted on the baseboard in an effort to make the room gayer.

The group teacher was a young woman who looked like a child herself. She had short curly brown hair and wore woolen slacks as all the teachers did. Her love and sympathy for the group resulted in great eagerness on the part of the children to please her.

The IQ's in this group ranged from 38 to 60. She told me with pride that after three months one child with a 38 IQ began to speak and to write.

Ko-Choung had the short arms, dry skin, and stubby fingers of a typical Mongoloid but he had an elfin charm just the same. This day he had a running nose, and the curly-headed teacher stopped very often to wipe it. The child obviously adored her. Miss Lee said that he was very possessive of his teacher, and if she disappeared for even a few minutes he would run around and ask everyone where *his* teacher was.

Perhaps in a few years we will know how to prevent Mongolism, an illness that may be due to many factors. In 1959 it was discovered that Mongoloids have 47 chromosomes instead of the customary 46. It is hoped that further research on chromosomal disorder may lead to a solution.

As we left the room, the teacher had distributed round green cards on a large rough wooden table. The cards had white squares in the center with letters in them. She had a duplicate set in her hand. She would call a name, the child would run up to her, receive a card, and run to the table to try and find its mate.

The principal kindly arranged for the senior teacher of the mildly retarded and the young teacher of the moderately retarded to accompany Miss Lee and me to the home of two retardates.

Miss Lee explained that they had chosen two homes, one where a child was accepted by his family and one where the child was rejected. A cab took us up to an alley so narrow that a car could not get through. We got out and began to walk.

Ragged children ran out of the houses calling "Topiga"—Taiwanese slang for American. A few of the low dwellings had cement floors but many of them had only earth. The odor of human waste and rotting food permeated the air.

We stopped before one of the low-slung houses. Outside the door was a board on wooden horses that served as a bench. There were five dark rooms inside, and we entered the main one. Open beams stared down from unpainted walls on which several picture calendars were tacked. The floor was cement, and in one corner was a worn round walnut table with six stools. An old sideboard was cluttered high with odds and ends. Near the door were two battered rattan chairs. At one side of the room a series of baskets bulged with eggs.

A little boy appeared and looked at us in bewilderment. It was the little Mongoloid, Ko-Choung.

Two grown boys and two girls stood around bowing and smiling. They seemed quite proud and happy that I had come to see them about Ko-Choung.

Ko-Choung's mother had lost her teeth. He hair hung lankly about her weathered face. She smiled pleasantly and appeared quite relaxed.

Through Miss Lee, she told me that she had been forty-four years old when she gave birth to Ko-Choung. Since he was her tenth child, the delivery was very fast, very normal.

She noticed a difference in Ko-Choung when he was only one month old. He didn't gain weight, couldn't breast-feed, and she literally had to pour milk down his throat. He didn't start to walk until he was four years of age, and until he was five he never said a single word.

Now, she said, proudly, he could write one or two numbers and say more than ten words. She is very indebted to the school for taking Ko-Choung. She bowed to the teacher and Miss Lee.

I asked if Ko-Choung made a great deal of work for the family. Oh, no, the mother shook her head. She drew Ko-Choung to her and kept her arm around him. Everyone adored him. If anything happened to her, it would be a fight as to who would get him. The other boys loved him dearly. As for her, it was no trouble to make the long walk to school twice a day. Four, six times a day would not be too much. And she alone took him on the school's many picnics, outings, and trips.

On a recent trip to this country, Miss Lee told me the gain on this investment of love and devotion. Ko-Choung had been retested and his IQ had risen from 38 to 60.

I said to the child, "What a lucky little boy you are, Ko-Choung, to have everyone love you so much." Ko-Choung did not understand me, of course. But neither did he understand why I was there in the first place with his teacher and Miss Lee. In exasperation, he stuck out his tongue. The whole family laughed as if he had done something enormously clever.

"Are the other children well?"

"Oh, yes," the mother nodded. "Three boys are at school. These two,"

she indicated the tall boys in the background, "work. The two daughters here work in the household and help with the eggs."

Apparently the mountains of eggs were a source of income.

I did some mental arithmetic. She had said ten children.

I hesitated. "And the other two?"

"They are girls. I gave them away."

We left the house in silence. At the end of the narrow, crowded alley,
we found a taxi. On the way, Miss Lee told me we were going to the
home of a general's lady. The child was Liang, the destructive boy in
the mildly retarded class at the Chungsan school.

"Liang's father is a general!"

Miss Lee smiled. "We have many generals in Taiwan."

The house lay behind a wall. We rang a bell and someone opened the
gate. We stepped in and something swung at me. The general's lady
apologized to me as she lifted the wet pants to allow me to pass.

Thin wooden poles were drawn out in awning fashion from the
front of the house. The remaining wash hung on some. By bending my
head I was able to escape the clammy contact. On other poles, flatly
ironed ducks and fish of varying sizes were drying.

This was a two-story house. There was a cement floor but it was
smooth, unlike the rough ungraded one at Ko-Choung's. The living
room was furnished in cheap modern. A small tin stand with red
netting held books. The only hint of beauty in the room was four
Chinese scrolls with famous proverbs that hung on a wall.

The house was freezing. The general's lady in warm slacks and
sweater left to get us some hot tea.

I asked Miss Lee how the general reacted to Liang.

"I know nothing about him, but his wife finds Liang a tremendous
hindrance to her in attendance at social functions."

"How does she manage?"

"She sends him to the movies. Sometimes he has to stay and see the
show three and four times, and since she goes so often and the pictures
change so seldom, no one knows how many times Liang sees the same
picture."

Liang's mother came in with the tea. She told us the family came
from Shanghai and fled before the Communists. She came to Taiwan
in a disturbed and unhappy state of pregnancy. There was no physical

difficulty at birth, but after fourteen days the boy had a very high fever.

Upon his recovery, they noticed nothing except that he slept a great deal. He did not walk until he was four and said only Mama and Papa. At the age of five, the parents discovered he was unstable. He could learn nothing. He moved constantly and was extremely restless and unpredictable. Sometimes he would learn something very easily, and the next moment he would flare up, it appeared, over almost nothing. He seemed to have no control over himself at all, either in school or at home. She simply could not understand him.

Many retarded, like the normal, have emotional problems. Liang may have developed permanent changes in the cortex of the brain because of the infection reaching his central nervous system. If this were true then there had been organic brain damage.

Symptoms vary in these children. Some of them seem highly distractable because they pay so much attention to irrelevant details that they cannot concentrate on the center of interest. Bright pictures, unexpected noises, and movements of other children are interferences to which the brain-injured child can offer little resistance.

These children have more than the usual difficulty in controlling their impulses. An important part of their training is to *teach them over and over again an acceptable pattern of behavior*. Sudden loss of control occurs when children are frustrated by their inability to achieve a certain goal or when some unexpected event disrupts their routine. Their explosive reaction is similar to a temper tantrum in a younger child. They may become quite violent for some trivial or unknown reason, and calm just as quickly when something diverts their attention.

Perhaps this is related to some abnormality of the biochemical metabolism (serotonin level) of the brain. However, certain of the tranquilizing pills may offer hope of modifying behavior. With or without their help, the emotions have to be dealt with. The professional maxim of patient indoctrination of controlled behavior is the only hope we now have. And we must use what we do have, not wait for magic.

Liang himself was eleven years old, tall and slim. He came and went several times. Sometimes he sat down on the floor, other times he stood, but always he kept peering intently into my face as if searching for the key to a riddle.

His mother continued her narrative.

Liang was sent to the primary school for one whole semester every day, but the teacher did not understand that he was retarded and punished him cruelly when he was troublesome. His mother went to school herself "to see" as she put it.

Liang was either at cross-purposes or fell asleep. There was no communication between the teacher and him.

Then Liang finally went into the second grade. According to his mother, this teacher had evidently been informed by the previous one that he would be difficult, and she, if anything, disliked him even more than her predecessor. She finally sent for his mother and told her that Liang was learning nothing and was disrupting the entire class and that she must remove him from the school.

"But I could not allow my son to leave school. To my husband and me it is very important that our children secure an education. I went to the school and tried to explain. They were unwilling to listen but when I insisted, for after all I do hold position in Taiwan, they finally placed him in another class.

"This teacher was very kind, very understanding. Liang became more stable. He began to learn his numbers, to read and to write."

Then came the news of Dr. Lin's experiment. She applied and Liang was accepted at the Chungsan school for the special class.

Through Miss Lee, I asked, "Is the situation any better at home now?"

"It is very difficult. My son and daughter sense that Liang makes me feel very guilty, very bad, and they hate him for it. I cannot leave him alone in the house with them. They hit him."

"And the neighboring children?"

"They dislike him and refuse to play with him. If he attempts to join them, they throw stones at him and call him names. Very, very bad names." She sighed. "He is very difficult. Eleven years old and still he tries to climb on my lap or my husband's."

"Do you permit it?"

She looked at me aghast. "An eleven-year-old boy?" There was a brief, brittle silence. "He is always asking me to buy something for him, or do something for him. Sometimes I try to love him but when I make affectionate advances, he pushes me away. I am a very nervous woman. I take tranquilizers every day. When Liang rejects me, I hit him!"

"Do you find it necessary to hit him at other times?"

"When he is bad, yes."

"And your husband?"

Liang's mother's eyes grew dark. "He hits him when he is at home. But that is seldom. For my husband, it is easy. He is away most of the time. He says it is the army. He must stay at the barracks. But there are other officers, other generals—they find time to come home to be with their families! I think he does not want to be bothered with Liang. It is a good way out for him. He can come and go as he pleases, but me—I am stuck, tied down, helpless! Unable to participate in the proper social functions for the wife of a general."

"You are never able to leave the house?"

"Only on very special occasions."

"How do you manage then?"

"I send Liang to the movies with my older son."

"And does this give you enough time?"

"They stay and see the movies a second and a third time when it is necessary." She added hastily. "This occurs only on very special occasions. Very, very special."

"There is nowhere else Liang can go—no one with whom he can stay—no one who ever wants him?"

She shook her head. "But he does go to visit his aunt sometimes."

"How does he behave there?"

She shook her head in bewilderment. "I do not understand it. His aunt, sometimes I think she is as foolish as Liang, the fuss she makes over him. Liang loves to go there. He would stay there forever, with an aunt, rather than with his natural mother." Her head continued to move from side to side broodingly. "I do not understand it. . . ."

On the ride back to the hotel, Miss Lee told me how the team coordinated the school program with their own efforts. The team consults with the teacher of the special classes once a week. If the child or parent becomes too difficult for the teacher, the parent is sent to Miss Lee, the psychiatric caseworker, and the child to Dr. Hsu, the psychiatrist, for individual treatment even while he continues to go to school.

There were several attempts to bring the general's wife to the center for consultation and treatment but she rejected all offers of assistance. When at the end of a year and a half of the experiment, Liang had made no advance in his behavior, and if anything grew worse, she finally called Miss Lee voluntarily seeking help. She has since been receiving treatment and it is to be hoped has succeeded in not only keeping herself but her son as well.

Miss Lee, incidentally, not only treats parents but also gives courses in how to make home visits, handle the children, and so on.

When I had my interview with Dr. Lin, he said that he had become interested in the mentally retarded fifteen years before he instituted the first classes for them within the Chungsan school. A team, whose services he had enlisted, made a house-to-house survey in the island's several provinces to get an accurate picture of the retarded—their numbers, status, and requirements—before he felt ready to plan what he hoped would be a truly constructive program.

In addition, he had to have an idea of their potential, of the kind of vocation that would be practicable for them, and of whether, after training, they could live alone and become independent in the community.

He was determined to go slowly in order to produce a soundly structured program.

"But fifteen years!"

Dr. Lin smiled. "The Chinese had done nothing for five thousand years. Fifteen years more was not too long to wait."

Some time later, Dr. Lin said he estimated that 6 to 7 percent are mentally retarded in Taiwan. In almost every country I visited, including our own, the percentage varied from 3 to 4 percent. The Taiwan figure seemed very high to me. But when a team member began to speak of *curing* retardates, it began to make more sense to me.

For instance, after one year of special education at the Chungsan school, 3 out of 30 children tested from 90 to 100 IQ who had previously tested only 70. These were really emotional or social retardates,* and Dr. Lin told me that there may be many of them on the island, accounting for the high statistics.

A true retardate can frequently be rehabilitated, trained to perform to his utmost potential, which can be amazing, but cured in the sense of restoring him to an undamaged state—no! Not with what we know at

---

* Social retardates are the result of economically and culturally deprived backgrounds.

present. The time may come, but to my knowledge it has not as yet arrived.

Frequently there is a correlation between retardation and emotional disturbance. Many of the emotionally disturbed function as retardates. When the emotional illness is properly diagnosed and correctly treated, the person may be restored to an undamaged intellectual state. If this is so, as has been suggested by the number who have made marked gains on retesting, then one might assume that Taiwan suffers no appreciably greater morbidity of retardation than the rest of the world.

Testing has been a great problem in the Orient, for the reasonably perfected Western tests, like Stanford-Binet, etc., are not culture-free. As an example, questions relating to certain musical instruments cannot be asked of an Oriental if such instruments are unknown to the Far East.

Dr. Lin now uses an IQ test which they find quite reliable and useful. He has already tested 3,000 children. One of his conclusions has been that males have a higher rate of mental deficiency than females, and secondly, that mental retardation is higher among the economically deprived—farmers, vendors and other small merchants, and laborers.*

Any parent may now come to the clinic for diagnosis. The fee is $10 Taiwan, which is approximately 25¢ U.S., for a visit. The cost of the test is $30 Taiwan, which is about 75¢. If the family is very poor, the consultation and test are free.

So far as I know, there is only one such clinic on the island.

The rehabilitation of retardates is a new concept to many people all over the world. They have had to learn about it, to test, to digest before admitting that it even exists.

The work in Taiwan is just beginning but it is going slowly and steadily forward. It took almost two years to prove conclusively that there was merit to further education, training, and psychiatric help as exemplified by Ko-Choung's successful retesting and by Liang's mother finally accepting therapy.

A few months ago I heard from Dr. Tsung yi-Lin. He wrote to me:

"Yes, things are moving fast here. The City Bureau of Education has already initiated the teachers' training program for the mentally re-

---

* The larger percentage of retardates lies in this group the world over.

tarded using our center (Taiwan University Hospital Neurological Division) and the special classes at the Chungsan primary school as the base. Six teachers will be enrolled in the first year during which they will spend six months in our center and six months at the Chungsan primary school. It is also planned that they will start new classes for the mentally retarded after their training."

As of 1968 forty new classes have been established for the retarded.

5

Hong Kong

As we walked out of the customs in Hong Kong, I saw a long aisle lined with smiling Chinese faces looking expectantly in our direction. They had not come for any celebrity, merely for us.

Suddenly two Chinese boys thrust a huge sheaf of flowers in my hands while their amah beamed up at me, and their father, gentleman-jockey Alex Lam, a former business associate of my husband's, spoke a few words of welcome. Then came a babel of brief introductions as my husband and I passed down the aisle into a waiting limousine

Hong Kong was ceded by China to the British in 1841. The 29-square-mile island of Hong Kong, which includes some smaller islands, is separated from Kowloon (approximately 3¾ square miles) on the mainland by one-half a mile of water. Beyond Kowloon lie the New Territories and some 235 small islands adding up to a grand total of 398 square miles for the British Crown Colony.

Kowloon with its New Territories lies at the doorstep of Communist China. It could be swallowed up by the Communists at any time. The chances are excellent that they will never avail themselves of the privilege. The Communists need the outlet for free trade cutting across bureaucratic rules and restrictions. For example, Americans can export to Hong Kong traders, and some American goods may be resold to Red China without the knowledge of the Americans, who are forbidden by law to trade with Red China directly or indirectly.

As we drove along under the glaring sun, I received my first sight of the immigrants who had poured into Hong Kong. Cheong sams, the knee-length dress of the women, cotton chien sam foos, the short jackets and trousers, and Western dress merged into a mass that flowed through the streets like endless churning rivers. Then we caught the view of the stunning harbor as a parade of a hundred ships glided through or lay at anchor in the purple waters. Both Hong Kong and Kowloon have little flat land. The mountains rise sharply from the sea. Of the total of 398 square miles, only 55 square miles are arable, and consequently people must be employed by industry in order to survive.

I phoned the USIS and discovered that Mrs. Arax Warner had been alerted to assist me. She is the wife of John Warner, head of Hong Kong's new art museum. Mr. and Mrs. Warner are both English.

Arax Warner spent two days arranging appointments for me.

A pleasant English lady received me at my first stop, the Department of Education. I soon discovered that public education for retarded children has not as yet been established. There has been no provision in the educational budget for the mentally retarded, and consequently there is not a single class for them in the public school system.

However, the Hong Kong school system has special problems. The population explosion, due partly to the influx of Chinese refugees, has made for a frantic scrabble by parents for school placement. There is no compulsory education in Hong Kong, but parents are anxious for their children to attend school, and they have instilled in their children a deep respect and eagerness for learning.

Three government colleges have been set up for teacher training. The plan is to provide for 33,000 new placements a year for the next three years. There has been a Herculean effort to get as many children as possible into the primary schools. There are 40 children to a class, and gradually the authorities are reaching their objective of finding a place for every child. The primary grades take in six- to twelve-year-olds.

With all this basic work to accomplish, plans for the care of mentally handicapped children are only now slowly being put into effect.

On my third day in Hong Kong, Arax Warner sent me to see Miss Daphne Ho at the Department of Social Welfare on Causeway Bay.

Miss Ho was sympathetic, patient, and cooperative. She confirmed that, as of 1963, there was no institution or school for the mentally retarded in Hong Kong. She reiterated what I had learned in Taiwan: The Chinese have a great love for their children, but when they get desperate beyond human hope they will abandon them. Most of these abandoned children end up at North Point Camp. Since my visit the Rehabilitation Center at Aberdeen has been completed, and the children are now being sent there.

Accompanied by an assistant of Miss Ho's, I visited North Point Camp. This government-supported center for the handicapped and displaced persons was organized in 1938, at the beginning of the Sino-Japanese War, and was designed to care for refugees from the mainland. It has nine dormitory-like huts, each housing about 35 people, clustered on a barren piece of property which the Chinese are now trying to beautify with trees and young shrubs.

The retarded-children center is set apart from the adult center. These children range in age from five to sixteen. Some have been abandoned as subnormal, others are children of divorced parents who are wanted by neither. Most of the retarded children in this center were considered trainable—moderately to severely retarded. Very few seemed really educable or mildly retarded, but because no standardized tests were as yet being used here, it was hard to be certain.

Retardates, numbering about 50, were divided into two groups, one for the totally dependent and one for the less severely retarded. Perhaps two or three children of the latter group will receive academic training of some kind; the rest will be given manual training in the hope that they will eventually be able to work. The totally dependent and 26 retarded children will eventually be transferred out of the center to Tung Wah Hospital. The 50 children are cared for by 5 amahs on day duty and 4 for the night shift. Always on call is the doctor in charge of the clinic and his assistant, a male dresser or orderly. Two nurses, soon to be assigned, will refer the inmates with serious illnesses to a regular hospital.

The children are taught to dress, feed, and care for themselves, to tie their shoelaces and wash their bowls after eating. In the classroom they are taught painting, drawing, response to music, and basket weaving. Only one or two of the children are able to learn the latter. One or two of the children are destructive; few have severe emotional problems.

Food is served five times a day. All the children have mattresses, and the very young have cots as well. I was assured they are living a better life than that of the average citizen in Hong Kong. But North Point Camp was severely overcrowded and sorely in need of a new center which was being built at Aberdeen to take care of the very severely and profoundly retarded children who will never be able to care for themselves.

It took three years before the new rehabilitation center was completed. The 253 residents of North Point Camp moved in on the last day of March, 1964. Aberdeen, the largest of the Department of Social Welfare institutions, has a capacity of 500.

North Point Camp keeps the mentally retarded as long as possible. Their dischargees usually ask for a hawker's license, for peddling is about the only way they can hope to earn a living. North Point tries to find them homes for their return to community living. Actually, however, very few of them are really able to leave the camp and earn their own living.

From the camp's grounds, I saw small, black-coated figures, protected from the sun by huge round hats, picking their way up a roadless mountainside to their crude huts. Across their shoulders they carried bamboo poles with pails of water suspended from either end. The little water carried such a difficult distance must serve the needs of entire families.

These people were refugees from the mainland. They exist on incredibly minimal wages.

I said to the social worker, "Those poor people, what do *they* do with their retarded children?"

"They hope for them to die, and most of them do. The family has only one meal a day, at night. What food there is is divided among the nonhandicapped. They just do not feed the retardate. They leave him to starve to death."

At the time I was in Hong Kong, North Point Camp was the only residential unit that could take any children at all. I inquired about a nonresidential unit and was told that just this fall a day care center had been established at the Old Tsan Yuk building.* My guide told me he would give me directions and a worker would meet me there the next day and show me around.

As we were leaving, I saw a small Chinese girl taking leave of a large Mongoloid boy. He stood there with two large tears rolling down his plain face.

My guide spoke to the girl in Chinese. The girl smiled a little, examined me minutely, then answered. My guide translated. "The boy is always sad when his sister leaves. But she is very good. She comes every week when it is possible to get a train from Shat-tin."

"Don't they run regularly?"

"Yes, but the people increase even more regularly. We have too many people, too many for the unskilled jobs available, for the homes, for the schools, and for the trains. When you go to Shat-tin, you will see what I mean. On Sundays and holidays they wait for half a day in a queue and cannot get on any train at all."

"What a devoted sister to make such a trip!"

"You know, she isn't his sister at all. A Buddhist monk found them after the war. They were both abandoned at roadsides. He took them home and raised them until he could no longer care for them. Then he brought them here. The girl, she was bright. She had already been taught a great deal. She completed her studies quickly and now teaches in Shat-tin. The boy, as you can see," he shrugged his shoulders. "But she has never forsaken him. She returns as often as possible, always bringing him little presents. . . ."

"I wonder what her real ambition is."

The guide spoke with the girl and reported, "She has only one ambition; to save enough money to make a real home for her brother."

"To sacrifice so much for someone who needs her!"

My guide translated. With a shake of her head, the girl said simply, "It is I who need him."

---

*On January 9, 1964, another such day center was opened called the Tung Tau Resettlement Estate with a capacity for 60 mentally retarded and the same kind of program as at Tsan Yuk Center. Additional classes were started in both centers on an experimental basis for 40 older children for training to develop manual dexterity as a prelude to vocational training.

The next day I took a taxi to the day-care center at Old Tsan Yuk. The lobby of the former hospital was dirt-encrusted, with peeling stairs leading upward. Standing wearily in the lobby were a number of Chinese—probably parents waiting for their children.

This center has been established since January 12, 1961. It caters to 40 retarded children living with their families. Children are divided into two classes in accordance with their social and emotional maturity levels. Transport is provided.

I was received by Miss Catherine Chang, the officer in charge of the Center. A trim, energetic woman who had studied in England, Miss Chang explained that the Tsan Yuk Center had been in operation only since the spring of 1962. Its 40 children do not have the benefit of a special diagnostic center. Mr. Ko Ki Chung, whom I had met at the Department of Welfare, does informal mental testing at no charge. The results are supplemented by information obtained by a social worker on the child's developmental history. The child guidance center of the University also does testing.

Miss Chang explained that it is impossible to diagnose accurately because there is still no culture-free test for the East, and these children came from widely varied cultural backgrounds. When the center opened, the registered cases were referred to them from the Department of Welfare at Causeway Bay. Some children came from public schools, some from families living in the huge flotilla of sampans in Hong Kong harbor.

Some sampan families are not as poverty-stricken as the refugees on the mountains in their wooden huts; many who could afford better homes ashore remain in their floating houses by choice. But even they learned quickly of the facilities at Tsan Yuk. The waiting list for admission is already too long.

The children attend the center from 9:00 to 3:30. The timetable includes habit, sensory, physical, and speech training, handwork, music, and movement training in simple domestic tasks. This training is supplemented by the parents who come to meetings regularly to receive instruction. Miss Chang said the parents are eager to learn, cooperative, and touchingly grateful.

As in Taipei at the Chungsan school, there is a classroom for the so-called trainables, roughly anyone with below 50 IQ and their educables with IQ's from 50 to 70.

Miss Chang brought me to the trainable class first. Like the rest of the building, the room with its peeling plaster and unpainted walls was in a state of disrepair but the teacher had attempted to brighten it with colored drawings made by the children.

My first impression was of a group of busy children at long low tables arranged in a U shape. After a few minutes the group began to become individualized. The children realized that they had a visitor, and even a blind child's face was turned in my direction. Soon one or two of them began to misbehave in an effort to get more attention.

One boy with a broad, empty face, suffering from Down's syndrome,* was very severely handicapped even for a Mongoloid. Like so many other Far Eastern children, he had suffered from brain damage during a high fever in his infancy. Perhaps as antibiotics and other medicines become available, this toll will be reduced.

Another boy with a bowl-shaped haircut sat at his table and laughed silently but incessantly. Miss Chang said he was completely out of contact with his surroundings. They are keeping him, hoping that some day soon they will be able to reach him in some way and to discover whether his problem is imbecility or is emotionally based. He, like others, recognizes his family when they call for him.

The preponderance of boys reminded me that on Taiwan there were more boy retardates than girls. Miss Chang's explanation for this apparent discrepancy was that the Oriental people are more concerned for their boy children and work harder at getting them placed in institutions where they will receive training.

At one of the tables the children were crayoning guide-lined outlines. Miss Chang said their progress was most interesting. At first the colors would run haphazardly over the entire page; then gradually, the children became aware of the outlines, and finally they were able to color quite accurately within the lines.

At another table, it was surprising to see how skillful they were at working jigsaw puzzles. These ranged from sets with large, simple pieces to sets of over a hundred small ones. And these moderate and severely retarded children were fitting them together. Miss Chang said

---

* Down's disease or Down's syndrome, so called after Dr. John Langdon Down of Great Britain, who in 1866 described the characteristics of Mongolism.

she started them off on the very simple puzzles and let each progress to the more complicated ones according to his own ability.

I noticed two toy telephones. Miss Chang said they encouraged the children who were without the power of speech. Just holding the receiver to the ear gave them pleasure.

Little attempt is made to teach the children academically, but music has proved a valuable tool and is used constantly. The children are taught to move to it, to sing, to respond to it in games such as musical chairs, which encourages them to run. In another good game, the teacher hides an object and the children look for it.

The approximated IQ's were no higher than those of many of the children at North Point Camp, and yet there was a difference. Unlike the abandoned residents of North Point Camp, these children at Tsan Yuk did not look lost. Indeed, as Miss Chang told me, most of them were happy and secure in the affection of their families.

The program for the educable or upward of 50 IQ group is more advanced. They are being taught to write numbers and letters, but Miss Chang said that so far they have met with little success. One of the work projects, the making of artificial flowers, has produced some realistic pussy willows.

In honor of my visit, the teacher called together the little band she had trained. She sat at the piano with five boys and three girls beside her. They played the cymbals, drums, and triangles with two sticks, swinging right along on key. Their obvious success made even the most impassive Oriental face flush with pleasure. I complimented the teacher on her accomplishments and asked if she had been specially trained to teach retarded children. She replied that all the teachers at Old Tsan Yuk were recruited from the Civil Service rosters and that no previous training in this work was required.

The children in both groups undress themselves for naps every day and have been taught to find their own pillows and blankets. Even the little blind boy knows how to find his way. In cold weather, they have their tea parties indoors and in summer they picnic out of doors. Their noon meal consists of rice, vegetables, and meat or fish. The midday meal is an essential part of the Center's training, providing teaching of good manners and consideration for others. The children may eat with chopsticks or a spoon. For many of them it is the only meal of the day, but in the afternoon they get a snack of milk and cookies. The children are ecstatic over this treat. Most of them have never even tasted anything so extravagant at home. At the end of the day, the children must wash their hands and faces, each with his own washcloth. No one may leave until all have passed inspection.

Tsan Yuk cares for children from the age of eight to fourteen. Then they are discharged. And what happens to them afterward? When I asked this question of Miss Chang, she sighed and shrugged.*

The next day I returned to the Magistracy at Causeway Bay. A social worker, Miss Lung, was assigned to accompany me on the family visits. In the taxi, Miss Lung told me that the Tam family lived in the third cubicle at Number One Moon Street. The description seemed an unusual one but soon proved to be extremely accurate.

On entering the long, low, barracks-like dwelling, we almost fell over a woman who sat sewing in the dark hallway. Four families occupied the hall, one right after another in dark, damp, narrow areas separated only by curtains. On the left of the hallway were the cement cubicles. We entered number three, which was approximately six by nine feet in size.

The room was almost filled by the "kang," a platform-bed traditional in China. Above this, a shelf about two and a half feet wide had been built for the retarded boy, who was twelve years old. The cement floor was littered with orange peels and crumpled papers. Pots and pans were piled on a wooden chest against one wall, and a wooden crate containing rice bowls and teacups stood near the bed. The small barred window provided the only ventilation and gave the cubicle a final prison-like touch.

I was told that Number One Moon Street had a single community kitchen in the rear, and that eight more families lived on a narrow balcony overhead. In a community that size, some families had to take their turns cooking at night in order to have a meal ready for the next day.

During my interview with the family of Cubicle No. 3, Ngai-Tsai

---

* Since the construction of the Center at Aberdeen, some retarded who are believed able to function in the community are trained there.

came in. He was a slender boy with a face that suggested vulnerability rather than retardation. He watched a little girl playing in the room. Did she belong to Mrs. Tam, too? Mrs. Tam shook her head. No, a neighbor paid her to take care of the girl; her own little girl was five years old and went to school.

And Ngai-Tsai, did he go to school too?

No school would take him.

Mr. Tam is a temporary worker who earns six Hong Kong dollars a day—about one U.S. dollar. But he is able to find work only about twenty days a month. The total income of the entire family is roughly $30 U.S.

The rent for the cubicle is $10 Hong Kong, and the family must pay $13 Hong Kong for the daughter's schooling. She is waiting to be admitted to a government school.

Ngai-Tsai was born on the mainland of China in a remote country village. To bear him, Mrs. Tam was in labor for over twenty-four hours. No doctor or nurse was available, only a midwife. During the difficult delivery the mother lost consciousness, but the father told afterward of how blue the baby's face had been, and of how long he had to be slapped to make him cry.

When Ngai-Tsai was one month old, the parents escaped to Hong Kong, leaving the boy in China with his grandmother. He remained there for two years and was fed only rice. Finally an aunt smuggled him out to Hong Kong.

The family soon realized that Ngai-Tsai was not normal. The first symptom they noticed was his crying; he cried often and for abnormally long periods. At the age of four, he still could not speak. He was five years old before he began to feed himself. He did not become toilet trained until he was seven. Both parents say the boy is slow to learn and that his memory is poor. They love him and are kind to him, but the outside world is cruel.

Children call Ngai-Tsai crazy; they ridicule and persecute him. When he goes into the public outhouse, the boys follow him and steal his pants; he emerges disgraced and ashamed. One day he wandered from home and the boys from his neighborhood followed him unseen. Finally they attacked him and tore off his clothes. Stark naked, he ran a gauntlet of pointed fingers, laughter, and obscene jeers until he found his way home. For days afterward, he cowered in the cubicle and refused to leave it.

As she told this story, Mrs. Tam broke down and cried. She said that she now feels obliged to stay constantly on the alert to protect Ngai-Tsai, and that this has made it impossible for her to seek work and to help supplement the meager family income.

Would one of the neighbors mind him?

She smiled bitterly as she explained to me that they were the worst offenders. They insulted her and her child daily. She dared not make scenes for fear that the landlord would ask her to leave as a troublemaker. Many families were waiting for this cubicle. If they left, it would mean returning to a wooden refugee hut on the top of a mountain.

With so much building going on in Hong Kong, was there no other place to move to?

Yes, a housing development was being erected for poor people, but the rental was high and already 19,000 families had already applied for 5,000 places.* There was no other place to go.

What did they do when her husband came from work?

"After supper, when the weather is cold, we go to sleep at eight o'clock. All poor people do. We have no light and nowhere to go."

"Can a place be found for Ngai-Tsai?"

She brightened. "There is great hope. He has been enrolled on the waiting list at Old Tsan Yuk. As soon as there is a place for him, he will go. Social Welfare will pay the fare."

I asked her if she would permit her son to live in an institution if one were available.

"An institution?" she shook her head violently. "Ngai-Tsai is a gentle boy. He is part of our family and we love him dearly. If only the neighbors would leave us in peace—"

As we rose to go, I asked the social worker who the handsome couple were in a framed picture on the chest. She told me they were Mr. and Mrs. Tam ten short years ago. There was only the faintest resemblance between that beautiful woman and the worn one who bade us good-bye.

---

* The government has embarked on one of the biggest housing programs in the world, but the rate of immigration has outraced the rate of construction.

A professor who knew of my interest in retarded children arranged for me to meet a family whose home was outside the city, in the rural village of Shat-tin. We parked at the waterfront, for the village lies close to the sea. An emaciated dog greeted us. Ragged children were everywhere, and people in native dress wearing long black pigtails.

We paused in a narrow street. Papaya melons, looking like oversized beads, were strung up to form a curtain. Orange and white Chinese signs blazed over food counters. Bean curds, prawns, orange and white Chinese potatoes were being cooked in vats of oil by street vendors. The aromas of frying foods mingled with the dark saline scent of the sea. Everyone was preparing for the Chinese New Year.

After some time and after several water buffaloes had passed, we drove out into the country, beyond a small bridge to a white stone house ornamented with carving. Mrs. Chouyen received us in a living room decorated with beautiful wall scrolls and furnished with a simple coffee table, a modern couch, and the inevitable maroon leatherette chairs. On the corner table flowers were gracefully arranged in a beautiful Ming vase. The Chouyens were not only highly educated but extremely wealthy, having large real estate holdings.

An exquisite young girl came in with a tall, handsome boy. Mrs. Chouyen introduced them to me. They were followed by sixteen-year-old Ching—poor Ching, with her rounded back, protruding teeth, and straight-cut black hair.

Ching was born normal in 1946 in Peking. At first she was an alert infant, brighter than most. She started to speak at ten months and showed a lively curiosity in everything. But at two she suffered a very high fever for three full days and nights. A year later, she had a similar attack.

It was after this that her curious behavior began. Intermittently she appeared very bright, then extraordinarily obtuse, stubborn, and aggressive.

She was sent to kindergarten but her difficult behavior caused serious problems. She was disobedient. She sought out other children but she was so destructive and messy that they refused to play with her. So she remained alone and miserable.

When Ching was four, one of the teachers pointed out to her parents that there was something very wrong with their child. Ching spent two more years in kindergarten, but her behavior grew more erratic. When asked to sing, she refused, but when everyone else had finished, she would begin. When she was sent to grade school, everyone began to learn to write and count except Ching. She failed in the first, second, and third grades. Mrs. Chouyen was forced to take her out, but Ching begged and begged to go back. The school agreed to accept her, but once again she disrupted the entire class.

One day in Ching's ninth year, the children made sport of her. They grabbed her and tossed her back and forth in the air. She was too frightened to cry out. Then they dropped her and she fell, breaking her leg.

After that incident, she was dropped from school entirely, and she has been at home. Without schooling, she has become progressively worse. An examination given her when she was ten seems to have established the fact that her intelligence is that of a six-year-old child. Her circulation and coordination are poor; she falls constantly.

I asked Mrs. Chouyen what effect Ching had on the lives of the other two children.

"They are very good. See how quiet they are. They let her have her way in everything. She is very demanding and they understand that. . . . When they were younger, they were teased unmercifully about having a sister like Ching. Now that their friends don't see Ching, it is better. They go to their friends' homes if there is any visiting to be done."

"And *your* friends? Do they come here?"

"I have almost forgotten what it is like to have friends. My husband and I have had to be content without many things.

"When Ching was eleven, she had convulsions. That was the worst time of all. Since then she can never be left alone. Not even for a moment. My other daughter goes to school during the day and the boy goes at night so that they can take turns staying with Ching. She is under constant medication, a thorazine concentrate. She takes it three times a day."

During this interchange Ching kept trying to climb onto her mother's lap. She whimpered constantly. Abruptly she cried out and pointed: "The foreign lady is talking about me. I want her to stop!" Then, "The lady has much makeup on—mascara, rouge, lipstick, and jewelry. If I had jewelry, I would be beautiful, too. Give me my ring!"

Her brother rushed out to get it for her.

Mrs. Chouyen, distressed, explained that the cold weather was very bad for Ching. She was much better in the summertime.

Suddenly Ching began to sing. It was a song she had learned in school long ago. Then she started to cry that she wanted to go to a schoolmate's house and began to enumerate all the places where she had once been. Her brother returned with the ring. She slipped it on and then fell quiet.

But soon she began once more. Mrs. Chouyen explained that Ching was complaining about the other two children, that she was intensely jealous of them, even though they petted her, complimented her, and gave her constant attention.

Since Ching had been normal in behavior, there was reason to believe that her problem resulted from specific brain damage. Her unpredictable behavior, lack of coordination, confusion of time, sudden loss of control and temper tantrums all follow the pattern of a brain-injured child. But brain-injured children are not necessarily retarded in all areas. Ching, with her sudden recall of incidents, songs, and conversations, did not display the behavior pattern of a true retardate. I suspected that Ching was a deeply disturbed emotional retardate.

Before I left Hong Kong, I went to the True Light Middle School to see Dr. Irene Chang, who had once been a member of the executive board of the World Federation for Mental Health. Dr. Chang was busy but gracious. She informed me that another American had preceded me who was also interested in the field of mental retardation. She thought I might know her: Mrs. Sargent Shriver, sister to the then President John F. Kennedy.

Dr. Chang has been agitating for her countrymen to assume educational responsibility for the less fortunate much in the tradition of her mother before her. The older Mrs. Chang was one of the founders of the Po Leung Kuk school, the first vocational training school for homeless young women and children. She had to beg, charm, and cajole people into donating funds for the school which still continues her work and profession. Her daughter is no less determined.

The True Light Middle School is a private Protestant school comparable to a mission school. The school receives a small government subsidy. More than 3,000 children attend, and alumni in the United

States send money to help keep it functioning. Dr. Chang herself believes in the teachings of Confucius, as did her mother before her. She told me she had consented to come to the True Light Middle School for only a few years. It was my impression that she wished to have the maximum time to devote to the needs of the mentally retarded.

In 1954, the Hong Kong Council of Social Services urged the Governor and Commander-in-Chief of Hong Kong to provide facilities for the mentally retarded. It was then that the government decided to place these mental retardates in the Residential Center of North Point Camp.

Dr. Chang urged social welfare institutions to assume responsibility for women and children needing care and protection, hounded the government to provide teachers for the retarded at North Point Camp, and then exerted additional pressure to bring the expert Dr. H. T. Hilliard from England in 1960 to organize and train these teachers.

Dr. Chang felt that the Medical Department should be responsible for the very severely and profoundly retarded who can do nothing whatsoever for themselves; Social Welfare should care for the less severely and moderately retarded (IQ's 25 to 50) who can learn self-care and some skills; and the Education Department should provide special classes in special schools for those with IQ's of 50 to 70, who can learn simple academic and vocational skills.

Dr. Chang is fighting for a school for retarded children in each district.

It is interesting to note the social and economic results of women's inferior status in the Far East. New multiple marriages have been ruled illegal in Hong Kong but polygamy established before 1960 is recognized. As a result there are still many families where Chinese men have several wives.

The poor women work unceasingly in Hong Kong. There is no middle class. The wives of the wealthy spend an enormous amount of time playing mah-jongg, often for prohibitive stakes. Some of them start at nine o'clock in the morning and end at midnight, with their husbands' knowledge and approval. The elaborate jewelry they wear is indicative of great personal fortunes.

The Chinese women of Hong Kong do little organization work as we know it in the United States, for example. It is only recently that

Dr. Chang helped organize groups, similar to our own National Association for Retarded Children and other organizations of parents of mentally retarded children. Hong Kong now has two parent groups, one on the east side of the island and the other on the west. They are now attempting to form a similar organization in Kowloon.

Dr. Chang has given extramural courses in special education and special services for welfare but she feels that education is sadly lacking in this field in Hong Kong. She lobbies constantly, and in 1959 a Chinese British subject was given a combined Kennedy Foundation Fellowship and Asian grant to come to America for two years of training. When he returned he was placed as a social welfare officer. There was much objection to his working solely for the retarded when there was so much need among normal children, so they finally compromised by having him work in both areas. Despite this extra work load he managed to establish two training centers and worked on plans for a third on Kowloon.

As I left, Dr. Chang, the indomitable humanist, quoted a saying of Confucius: "Thoughtful people cannot always be made to understand, but they can always be persuaded that it is reasonable to follow. And when they follow the wise and the good, they are happy."

6

Thailand

TODAY IN THAILAND, WORK WITH RETARDED CHILDREN BEGINS AND ENDS in one place—the hospital on Ding Dang Road in the capital city of Bangkok. This nation, formerly known as Siam, was opened to Western trade almost a century before Japan was; but its progress since has been slower and harder. It was not until the second half of the nineteenth century that the country embarked on a concentrated program of modernization, and it was not until 1932 that Siam became a constitutional monarchy under the name Thailand, from the Thai meaning "free people." The present King and Queen are enlightened and progressive monarchs who have contributed generously toward the building of the first hospital for mental retardates on Ding Dang Road.

The care of retardates is under the supervision of Dr. Phon Sang Sing Keo, Undersecretary to the Minister of Health. Dr. Rosjong Dasnanjali is the Director of the Institute for Mental Deficiency on Ding Dang Road. Dr. Rosjong suggested that I drop his surname because of the difficulty of pronouncing it. The building itself is a glistening glass structure—a modern anomaly from the Western world set down on a barren patch of Thailand.

On my visit to the hospital I was escorted up shiny stairs to a sunfilled room to wait for Dr. Rosjong. On a blackboard up front was written this brave organizational outline:

Ministry of Health
Department of Medical Services
Division of Mental Hospitals
Mental Deficiency Hospital

3 Sections

ADMINISTRATIVE	MEDICAL	SCHOOL
CORRESPONDENCE	EXAMINATION AND DIAGNOSIS	CLASSES
ACCOUNT AND FINANCE		WORKSHOP
MEDICAL EQUIPMENT	INTELLIGENCE TEST	GARDENING
		FARMING
TEACHING EQUIPMENT	SPECIAL APTITUDE TEST	MUSIC
KITCHEN AND LAUNDRY		
		PLAY
	RESEARCH	SIGHTSEEING

Dr. Rosjong, who had spent a year studying mental retardation in England, soon arrived to show me around. He told me in English that his colleagues divide retardates into three categories: nontrainable, trainable, and educable. The 150 children at the hospital ranged from seven to eighteen years of age. There is not a single nursery school for the retardates in all Thailand, and the doctor explained that if the family cannot cope with the child, he is committed to the general hospital or the Hospital for the Mentally Ill. For years Buddhist monasteries were the only sanctuaries for the retardates. Unfortunately these monasteries had meager funds, and when they could no longer afford to care for their retardates, the children were sent home. If the home had disappeared, they were put out on the streets.

I asked Dr. Rosjong what psychological impact a retarded child had on Thai parents. He replied that most families accepted the hardship without complaint. In their culture, every child was a blessing, even a retarded one. And the average family had five children.

We walked out into a corridor that led past sunny, spacious classrooms. Because of the difficulty in obtaining teachers, the hospital's 8 trained nurses were working with the children in a teaching capacity. One nurse was working with a boy to teach him to tie his shoelaces.

There were 5 full-time teachers. I saw a young man teaching carpentry—showing the children how to cut and assemble wooden horses. This was the beginning of the first vocational training workshop.

I asked what academic training the children received. Dr. Rosjong said they were being taught to distinguish colors, to read, and to write. He hoped that eventually some would reach the fourth grade level. The program was still too new to tell how successful it would be.

As the children ate in a large, airy dining room, they gave no outward manifestation of emotional problems. They were clean and well cared for and seemed to be contented. All told, they numbered 200 inpatients and 50 day ones. Dr. Rosjong planned to care for 400 here, and a separated special home was preparing a 40-bed unit for the care of the "very severely" and "profoundly" retarded.

On the main floor of the hospital was a suite of offices. Here a single social worker was testing several children, using variations of the Binet, Wechsler, and other IQ tests. Here too the nurses and the hospital's 5 physicians gave the children periodic physical examinations. Soon the staff would be increased by a physiotherapist and a therapist to help the children with speech, art, and play training.

In the corridor a young girl came by with a tall, dark boy of about sixteen. They were brother and sister. She had brought him in for testing. She said that the boy, Chaiporn, had been delivered without difficulty. But he had had a high fever during infancy, and at the age of three he suffered from severe convulsions.

The boy stood very still. I was told that he seemed to have the ability of a child of seven or eight. His sister said that he helped at home with the household chores but did so only in response to commands. The only child he played or associated with was his younger brother, on whom he lavished great affection.

Chaiporn never went to school despite the fact that in Thailand seven years of elementary education is now compulsory. Ten years ago, 70 percent of the population could read and write. The fine for keeping a child at home is 100 to 500 bahts—$5 to $25 U.S. But, as in many countries of the world, the retarded child is permitted to stay at home.

So Chaiporn had been taught nothing—neither academically nor vocationally. There had been no place for him.

The sister turned to the doctor. "What are we to do with this boy?"

What indeed?

Dr. Rosjong arranged for his wife and a social worker to accompany me to the home of a family with a retarded child. On the way to the car, he told me how desperately he needed personnel. His little staff could not care adequately for its 250 charges, yet countless other children needed help—and there was not another trained person in the whole country.

Anxiously but not hopefully I suggested that he appeal to the United States Information Service and to his own government. He shook his head sadly. "So much red tape. So much time is consumed. And in the end so little can be done." *

Dr. Rosjong gave directions to his wife, worker, and chauffeur and we drove off.

---

* Dr. Rosjong did beleaguer his government, which granted him funds for a trip to Europe, the United States, and Australia so that he could learn more of the needs of the mentally retarded.

The route we took passed between dense clusters of shacks perched on wooden stilts in sodden fields. Finally the car stopped on the road and we got out. Wooden planks formed the only path on which to cross the deep muddy flats. We made our way gingerly to one house and entered.

There, directly before me, in a wicker basket swinging on ropes from the rafters, lay the retarded child, sleeping. A fly lit on his cheek; the mother, Mrs. Chanko, automatically stuck out her foot and sent the basket into motion, then turned away.

We took seats on benches and boxes among Mrs. Chanko's several visitors, all of whom sat motionless and stared at us steadily. Mrs. Chanko, established at a sewing machine with a small baby girl on her knee, wore a loose yellow print blouse and red cotton skirt. Her feet were bare.

With Mrs. Rosjong serving as interpreter, the interview began. Mrs. Chanko said she had had four children. One of them had died. The delivery of the retarded child had been quite normal. Three or four days after his birth, he contracted jaundice, but she noticed no after-effects. He was breast-fed and was a quiet child. At the age of eight months, however, he had a very high fever. She began to notice something different. He cried but never smiled. Mostly he just lay there as he was lying now. She said he was asleep, but this kind of sleep was more like a stupor. It made him appear to be a most profound retardate, almost completely out of touch with his environment.

By now the doorway was filled with children, dirty, ragged, and bursting with curiosity. The littlest ones walked around completely naked. No one chased them away. Mrs. Chanko, noticing that another fly had settled on her sleeping child, again set the basket in motion. Then she reached under her blouse and drew out a drooping breast and impersonally gave it to the child on her knee.

Had the retarded child proved to be much of a hardship? The mother pondered, then suddenly burst forth. The child causes a great deal of work. He cannot feed himself. Everything must be done for him. He is able to walk but must be kept indoors most of the time. He cries a great deal and often at night.

What does she do then?

Sometimes she rocks him. Other times she turns over and lets him cry.

The child ties her down. She and her husband have gone to the movies only once in three years. They always went together before this. Now they must take turns going alone. And the medicine for him is so costly, she cannot even buy a silver bracelet for herself or her little girl!

Does her husband resent this child?

No, her husband loves this child above the others. He is very devoted to him.

And the neighbors. Are they unkind to the child?

No, the neighbors are very kind, very helpful and sympathetic. They understand. It is the oldest boy who does not. He hates the retarded child and hits him constantly. She would like to be relieved of this child, but the government will not take him until he is seven. As if sensing a possible disapproval, she cradled the little girl in her arms. "What else can the mother do? The government will not sterilize you until after you have had five children. And for a poor woman five is too many."

I noticed that the little girl was wearing a silver chain with a mesh locket around her neck. I admired it.

"It is only silver," Mrs. Chanko said quickly. "People of consequence have gold. But with that child"—she glanced over at the one sleeping in the basket—"it will never be possible. My husband works as a custodian and makes only 400 to 500 bahts a month ($20 to $30 U.S.), and with that five people plus grandparents must be fed. I sew to make some extra, but even with that it will be many years before I can have a gold bracelet." She jogged the cradle and added discouragedly, "If ever."

At the suggestion of Mrs. Jensen of the United States Information Service, I telephoned the Princess Prem to ask for an interview. Though the Princess kept busy working on innumerable committees for public welfare, she gave me an appointment. The next day I took a taxi to 77 Rama Road.

Her Highness received me cordially and ushered me into a living room furnished in Western style with a low-slung leatherette couch and chairs. Her concern for the physically and mentally handicapped takes practical form. She employs a blind boy to answer the phone, which seemed to be ringing constantly, a crippled man who types, and a retarded houseboy whose father is a schoolteacher.

The Princess told me that of the 26 million people in Thailand
200,000 are mentally retarded. Quite seriously she said, "It is too much."

I told her that it was far too much everywhere in the world—that in
fact, because the percentage of mentally handicapped varies little from
country to country, a thorough survey of Thailand would probably add
another million to that 200,000.

The Princess looked at me with incredulity but was too polite to
dispute me.

Up to a year ago, she told me, Thailand had done nothing for retardates. The children simply stayed at home. When they became too
burdensome they were sent to the Hospital for Mental Diseases. Dr.
Phon, Minister of Health, was the first to urge acceptance of the fact
that retardates were not psychotic. The Princess does all she can to
help. Since the King gave his contribution toward the building of the
hospital on Ding Dang Road, she has labored not only to raise additional funds but also to enlist volunteer workers to relieve the hospital's
overburdened staff.

We talked for perhaps a half hour. As I departed, Her Highness informed me she had been invited to the United States to see what we
were doing for our mentally and physically handicapped. She felt
certain that American methods would help accelerate her country's
program.

I phoned the United States Information Service before I left, stressing
Thailand's need for teaching aids and trained personnel, plus the
advisability of either importing an expert in the field as the British had
done in Hong Kong or sending one of their own people to learn of
the planned progress in other lands.

I left Thailand with mixed feelings. Most people, and not only those
in the Far East, were much like the Princess Prem. On the positive side
they were sympathetic and well-intentioned, and they were newly
aware of mental retardation. And yet it was discouraging to see that
they barely grasped the immensity of the problem.

Within a year after my visit to Thailand, Dr. Rosjong received his
government subsidy to attend the International Congress for the Mentally Handicapped at Brussels. He routed himself back through the
United States where he spent a precious few frantic days traveling to

centers in the Bronx, Brooklyn, and Manhattan and even rode the train
three hours each way to visit the Seaside Regional Center near New
London, Connecticut.

Things will happen faster now, I know, for Dr. Rosjong visited me
before he left New York. He was enormously impressed with all that
he had seen here and abroad. His mind seemed to be like an old-
fashioned roller desk, full of cubicles with precious projects stored
away in each. He will be the peduncle—the sturdy stalk from which
many plans will flower.

7

Israel

THE FEELING OF SHAME AND GUILT THAT OFTEN UNJUSTIFIABLY HAUNTS
parents of retardates has run unusually high in the people of Israel.
The need to remove it was one object of AKIM,* a national organization founded to work with the mentally retarded, to help them achieve
independence through training and guidance and regain their pride
and self-respect.

Mr. and Mrs. James MacFarland, two of the best USIS people abroad,
arrived at the hotel with Mrs. Ethel Greenberg of AKIM. The Mac-
Farlands had asked to be assigned to me because of their long-time
interest and hard work in the field of mental retardation. Mrs. Greenberg, an American college and law school graduate, is married to an
Israeli and has three children. Her middle child is profoundly retarded.
She gave me a brief résumé of the mental retardation movement.

---

* *Aguda Lekimum Mefagrim* (Association for Rehabilitation of Mentally
Handicapped).

Israel is a potpourri of peoples. Great numbers arrived destitute from such countries as Syria, Lebanon, and Iraq in the Middle East and from Morocco, Tunisia, Algeria, and Libya in North Africa. Many had lived as a minority in Arab communities in the *mellah* (Jewish quarter). Culturally and economically deprived, they had adopted some of the naïve philosophy native to the country of their origin. For instance, a thirty-eight-year-old Yemenite father arrived with his seven children, fully expecting to retire and have them support him. His one retarded child, whom he did not identify as such because the boy was not a profound case, was also expected to work and help support the idle father. To the Israelis, struggling with their manpower shortage and feeling of responsibility for education and rehabilitation, this philosophy of early retirement from work has proved a problem.

Tests could not be applied to many young immigrants to determine accurate degrees of retardation. A child coming from, let us say, Kurdistan, having lived primitively in a family of ten in a single room, and economically, culturally, and perhaps emotionally deprived, could not possibly perform on a test to his maximum potential. The child might be functioning as a severe or moderate retardate, but in reality might be only mildly retarded, if at all.

The reactions of the families differed widely when a retarded child was recognized as such. Some parents would not part with their retardates; others tried frantically to find someone to take them off their hands; and a third group, in a panic of ignorance and fear, locked the children up so no one would ever see them.

Before the advent of AKIM it seemed that nothing could be done. A member of AKIM, hearing Dr. Abraham Jacobs of Columbia University in New York read a paper at an International Conference of Psychologists and Guidance Counselors in Israel on retardation and rehabilitation, approached him to set up a comprehensive program in Israel. If the United Nations Technical Assistance Program would approve the assignment, he assured the Israelis, he would be happy to come.

AKIM applied to the Department of Health, which submitted the necessary papers to the Prime Minister's office, Department of Technical Assistance. They in turn tendered the request to the Rehabilitation Unit Bureau of Social Affairs, Department of Economic and Social Affairs, of the United Nations Technical Assistance Program.

The World Health Organization, satisfied with Dr. Jacobs' broad qualifications in mental retardation, psychology, guidance, and vocational rehabilitation, assigned him to Israel.

Dr. Jacobs and his wife spent six months establishing a program which started with nursery school classes and ended with the establishment of a workshop in Jerusalem. Eight teachers a week were permitted to visit and observe, and at the end of a four-week period, 32 teachers had had training in the teaching of the mentally retarded.

The inception of the program had been at Swedish Village in Jerusalem. My husband and I hired a car and chauffeur and arranged to visit there the next day.

The chauffeur turned out to be an excellent guide. He told us that the road we were traveling from Tel Aviv to Jerusalem was originally called the Burma Road because it circumvented the main road and went through the hills. In the War of Independence, it became known as the Road of Courage, and so it has remained.

After the UN declaration on partition of Palestine in 1947, the Arabs refused to accept the majority vote and waged war on the Israelis. Jerusalem was besieged, and the people were completely cut off from food and supplies to be starved into submission.

Elderly men, Orthodox Jews who would not kill, old women, and children carrying stones in their bare hands built the road at night under fire from the attacking Arabs. The Israeli soldiers traveled the road in trucks and jeeps in an effort to alleviate the suffering of the people in Jerusalem. Ambushed and machine-gunned jeeps still stood at the side of the road, an eloquent testimony to the price Israel paid. But the Israeli soldiers had moved steadily past their fallen comrades until they climbed the mountain and brought help to their beleaguered people.

I considered the courage, stamina, and strength of purpose of the Israelis, who in their dedication to a democratic ideal never faltered in their responsibility to one another. This was no prestigious commonalty. Here was a tiny country, struggling to survive, providing education and rehabilitation not only for its élite, but for its blind, deaf, physically handicapped, and mentally retarded as well.

Our car drove up to the Department of Social Welfare, and Mrs. Kahn, then head of international relations within that department, assigned a social worker, Mr. Rosenberg, to accompany us to Swedish

Village. (Mr. Rosenberg was later appointed director of mental retardation in the Department of Social Welfare.)

Mr. Rosenberg told us that Swedish Village was donated to Israel by the Swedish branch of Save the Children Federation to care for orphans who were pouring in from all over the world. When the Israelis decided to found a refuge for the mentally retarded, they combed the country for the most beautiful spot they could find, and that is how Swedish Village was reorganized to care for the retarded. The financial responsibility belongs to the Minister of Social Welfare. The welfare worker taxes the family according to its ability to pay.

There is a long list waiting to enter.

Swedish Village is one of 5 public institutions. There are 13 private ones as well.

With the help of the Department of Social Welfare and Hadassah, Swedish Village has been trying to establish a complete treatment center. In addition to the diagnostic center and psychological and physical therapists, the department was negotiating for speech and art therapists. The center is looking ahead toward long-range results, so the retardates, living in, can attend classes while they are receiving treatment.

The Village cares for all age groups and degrees of retardation. With the help of Columbia University's Dr. Jacobs, some academic classes had already been set up.

The program concerns itself with the profoundly and severely retarded who, unable to help themselves, require nursing care; it also provides training and self-help and some workshop participation for the moderately retarded, and vocational training and placement in private industry for the mildly retarded. Mr. Rosenberg added that he was being sent abroad to explore further means of enriching the program.

We finally arrived at Swedish Village, which is a community of prefabricated buildings surrounded by attractive gardens. It is high on a mountaintop overlooking a deep, fertile valley with beehive roofs and mosque-type monasteries. In the office we met Mr. Eleazer Cohen, the fiery, dedicated director, learner, and teacher.

In Israel, he told me philosophically, there are two basic approaches to retardation. One is pessimistic and the other optimistic. The pessimistic group feels that the cases are not medical and need only the physical custodial care of the Department of Welfare and nothing from the Department of Health. The optimistic group includes doctors and educators who feel that the problem concerns such things as correction of dietary idiosyncrasies, antidotes to certain types of physical illness, and the enormous possibilities of rehabilitation. They became involved.

When Swedish Village was started, the Department of Social Welfare assigned a doctor for one-half hour a week. Now the Village has one full-time doctor who carries a very heavy load. She is not a psychiatrist. She has two jobs, one the treatment of illness and the other the summoning of physicians from Hadassah Medical Center when necessary.

These physicians from the Medical Center specialize in neurology, physiotherapy, and rehabilitation. Apart from the times when they are called in for special consultation, they visit the Village regularly twice a month. Each specialist has his own case load, studies the individual reports, gives a prognosis, and recommends treatment. This builds up a tremendous follow-up job for the one full-time physician.

The visiting physicians found that most of the retarded at Swedish Village were having trouble with their gums, and imported a new drug from the Lukini Company in Switzerland to counteract it.

Another area of vast interest has been epilepsy, and the records of Swedish Village show that application of their research findings in this field has considerably diminished the frequency of patients' seizures.

Symptoms of retardation can be puzzling and sometimes result in mistaken diagnosis. One such error occurred with a child who became very aggressive and appeared to have every symptom of madness. This mistaken impression seemed confirmed when the files were reviewed and it was discovered that the mother was in a hospital for the mentally ill. The child was sent away for several months' observation, and he was discovered to be a retardate. He was not insane at all.

In another instance a boy was committed as retarded, but his behavior was at variance with the diagnosis. After further testing, the doctors discovered that the boy's condition was due to lack of communication: he had no peers to talk to. They placed the boy among children of considerably higher IQ's, and he is now undergoing a complete rehabilitation which will enable him to compete successfully in the outside world.

And then there was Gabby. He was brought in as a nontrainable, severe retardate. He could not sit or walk, could only crawl, and that not too well. But the directors of Swedish Village detected signs of higher intelligence in him. Close examination suggested that his problem was partly physical, and the doctors performed an orthopedic operation. Now Gabby is not only able to sit but can also walk. He attends a hospital for physiotherapy and will shortly be returned to his own home. The boy tested 30 IQ before the operation—and 60 after it. His IQ is now thought to be much higher even than that.

In sum, Mr. Cohen said, Swedish Village has found that each retarded child—like any normal one—has a potential of his own that must be accurately evaluated and then developed by every technique, from surgery to vocational training.

The Village has several buildings, including an administrative building and a new kitchen equipped to serve about 500 people a day. Food for the nonambulatory cases is brought to the buildings where attendants serve these children. Residents receive five meals a day: breakfast, tea and bread and butter at 10:00 A.M., lunch, a snack at 5:00 P.M., and dinner around 7:00.

A new school building, to house 10 classes, was being built along with a new dormitory.

The Village had room for 150 in-resident children, and it was filled up. Of the 150, 32 were profound or nontrainable retardates; 80 to 90 were severely to moderately retardate, and the last was an adult group of varying degrees of retardation from twenty to forty-four years of age.

I looked in on the dining room. The shortage of water in Israel had not affected its cleanliness. More important, there was an air of warmth and well-being. Whether it was due to the smell of European cooking that hovered tantalizingly over gleaming white-oilcloth-covered tables, or to the children who sat close to the staff and hugged them, or whether it was the teachers' and attendants' seemingly personal concern with the individual children, I don't know, but it was there.

After lunch, we went through the buildings. I was told that a great deal of money was used to install ramps inside and out, for the use particularly of the nonambulatory cases. In two of the rooms, we saw the profound group who appeared to have visual and auditory as well as mental handicaps. There is reason to believe that such children might prove more intelligent than we suspect—if only we could reach them.

In two other rooms, prenursery rooms, which Mrs. Jacobs and her husband had had painted yellow and blue, there were various balls, hoops of varying sizes, and so forth, which were used to teach matching of color, shape, and texture. Many Montessori toys, graduated blocks, brooms, sponges, mops, pots, and pans were on the shelves.

Mrs. Jacobs later told me that the children could play with whatever they wished. Sometimes they took a toy to their living unit and were allowed to keep it for a week and even two. Circular, square, and triangular objects were handled constantly by the children in order to acquaint them with shapes. It is Mrs. Jacobs' contention that children cannot learn to read and write unless they are well aware of shapes.

The shortage of supplies in Israel was a challenge to the ingenuity of the teachers. Finger paint was made with vegetable coloring. Flour and water made a putty for molding.

As in other countries, in addition to the painting there was a great deal of use made of music, musical instruments, and response to rhythm.

Mrs. Jacobs, along with an Israeli teacher, Rena, took the middle group of retardates, that is, the moderate IQ range from 25 to 50, and in one month taught them to wash their hands and faces and clean their teeth; to know their own towels and belongings, and not to put their hands in the bowls of food, but wait and eat it with the proper utensils.

I asked Mrs. Jacobs what had been the most moving moment at Swedish Village. She answered that it was when a Middle Eastern Negroid Mongoloid child, paralyzed on one side, learned to use her good hand and drew a perfect circle with a wet sponge on the blackboard, and then turned to face the class.

Most play slides for children have a steep flight of steps, and when the child comes down, an adult often has to be there to catch him. Before Mrs. Jacobs left Swedish Village she had a slide built to her own specifications. The steps were very shallow, then came a bridge like a wide gangplank, and then the slide with a long sweep which forced the children to a complete stop before they got off. It has proved to be very successful.

Mrs. Jacobs said she learned something important from her Israeli assistant, Rena, who taught very objectively and refused to wait for the so-called readiness to learn. She made the child do something over and over again until he was successful. Rena refused to succumb to emotion. She felt too much compassion in teaching retardates drastically delayed learning.

We finally drove down the mountain to a sheltered workshop in the heart of Jerusalem. Dr. Jacobs, with the support of AKIM, canvassed Jerusalem until he found a suitable area for a workshop, an empty loft in the center of an industrial area. He approached five different industrial concerns nearby and asked if they would award contracts to a working group of retardates if a shop were established in this vicinity. They gave their promise, and the first sheltered workshop in Israel was formed.

AKIM works unceasingly for the workshop. They make up any financial deficit incurred.

When we arrived, we were greeted by the man in charge, a Scotsman with a thick burr. He was our guide through the establishment.

The IQ range in the workshop was from 30 to 55 at that time. The workers earned from one to three Israeli pounds per day—the United States equivalent of 33 cents to one dollar. Before the highest earner in the shop started his training, he was able to earn only half a pound—17 cents a day. With training, his wages jumped to 4 pounds —$1.32 U.S.—a day. When a worker is able to earn that much, he is deemed capable of competing in industry, and the shop finds him a job.

The caliber of the work being done in this shop was unusually high. The retardates who were physically handicapped had special chairs built for them. Some were assembling wheels for baby carriages, which meant putting spokes in a rim and fitting hubs and pins into place. Others were packing steel wool; still others were cleaning parts of electric motors, or enclosing plastic spoons and knives in cellophane for the El Al Airlines, or placing small knobs on metal clothes hangers.

As the air of diligence and concentration attested, this workshop has been enormously successful. Due to its lack of space and its inadequate staff, surplus contracts have been farmed out to the workshop in

Tel Aviv, Swedish Village, and to another institution privately run by Malben.* The work center is now named the Dr. Abraham Jacobs Workshop in honor of its late founder, who died suddenly in May, 1964, at the age of fifty-two.

An outstanding weaving workshop founded by the Jerusalem branch of AKIM provides vocational training and employment, with programs for retardates at AKIM's Rachel Straus House. Beautiful gifts made there have a ready market, giving the men and women employed there the satisfaction of being wage earners.

Before we left Jerusalem, we drove through that small part of the Old City which was then in Israeli hands. The streets were no more than narrow passageways. We stopped at the Mandelbaum Gate† where so much drama has been enacted. It was merely a wooden barrier such as railroads use to halt traffic. On the other side lay a meadow, split down the middle by a barbed-wire fence. This was ancient Israel divided between Israel and Jordan.

In Tel Aviv, the Minister of Social Welfare and the Minister of Health, in cooperation with AKIM and Malben, set up a diagnostic clinic to work with doctors, neurologists, and physiotherapists from the Tel Hashimi Hospital. This medical group, in conjunction with a psychologist and social worker, test the child and make recommendations and referrals.

The Day Center connected with the diagnostic clinic in Tel Aviv was chosen for its proximity to available transportation. The retardates have been taught to travel by bus. It has taken time to train some of them, but the Center has been successful with every single candidate.

Five rooms, including a well-equipped kitchen, comprise the school and workshop. They call it the GIL workshop. The work program, which includes training the girls in every phase of household work and both boys and girls in work similar to that at Swedish Village, occupies the mornings.

Most of the girls had to be taught the most elementary living habits —bathing, shampooing, hair styling, dressing, and proper deportment.

---

* Malben is the Israeli organization of the American Jewish Joint Distribution Committee for service to the Handicapped Immigrants.

† The Mandelbaum Gate was removed in September, 1967, after the six-day June War.

Now the girls are not only very clean themselves, but keep the quarters immaculate as well.

In the afternoon a teacher comes to teach reading, writing, and arithmetic.

The social welfare worker who had been assigned to accompany me told of a frantic family who brought a very low-grade Mongoloid to the diagnostic clinic.

The mother wept bitterly. "He would be better off dead. There's nothing anyone can do for him, and nothing he can do for himself."

The Department of Social Welfare took charge of the boy and, in this country where there is a tremendous manpower shortage, taught him to take care of 15 cows.

I was shown some astonishing examples of hand-embroidered cloths and napkins done by girls whose IQ's were under 40. Since the Center was founded two and a half years ago, it has placed 18 girls in industry.

As we stood there talking, a grinning young Yemenite girl named Ahuva came in to display her work. She was dark, small, and thin, with woolly hair and oversized mouth, hands, and feet. She was nineteen but appeared to be twelve.

The social worker asked if I would like to visit Ahuva's family and I accepted with alacrity. Ahuva was so pleased that she danced in front of us all the way to her home.

The house turned out to be a barrack-like hut, built of tar paper on wood, painted white.

There a charming girl, Ahuva's sister, came to the door to greet us. The interior of the house had also been painted white. Ahuva's sister, who is twenty, works half days in a greenhouse. There was a large, unusual plant on the bookcase and green life in all corners of the house. The bookcase was filled with volumes on plant life, and the girl smilingly admitted that her greatest joy in life was to watch things grow.

From the well-scrubbed Arabian tile floors to the shining windows, the house bespoke loving care. The father has been dead for some time, and the mother is a cleaning woman. Before they came to this home, they all lived in one room, the mother, four sisters, and one brother. As soon as the children were able to work, they pooled all their money and rented this house. It is their castle.

Through the worker, I asked where the rest of the family was. The sister replied that one sister taught, the other worked as a domestic, and the brother was a soldier. They all would come home for the evening meal.

How did Ahuva get along with the family?

The sister shrugged. "When she is not aggressive, we like her very much. When she is moody we don't like her at all. And when she becomes impossible, we hit her."

During the entire interview, Ahuva's bright black eyes danced in her head. I felt that she not only understood what was going on, but also had a keen appreciation of the fact that she sometimes deliberately goaded her family beyond endurance.

The social worker interrupted to tell me in English that the sister who worked as a domestic was slightly retarded. It was with her that Ahuva fought, if she quarreled at all.

When the family lived in one room, the children in that neighborhood taunted Ahuva unmercifully. They called her names, chased her up and down the streets, and threw stones at her if she ventured anywhere near them when they were playing.

During all those years Ahuva was as savage as Itard's wild boy of Aveyron. She grabbed food and wolfed it from her hands, had practically no speech, and could not wash or dress herself. She was always filthy, her eyes and nose ran constantly, and she made no attempt to wipe either. The family was in despair. When she was seven, her mother had no alternative but to put her in an institution.

Ahuva stayed there for three years but kept running away. The last time was a frightening one for everyone concerned until the police finally found her. The mother could not bear to see her so unhappy so she brought her home again and decided to try to teach her to care for the house.

It was a brave decision, but it failed. Freed from the hateful institution, Ahuva was wilder than ever. This uncontrolled behavior went on for six or seven years more. She became so destructive that she was finally brought to the attention of AKIM. A social worker was assigned to her case and then the day came when she told Ahuva she had been accepted at the school and workshop.

The worker said the tears came to Ahuva's eyes, she gave a series of staccato laughs, and trembled violently. The laughing and crying had alternated with her questioning. She could not believe that she was going to go to school—to learn to do things like everyone else.

When the worker told her there would be a place for her in two months' time, Ahuva had answered that two months was not too long a time to wait. Had she not already waited for so long?

As the worker told the story, Ahuva started to laugh and cry again. In between she kept shaking her head at me as if to say, "Yes, it is true, all of it." Then she walked out of the room. In a few minutes she was back bearing cups of tea for us all.

The sister smiled fondly at her in approval. She added, "Before Ahuva went to the Center, she couldn't comb her hair, dress, or sit still. Now she can set the table, eat well with her utensils, and even waits for everyone to start before she begins. She also washes, irons, cleans shoes, and does other household chores. All this she has accomplished in two short years. AKIM has been wonderful to us."

Ahuva interrupted. "Now everyone likes me. Before no one did. You have seen my hand embroidery? Would you like to see my room?"

I rose and followed her. The room was tiny, barely large enough for a makeshift chest and a cot bed. There was a pretty cotton spread on it and draperies to match at the window.

"Did your mother teach you to do that?"

Ahuva shook her head and grinned broadly at the social worker who had accompanied us here from the school.

Once AKIM took over, the members of the whole family redoubled their efforts to help Ahuva. The mother came to the workshop to check on her progress report. The family found that Ahuva needed a great deal of love, attention, and praise—and she received all she needed.

Ahuva's family did not indulge in fancy dialectics about the nature of love. They knew only that one of their own was in need, and they helped with the only thing they had to give, part of themselves. They learned to love and accept Ahuva; in turn she, in her need for emotional reinforcement, brought out the best in her family. They keep encouraging her to learn. Her slightest improvement is lovingly praised by them all. They know she can never be as they are, but they accept

Ahuva's retardation as an illness which cannot be helped but need not be hidden out of shame. Rather, they are now truly proud of her progress.

On the way back to my hotel I discussed Ahuva and her family with the social worker. Finally I said, "The family is so emotionally healthy. But it must be very sad for you to go into the homes of these handicapped children day after day."

"Not half so sad as going into my own," she said.

Then after a moment she told me she had a son. "The doctors think he is brain-damaged. Some things he can do well and at other things he is quite hopeless. The difficult part has been his temper tantrums. He becomes violent over the most trivial things. He cannot control himself. Yet as soon as something diverts his attention, it is like a summer storm that has passed and all is calm again."

I murmured something about how difficult it was.

"Difficult!" She turned and stared at me. "I speak seven languages. I know of no words to describe the havoc my son has made of my home."

She went on to say that she had a daughter of sixteen. She could bring no one into the house. None of them could. If the daughter went out, he would run after her and scream at her in the street. One day the mother came home and found the girl crying hysterically.

"Let me out of here. *Let me out of here!*" The mother tried to calm her but she kept crying and begging. "Please. Send me away. Anywhere. To the desert. To the kibbutz. Lie about my age and send me to the army. Anywhere, but *let me out of here!*"

She said she knew then that she had to send her son away and made the decision.

"Did it help?"

She answered that her daughter had become quieter, a better student. She began to bring friends home, to live like other girls her age. But there seemed to be a sense of guilt for them both. The mother said she especially felt it.

Every week when she visited the school there was a terrible scene when she had to go home. She finally asked the school if her son might come home weekends. They agreed and the boy came—and his poor behavior started all over again. She had to threaten him that he could not

come at all and actually at one time she did not permit him to come
home for a month.

She turned suddenly to me. "How old do you think I am?" Before
I could make even a polite guess, she said quietly, "No matter. Years
do not really count. It is inside. Each time my son has to return to the
school, I age another year or two.

"But my son is better. The school has done wonders with him. I
should have entered him long before. The scenes are no longer as
painful. One day when my daughter is married, perhaps he can come
home to stay, my poor son, my poor, poor son. . . ."

And then there was Shoshana, a beautiful and profoundly retarded
girl. Her skin had the sheen of pale honey, her brown eyes were round
and large. Her straight, silky brown hair was caught up from her forehead with a bobby pin, giving her a look of clear innocence.

Shoshana, at the age of ten, probably had the IQ of a four-month-old
child. A victim of cerebral palsy, she sat twisted to one side, her hand
held in spastic fashion. Her chair was a specially constructed one, helping her to stay erect. She had to be fed, clothed, carried to the toilet.
She occasionally whimpered or cried out, but for reasons that no one
could determine: she was completely speechless. There she sat, day
after day, alive and breathing, but completely out of contact with
everything and everyone.

Shoshana cried normally at birth, but being a premature infant she
had been placed in an incubator.

When Shoshana was four days old she developed a high fever. When
she was ready to go home, the doctor recommended that she be given
over to a woman who specialized in the care of premature babies.
Three months later, when Shoshana's mother paid her a visit, she
found dirt encrusted in the creases of the baby's arms and legs. She
removed her immediately, brought her home, and began to nurse her
herself.

Shoshana was one year old when her mother began to realize that
something was very seriously wrong. The mother started the tragic
round of doctors, and her worst fears were confirmed.

I visited Shoshana and her family in their Arab-style house. The
rooms are large and airy with mosaic tile floors and old-fashioned
comfortable Western-style furniture. The other children were there, a

handsome, lively boy and another daughter whose grave, sweet expression made her a sister to Ching's younger sister in Hong Kong. I asked about the family's relationship to Shoshana.

The mother replied: "The ability to live through something like this is a strong test of marriage. This one has withstood it. My daughter is always gentle with Shoshana. As for my son, I can only tell you this story.

"One day we decided to go for a ride. The amah was here to care for Shoshana and we thought we would leave her home. We got into the car. Shoshana looked after us. Whether she understood or not, I do not know. Of course she could give us no sign. As we started to drive away, my boy began to sob. He cried that he would miss his sister, and it wasn't fair for her to be left at home when we were all going to have a good time. We turned around and brought Shoshana with us."

And that is how it is. The family take Shoshana with them whenever they go on an outing.

I inquired about their social life. The mother answered that her social life, as I called it, was in her work for cerebral palsied, much of which she could do at home. She added that many cerebral palsy cases were not retarded at all. With patience and understanding they can begin to function in society—to live. She said she felt society owed them that chance.

Her quiet voice was warm. "If you could see the joy of these mothers at every step of the child's progress. It is like taking wine—it is such a feeling of intoxication."

Then, as if she were reading my mind, she said, "You are thinking of Shoshana—that she understands nothing, feels nothing, will never take a step anywhere?" She shrugged. "One lives with the haunting feeling that perhaps she does and cannot tell us."

Hesitantly I asked, "Couldn't you bring yourself to send her to a place like Swedish Village? Perhaps they could find a way to help her, and certainly she would be well cared for."

"Perhaps one day I will bring myself to it." She looked at me quite directly. "You see, I know when I do she will never come back."

Mrs. Eva Michaelis-Stern, in charge of promotion for AKIM, took us to visit Miss Irene Gaster in her small apartment in Jerusalem. This indomitable Englishwoman, who was physically incapacitated in

World War I when she worked in an open-air military hospital at the front, came to Israel in pursuit of her life's work with retardates.

Since my visit to Israel, the Irene Gaster Vocational Training School has been named in her honor.

In her own words, Irene Gaster was the cheeky, independent daughter of the chief rabbi of London and granddaughter of the rabbi who headed the Jewish College in England.

The memories of her childhood included a large house open to scholars, Jew and Gentile alike, but it also held an army of governesses and maids and, due to lack of parental companionship, of great loneliness as well.

As one of thirteen children (seven brothers and six sisters) she was permitted to have dinner with her parents only on Friday and special holiday nights.

One day, she succeeded in frightening one of her brothers very badly. Her father tried to make her promise never to do it again. She would only promise to *try* not to do it again. Despite the thorough thrashing, she never would promise and said she learned from that lesson never to make a child promise to do anything.

During the war, a devout Protestant family next door trained a group in first aid. Irene was permitted to participate, and she then joined the St. John's Ambulance Brigade. It was in this service that both her hands and feet became frostbitten.

After the war, an aunt paid for her journey to Romania for a visit. Bored with embroidery and dressing for tea, she located the American Red Cross and worked with the gypsies and peasants at the clinic and out in the field. Without knowing Romanian, she did the translating, for, as she said, proficiency in words is not important in understanding people's needs.

All her life Irene lived in great fear of her father, and when the Queen of Romania sent a special train to bring him to Romania for a series of lectures, Irene fled to Germany. There she worked with retarded adults at the Deuerheim for three years and then returned to England when she became fed up with Naziism.

Back home she applied to the Central Association for Mental Welfare from which she received her appointment to Croydon where she spent many happy and productive years, and became convinced that the earlier you start training retarded people, the better they will learn.

Deciding to leave Croydon and broaden her horizons, she wrote to Henrietta Szold and said, "Since no one is doing anything for the retarded in Palestine, what are the chances of my being admitted?" Miss Szold wrote back, "With your physical disability, no connections, and no money—none!"

The saga of how Miss Gaster managed not only to get to Palestine but to get a permit to stay there is a story unto itself.

She started a home for two children, one of whom paid and the other did not. The number of her charges rose swiftly to 70, and the proportion of payment remained the same. Sometimes when the appearance of a child was too horrible for the parents to endure, she took babies even at only three days old.

Miss Gaster trained some of the retardates to help her with washing, cleaning, and feeding. She herself slept with three retarded children in the same room.

During the war for independence, she and her group were left in Haifa after the city was evacuated. Under bombardment and steady fire, the children became very frightened. She promised she would watch over them even while they were sleeping and did not get undressed for two straight weeks.

When the food shortage became so acute that it was necessary for her to go out and forage for food, she took all the children to the basement and told them to sit against the wall until she came back; that they were not to be frightened for when the guns went boom boom-boom, she would come back.

While she was gathering what food she could find, the fighting started. No one could restrain her, and under heavy crossfire she made her way back to the house. As she entered the basement, the children started to cry and clap their hands. "See—see," they shouted, "she said when the guns went boom-boom-boom, she would come back, and she came—she came. . . ."

I asked Miss Gaster how she felt she had most profited in her years of working with the retarded. She thought a moment and said, "From the mistakes of other people rather than their brains."

Her most satisfying accomplishment? When she made her first retarded child laugh.

How about institutional care? Miss Gaster preferred a family home type of situation but her true anathema was people who ran private institutions for the care of the retarded for profit. She said quite sternly that there should be no bargaining with human life.

Had her Orthodox background affected her life in any way?

She answered that her professional, political, and religious beliefs were all one—humanity.

8

Turkey

MR. SALIH ILGIN, DIRECTOR OF THE CLINIC IN ISTANBUL, COULD HAVE been an Arab, Italian, Catholic, or Jew as well as a Turk, since all these people originated near the Mediterranean and have great similarity of coloring and features. Being Turkish, he was Moslem; 99 percent of the Turks are Mohammedans.

Miss Ayse Sarialp, the knowledgeable, understanding, and diplomatic Turkish assistant to the head of the USIS, had located the clinic for me and then had come along to act as my interpreter.

Mr. Ilgin introduced me to his staff and we sat down in a semicircle. "There are no workshops or training centers as such for the retarded in Turkey; no special schools; the cities of Ankara and Istanbul have 15 classes for the mildly retarded whose IQ's range from 50 to 70, where they are taught some handicraft and weaving. The classes are limited to 15. They are learning the value of visual and mechanical aid. The schools are requesting support for these aids for the children

from the clinics and the clinics are attempting to purchase them."
"What about the moderate, severe, and profound retardates?"
He shook his head. "Plans are in progress to open some classes for
the moderately retarded. As for the others," he shrugged, "they remain
at home. If the child becomes too emotionally disturbed for the family
to cope with, he is sent to a mental institution. There is no state training
school for the retarded. Plans are in progress to organize 17 classes for
them; a large grant of 60 acres has been set aside for a retardation center, but thus far plans are only on paper." He sighed. "There is so much
to be done."

On the ride over from the modern, or European, half of Istanbul to
the old and more colorful section with its hidden courtyards and
narrow, tortuous streets paved with cobblestones and overhung with
balconied wooden houses, I tried to recall what I knew of the land.

Present-day Turkey is the remnant of the vast Ottoman Empire,
which in the early part of the sixteenth century was one of the principal
empires of the Western world. Its history is one of internal and external
wars, massacres, and oppressions. In 1912 its oppression of the Chris-
tians gave other European countries an excuse to intervene and attack,
and when the peace was signed in 1913, Turkey was forced to give up
practically all of her European territory.

Turkey was on the German side during World War I, and when the
war was lost she was reduced to little more than one-third of her size.*
Illiteracy has always been high, but when the country became a repub-
lic in 1922, education was made compulsory from the ages of seven to
fourteen. Despite this, according to the Turkish Information Bureau,
the literacy rate is only 30.6 percent, the remaining 69.4 percent are il-
literate. Turkey is largely agricultural, and the facilities and standards
of the country schools fall far below those of the cities.

The clinic wherein I sat had been in existence only four years. Our
meeting lasted all afternoon. But it did not seem that long, for in spite
of the language barrier, I was eager to absorb as much as I could,
since my stay in both Turkey and Greece was to be much too short.

---

* She has since regained some of her territory, but it is still less than
half of what it was.

The staff appeared as interested as I, and I only wish I could have been in a position to give them more helpful information, so eager were they to learn and share.

Mr. Ilgin said that when the mildly retarded children are ready to leave school, the guidance people work hard to get them jobs in private industry. Plans are in progress to educate employers of this reservoir of potential employment, but it is very difficult to persuade employers of this. Through Miss Sarialp, I assured Mr. Ilgin that the problem of convincing employers was not peculiar to Turkey.

Mr. Ilgin went on to say that most of the poorer families themselves would gladly give their retardates away if there were some place to take them. They do not understand how much rehabilitation can take place. "Before we can undertake the wholesale instruction of employers," he added, "we must first concentrate on educating the family itself."

I asked if economics played a large part in formulating family attitudes.

He answered that the educational level of the family, rather than the economic one, was the dominant factor. The poorly educated, better than half of the population, treated retardates inhumanely. They beat and punished the children in the mistaken notion that they were bad without admitting or understanding their affliction. When and if the case came to the attention of the clinics, the situation was explained to the family and generally a change of attitude was effected. Of the 233 cases treated per year at this clinic, 25 percent came from poverty-stricken, 39 percent from poor, 28 percent from average, and 8 percent from wealthy homes.

It is legal for retardates to marry in Turkey.

There are now six major cities—Istanbul, Ankara, Izmir, Eskisehir, Adana, and Erzurum—which have child guidance clinics for testing and diagnosis. Some others are located in pediatric and university hospitals, bringing the total to approximately a dozen for a country of 296,500 square miles, slightly larger than our own state of Texas, with a population of approximately 30 million. But, as I understand it, these clinics are all-encompassing and do not specialize only in retardation.

There is only one social worker at the clinic in Istanbul who works solely with the retarded. But there is an assistant responsible for investigating the situations of the children who are deprived of home life. This assistant works in the Special Education Department of the Ministry of Education.

While primary education is compulsory up until the age of fourteen, children may go until they are fifteen without cost. This same opportunity is extended to retardates.

It is of interest that secondary education is free only to the blind.

Psychologists are attached to the hospitals but not necessarily to the clinics. Nor do the clinics have pediatricians. Children are referred to hospital pediatricians when there is a specific urgency.

Each child entering a clinic gets a complete physical, including orthopedic and neurological examinations, dental X rays, and laboratory checkups. There are no nurses at the clinics. Very little physiotherapy is used and no art or play therapy, and there is only one speech therapist who works within the confines of the clinic.

A psychiatrist works in the clinic, evaluating the child and offering some therapy to him. None is available to the parents.

An educational consultant is connected with the clinic, but, as I mentioned before, there are no sheltered workshops either within or without the clinic domain.

Whatever is available is free. There is no fee at the child-guidance clinics.

The dull normal children, 70-90 IQ, go to regular schools and attend normal classes with requests to the teacher for particular attention.*

Dr. Ilgin's team told me that no statistical scale had as yet been formed for the number of retardates in Turkey. They know only that there is an overwhelming need.

Because my time in Turkey was so limited, the clinic team was kind enough to review two of their cases with me.

Oya was ten years old. Her father was a primary school graduate as was her mother. They both have normal intelligence, are articulate, and there is no history of mental retardation in the family. The preg-

---

* In the United States, the dull normal are in the 75–90 range. Anyone below 75 is considered eligible for institutional retardation care.

nancy was normal except for albumin in the urine of the mother, and this was treated very promptly. There was no other medical checkup, and the child was delivered by a midwife.

Only one abnormality occurred during the pregnancy. There was an earthquake, and the mother was badly frightened by it.

Oya had no high fever, her physical development followed a normal course, and she was breast-fed until the age of two. She had to be helped to sit up, but sat alone at the age of one year. On the other hand, she could indicate that she was wet at the age of nine months. She walked unaided at the age of fourteen months.

Oya had whooping cough when she was a year old and it lasted two months. When she was two, she had the measles. In all these years, she had only one minor accident. She fell on glass and cut her cheek.

At the age of ten, Oya cannot eat properly by herself.

The caseworker states that the parents are very kind to the child. The father is particularly understanding. He is a peddler, works hard, does not drink, and gets along very well with his wife.

There is another child of three and a half who is completely normal.

Istanbul has adapted the Stanford-Binet test for their own use. They have done the same with the Otis Beta and Thurston achievement tests, and the interesting part of this case is that Oya was given a Stanford-Binet in 1958. Her IQ was 78. She was given a maximum amount of assistance and, greatly encouraged by such understanding parents, the clinic decided to test her again six months later. Her IQ tested thirteen points *lower!* It was now 65 against the former test on which she had scored 78.

What is Oya and where is she? Are we already too late? Is she so successfully hidden that we will never find her?

Dr. Katherine Woodward has this to say about a case such as Oya's:

"In our study of preschool children with retarded functioning, we find a rather large percentage who are clearly mentally ill, but to all appearances are functioning at a retarded level. These children have basic problems in social relationships. They relate to objects rather than people and live in a fantasy world to the exclusion of the real world. Yet some of them can be salvaged by appropriate measures which may differ from those appropriate for the organically damaged child. Placement in a good in-residence school geared for their type of problem may be more successful than the rehabilitation programs, though many of these children may be found in those programs. I am not sure that Oya may not be one of these, but this kind of behavior may be seen in mentally ill children. In such cases, the IQ has very little meaning. The children may have good intelligence if we can help them to use it."

Ayse was a nervous, disobedient, undisciplined, unceasingly hyperactive, and very destructive child. She had what she called toy days in which she broke every toy in sight.

These are characteristics of brain-damaged children who flit from one object to another without any real perception of its function or value.

The mother, sorely disappointed in this child, criticizes her constantly and compares her to other children. The mother herself is nervous, severe, and contradictory in her decisions with the child.

The family lives in a small two-room house which they own. The father is hard-working and tries to protect the child against the mother. They say they do not quarrel in the presence of the child but the worker says they contradict each other constantly.

Ayse has been consistently subject to the ridicule and jeering of the neighborhood children. As a result, she is forced to play with those children younger than herself who will tolerate her.

Ayse's speech is very normal, she adapts herself easily, and can be very gay. She also appears to be a very sincere little girl who is eight years old, but tests six years and eight months. Yet she uttered her first word at the age of seven months. She is in a special class in the first grade of primary school.

The mother, as in the previous case, had albumin in the urine and also a very frightening experience during the pregnancy. There was no explanation of what it was. There was no other record of any destructive medical experience for the child.

The medical diagnosis for Ayse was congenital encephalopathy plus a slight thyroid condition. Thyroid treatment was given to Ayse, and she was then able to enter and profit from the special class she is now in.

Thyroid treatment does not increase the IQ but does allow the existing mental ability to develop and function properly.

A social worker from the clinic was assigned to enlighten the mother about how to treat this child.

Enlightenment cannot change a child's IQ, but it can enable the parents to increase their understanding and communication, thus helping the child perform to his utmost potential. And who is there to say what that functioning level might be?

9

Greece

ATHENS' ACROPOLIS RISES HIGH ON A HILL. AS YOU STAND AMID THIS city's staggering architectural accomplishments, there is an overwhelming realization of how many thousands of years ago man could courageously and brilliantly execute one of the greatest wonders of the world and, conversely, is still unable to make proportionate strides in human help and understanding.

The Temple of the Vestal Virgins, whose duty it was to keep the sacred fires of the hearth burning, overlooks a harbor; flaming in the sun, the light from that fire was the first beacon the sailors sought as they sailed into port.

Parts of the marble friezes of the Parthenon were purchased and carried off to England by Lord Elgin where, preserved in the British Museum, they are referred to as the Elgin Marbles. Arguments have been waged through the years as to whether this should have been done.

For many years, guides have thrown rocks at the statues, friezes, and columns of the Parthenon and other structures in order to whittle away souvenir stones for tourists to disperse all over the world and to be lost to us forever.

Today, the progress and preservation of a country's culture, economics, and education is no longer the responsibility of its citizens alone. We are learning to share it. Perhaps Lord Elgin was in advance of his time in preserving what he could for posterity.

The centuries have destroyed much of the glory that was Greece, a country now a little more than a few hundred square miles larger than New York State. According to the representative from the USIS, there has not been much known movement in the field of retardation. I spent two of my precious twenty-four hours in Greece with him and arranged to visit a psychiatrist friend of his who would be able to sum up what, if anything, was being done.

The psychiatrist and his wife were charming, and were able to give me the following facts:

There were no government hospitals or institutions for the mentally retarded in Greece. When a mental retardate is also severely disturbed, as in Turkey, he is relegated to a colony for mentally sick patients. For example, in a 200-bed hospital for the mentally ill, there were 50 mentally retarded cases with backgrounds of organic brain damage. Child guidance clinics are being organized for testing, but there is little available in the entire country for education and treatment.

Within the confines of the state hospital for the insane, a school was formed for retardates. Those children with 60 IQ and above are eligible to attend. Those with an IQ range of 50–60 work out a garden activity program. For those with IQ's below 50, there is nothing governmentally sponsored. They merely stay at home. There is no social, medical, or educational service of any kind for them provided by the government.

During the course of my visit, my host had a caller who was not only a psychiatrist but was also head of a mental institution. Quite seriously he said, "You know it is impossible to teach anyone with an IQ below 50."

I stared at him, appalled. "You might be interested to know I have just come from Israel, Doctor. There are two workshops in operation. They are weaving, embroidering, running machines, packing, and sealing." I paused. "The *average* IQ is well below 50."

The doctor was well mannered. He responded by looking sympathetic, completely unbelieving, and exasperatingly handsome.

I returned to the hotel where another young, specious Greek was our host for the evening. Dinner was to be out in the country. As we drove through Athens, I noted the number and size of the expensive modern apartment houses along the way, although Greece is not industrialized, and economic conditions for the country as a whole are rather poor. It seems to be a land of rich or poor with an almost nonexistent middle class.

The next morning, I was given all the information the USIS had been able to gather on mental retardation: (1) there were no available statistics; (2) there was but one semiprivate school in all Athens; (3) there was a small private school run by a pioneer in the field, a young female psychiatrist, Dr. Maria Paleologo.*

Swayed by predilection, I decided to visit the young doctor, although I realized later that if I had had any idea of her school's location, my enthusiasm might have been less buoyant.

Because of a little international misunderstanding I landed at the home, instead of the school, of Dr. Paleologo. Her mother and I attempted an ineffective conversation while the precious minutes flew by until plane time. Fate, which had sent this worthy woman to school in Germany for several years, came to my rescue. German had been my minor at college for no other useful reason than that I had received the only A I ever got in my very first term, and when I discovered she

_____

* Other private ventures in Greece include the Neuropsychiatric Clinic at Penteli, the Psychiatric Clinic of Mr. Polymenakou at Marousi, the Special Training Institution of Mrs. Almaliotou, the Psychological Center of Northern Greece and the Special Training Center "Stoupathion," a school for mentally retarded children at 141 Pentelis St. Malandri, Athens. The last named is supported by the Union of Parents and Guardians of Retarded Children. The President is Mr. V. Avyeropulos, Phidu 2, Athens.

Recently I learned of the Kaisariani Special School, 62 Solomonidou, Kaisari, Athens, which has about fifty youngsters. Mr. Demetrius Meveliotis is the director. It is the only public day school in Athens and, so far as is known, in all Greece.

The Hellenic Society for Disabled Children, 16 Kononos Street, Pangrati, Athens, has set up a special class for cerebral palsied children who are also retarded.

In 1963 the USIS had no information on the "Stoupathion."

was able to speak German, we were finally able to communicate. The school was in an outlying area of the city. Mrs. Paleologo called there and informed me that her daughter would be waiting on the main street for me and would guide me to the school. It all sounded quite vague and ominous, but I agreed to try.

The taxi ride was flat and uneventful, but frighteningly long. I was trying to remember what color country lay north of Greece on the map and how I would get a plane out of there, when a worried-looking young woman hailed the cab and stuck her attractive dark head inside. Dr. Paleologo climbed in, and then we turned a corner and drew up before a small whitewashed adobe-type building with barbed wire around it.

The yard was unplanted and the premises showed every sign of incompletion. The young doctor explained that she was more interested in the inside than the outside, with which opinion I heartily concurred. Still, I could not help but hope that there might soon be time to plant a few flowers or shrubs to deemphasize the ugly barbed wire.

Dr. Paleologo had founded the School Under Child-Psychiatric Supervision under her own initiative in September, 1960. In the interim, she scraped some money together and miraculously put up this building to which she transported her entire school in September, 1961, calling it "Idryma Paleologo." She now considers this a comprehensive child-psychiatric clinic. The program runs from nine to six. Some of the patients live in. Others go home on a bus accompanied by a teacher who utilizes this opportunity to keep in close touch with the family.

Dr. Paleologo has 12 children in the school. One small, wistful boy kept asking who I was. The doctor touched his face tenderly each time she explained my identity. He repeated the question during the whole time I was there. Never once did this amazing young woman lose her patience. She was concerned with my possible discomfort and explained apologetically, like a loving parent, that the child was a schizophrenic, as if he had a cold of which he would soon be cured.

Among emotional disorders, I understand that schizophrenia can be one of the most hopeless. Dr. Katherine Woodward has this to add: "Some are not so hopeless if we accept some limitation of goals. One of the children we have followed since age two and one-half is

now in a normal school, although he may be considered a somewhat
peculiar child. Some others may be quite educable although they continue to have social problems."

Heretofore there was little hope for the retarded in Greece, and the
feeling was prevalent that money for rehabilitation would be wasted.
Dr. Paleologo explained that her school had to be licensed as a hospital
by the Minister of Social Welfare. That is how she sometimes gets
paid. Apparently there is a great deal of opposition to the school, and
she said that the Health Insurance personnel try their best to dissuade
parents from enrolling their children there.

The young doctor said that there was one government school in
Athens where children are admitted but it is limited to those with IQ's
of from 60 to 70. She estimated about 40,000 retardates in Greece, but
admitted it was only a guess. Judging from the population of the
country, I would say the figure must be higher.

At her own expense, Dr. Paleologo has traveled and sought out advances made by other countries. She has constructed her own program
to fit the needs of the mentally handicapped children of Greece.

All the children in Idryma Paleologo are under child-psychiatric
observation and receive therapy according to their therapeutic needs.

The educational program is as follows: 9:00 to 11:00 o'clock—forming letters, spelling, writing, arithmetic (mainly numbers), and religion; 11:00 to 12:00 o'clock—the children are given plastic gymnastics
for the fingers to help them hold a pencil or a needle. Then they have
rhythmic gymnastics moving to the time beat of a piano. This is followed by some Swedish gymnastics without music. From 12:00 to
1:00 o'clock, they have speech therapy. One child at a time is taken and
the rest spend some of the time in singing. Lunch is served between
1:00 and 2:00 P.M.

Toys and dolls are at the disposal of the children and there is an inside court where a limited sports program is given.

Occupational therapy is taught in the afternoon, between 2:00 and
6:00, with emphasis on carpentry for boys and sewing for girls.

Like administrators in many schools in the United States, Dr.
Paleologo believes that instructive excursions are one of the best ways
of preparing for community living. Once a week, the children visit

different parts of the city: a church, a market, shops, the harbor, and so on. She calls this practical visual instruction, a way of learning by seeing.

Three times a year, the children present a social program for their parents and friends of the clinic. The children sing songs, recite poetry, and present sketches and *tableaux vivants*. An exposition of the children's handiwork is presented.

Dr. Paleologo has been making an effort through the Ministry of Education to invite teachers and students of normal schools to observe the programs that have been built up for these retarded children.

In the doctor's own English I quote: "The purpose of this effort is to give the idea to the teachers and students not to laugh anymore at mental illnesses but to consider that the children at this clinic may be returned to society one day and that same society should accept them and consider them with the same rights in life as normal people."

One must mention that the extensive use of music is made possible because it is provided free of charge by Dr. Paleologo's aged mother.

I asked about one older boy whose attractive appearance and gentle manner interested me especially. I learned that he was a student in the school and came from a highly educated and wealthy family to whom he had become an embarrassing intrusion. The father suspected the mother of taking on an outside alliance, which might have been her form of escape, and he beat her unmercifully. The wife in turn released her resentments and frustrations by neglecting and beating the boy.

Stunned and frightened, functioning like a severely retarded when he came, he is now not only learning to read and write, but piano playing and English as well. He is very helpful with the other children and extraordinarily kind. The parents seem relieved to be rid of him and the boy shows no inclination to return home.

As I left, I passed through a classroom. A teacher and four brain-damaged children were seated around a table. When brain-damaged children are not hyperactive, they are generally passive; but here there was a satisfied kind of silence, approaching tranquillity, that held the promise of peace to come.

After my return to the United States, I submitted a questionnaire to the various countries I visited. Ef. El. Mavroulidis, Director of the Greek Ministry of Social Welfare, was kind enough to send me the following information:

In the city of Athens, or its vicinity, there are 2 mental health centers acting as family guidance centers offering diagnosis and guidance to mental defectives as well as the emotionally disturbed, plus 4 child guidance clinics with the same facilities.

There is 1 out-patient clinic of the General Neuropsychiatric Hospital for Children.

In the big cities, Piraeus and Thessaloniki, there are at least 1 or 2 child guidance clinics, but in the other towns there are no centers for the diagnosis of the mentally retarded. As a matter of fact, there are no more than 12 clinics in the entire country.

Psychologists are attached to each clinic. In the above-mentioned 2 mental health clinics, health visitors are employed as active specialized members of the psychiatric team. But it is the psychologists who test the emotional, social, and mental development of the child.

A pediatrician is now always available as the child's doctor throughout his stay at the clinic. As in Thailand and Turkey, there are no play or art therapists as yet. There is a physiotherapist in one of the clinics and a speech therapist.

Individual psychotherapy is offered to both parents and children. Some group therapy is open for the children, but none as yet for the parents.

Since there are only two schools with limited possibilities open to retardates, no educational consultation has thus far been considered necessary, for obviously there is no place for the retarded children to go.

In those two schools there is an attempt made to teach the educables, or mildly retarded, to read, write, and do some essential work.

In Greece, there are no workshops to train retardates for manual skills.

Testing of retardates is free for the indigent and nominal for the wealthy.

There is no law in Greece prohibiting the marriage of the mentally retarded.

10

Italy

"WE HAVE NO RETARDED PERSONS IN OUR PROVINCE." THUS STATED MANY government forms returned to the Minister of Health in Italy.

Whether they would not or could not recognize the condition, or were too apathetic to bother reporting it, is open to conjecture. But this refusal to recognize the condition has been one of Italy's problems in its stinted provision for the education and training of its mentally handicapped.

Education is compulsory up to the age of fourteen, but heretofore retarded children were not permitted to enter the schools. This despite the important contributions made in this field by Maria Montessori and Sante Di Sanctis over fifty years ago.

In 1898, Maria Montessori, the first woman to obtain a degree in medicine in Italy, became the principal of a school for defective children in Rome. Practicing the techniques of the great Edouard Seguin in the teaching of the mentally handicapped, she evolved the revolutionary Montessori method of teaching, which she applied with tremendous success to the training of normal children. It became her life's work and she became Italy's Government Inspector of Schools in 1922.

The Montessori system * is based on individual freedom and the doctrine that the senses are the bases of higher life in man, and require cultivation in the early years. She carried this doctrine out by having the teacher pay attention to the child rather than vice versa, by allowing free movement in the classroom, and by training through special apparatus. The Montessori schools have been mainly organized for the

---

* Recently there has been a great revival of the Montessori system in schools. Since 1958, over 100 Montessori schools have been opened in this country. Articles concerning the Montesssori system have appeared in the *Saturday Review* and *Look* magazine.

preschool child. A typical classroom situation as quoted by Edward Wokin in the *Saturday Review,* November 21, 1961, consisted of a boy who sat at his desk endlessly tracing circles within the boundaries of a metal inset and filling in the circles with parallel lines; he was learning to handle a pencil as he became familiar with geometric shapes. A girl sat on her personal rug filling the countries of Europe into a metal jigsaw puzzle. Another fitted pegs of various sizes into holes of matching sizes. They were using self-correcting materials. Others formed words with colored letters, used red and blue rods to grasp addition and subtraction, beads for counting, boxes with compartments numbered 0 to 9 that contained corresponding numbers of sticks.

The approach of combining the engagement of the child's muscles and tactile senses in the learning process is of infinite value in the training of retardates.

Much of the Montessori system is still being used all over the world, as well as at the only school supported by the Board of Education in Rome for the education and training of retardates called the Special School for Subnormal Children at Via dei Genovesi No. 30.

There is a teacher-training school within the school where they are taught the Montessori-Montesano method of education. It is called "Scuola Magistrate Ortofrenica."

In the special school, besides dressing themselves, the children are taught elementary reading and writing. Each grade is repeated two years. There are 12 children to a class, a total of 20 classes bringing the school enrollment up to 240 children. Two volunteers come in to help enrich the curriculum. One teaches ceramics, the other sewing.

If Montessori has been remembered in history, Di Sanctis has been retained in the heart of those who knew him.

Sante Di Sanctis founded the first school for retardates about fifty years ago, and dedicated his life to the cause of the less fortunate. He had very modern ideas on education which the people were not yet ready to accept and as a result had very little support and no public interest. He believed in teaching children the skills that would help them function better as individuals and did not emphasize academic learning. Eventually, he opened 5 schools, but since he was often not paid, and the government would have no part of them, the schools barely existed through private collections. Today the government pays the salaries of the teachers at the 5 schools. Di Sanctis' son, Professor Carlo di Sanctis, has been named head of the medical services.

In a large municipal school in Milan, a special section for children with Mongolism has been in existence for more than twenty years. Was this due to the Di Sanctis influence in northern Italy? It may very well have been.

What then has happened to retardates in Italy all these years?

Profoundly retarded children were accepted by religious hospitals where there was room.* Other retarded were accepted by psychiatric institutions. The few who were only mildly retarded and could slip into the government schools were permitted to remain until they were fourteen. A new law has just been passed extending permission for retardates to remain until sixteen years of age but, since so few ever gain admission to a school, it is scarcely much help.

Oddly enough, with the amazing lack of facilities and attention provided for retardates all these years, there is a law in Rome that every employer of over 100 people must absorb 1 to 2 percent handicapped. One would think that with this kind of progressive thinking this provision would have included the mentally as well as the physically handicapped.

Through the auspices of a Dr. Negri, I was put in touch with Dr. Maria Luisa Menegotto, the head of the newly formed national association of parents of the retarded: Associazione Nazionale Famiglie di Faciulli Sub-Normali, at Via Benaco No. 15, Rome.†

A teacher at the Special School for Subnormal Children was kind enough to drive me to Mrs. Menegotto's and remained with me during my visit.

There is effective splendor in the marble floors that the Romans accept as standard apartment-house accoutrements. But the mark of home was in the floury hands Mrs. Menegotto waved at us as she invited us into the kitchen where she was baking cakes for a Catholic

---

* Today, Dr. Adelaide Gusson-Colli of the neurological institute "C. Besta" is also consultant to the organization "La Nostra Famiglia" which has compiled a number of quite good residential homes, specializing in children with motor and mental handicaps.

† Since 1963, 40 more local parent groups have been formed. They have displayed remarkable initiative in creating schools and training centers.

holiday. We sat there and chatted until she finished rolling her pastry.

Mrs. Menegotto, of French extraction, holds a Ph.D. Her graying hair above the pink and white perfection of her skin is vastly becoming. Anxiety has etched a faint pathless journey on her face, but it served only to make it soft. She is a woman of great charm and erudition.

We conversed in French and in English.

When the pastry was finished, she led us into her living room. I was conscious of blues blending with beiges, some fine paintings, a handsome inlaid desk, and the warmth of an open fire. The aroma of fresh baking wafted its way in and hung lightly suspended as we settled into enticing empathy.

While we were there, I met her son who came in with a friend. Both boys are retarded. They shook hands with us and went in to set the table for dinner. "He can do so many chores about the house," Mrs. Menegotto explained, "and I ask him to do anything that I think lies within his capabilities."

We spoke of her enormously attractive-looking retarded boy for some time.

"I knew this pregnancy was unlike the others. Day after day, nausea wound its way inside me until I could scarcely breathe or eat. Only oranges escaped that vise. I ate hundreds of them. The vomiting persisted."

"There was none with the other children?"

"Only with one, but not nearly so bad."

"And how is he?"

"Perfectly normal." She hesitated. "I can't explain it, but I knew something was wrong. When it came to the delivery, the nurse had to pull him out. Still he seemed wholly normal. Then he had convulsions, and when he was a year and a half old, he lost consciousness for a few minutes. I thought surely the end had come."

"The years dragged on and he became worse. The other children were so good, so quiet—too good and too quiet—and frightened. My conscience had been trying to speak to me for some time, and we finally sat down, my conscience and I, and had a good talk. Someone had to teach this boy something. I could not. I made the decision and placed him in an institution. We didn't talk about it at home, but my prayers were not confined to Mass.

"My boy was learning to do things for himself and it was easier at home now, but the institution personnel were so inadequate and my boy was so unhappy. . . .

"One night I was putting my younger son to sleep. He looked across at the accusing emptiness of the unoccupied bed and said wistfully, 'Mama, isn't it too bad that my brother can't be home with me? Like other boys' brothers?'

"It took a long moment for me to reply. I thought my heart would burst, it was so full of unshed tears.

"That night, my conscience, which had never left my side, my common sense, and I had a long talk. That I would bring my boy home was only a small part of this three-way discussion, for despite the government's inactivity, surely there was something more *I* could do for him than just despair.

"I hired a private tutor trained in the Montessori method and wrote to my family in France for any new educational visual aids.*

"My boy began to identify objects, to count, to recognize letters. Only someone who has suffered for his deprived child can understand the strength of the happiness created by each new small accomplishment. But the days were still too long. My other children were kind but they were busy with their homework. They seldom brought friends home, but when they did, they could not include him. It is hard to say who suffered the most—he, my other children, my husband, or myself.

"But my son's small successes began to motivate me as never before. One day I approached a newspaperman and enlisted his attention and sympathy. He wrote the first of a series of articles on the heretofore unmentionable subject of mental retardation. Then I myself wrote an open letter to another paper, but I did not write my letter for specialists; I wrote it for the people.

"My newspaperman friend continued to support me, and one day the two of us presented our problem to the Lord Mayor of Rome. He listened sympathetically and ended by offering me two prefabricated buildings, but the rest would be up to me.

"Now what could I, as a single individual without staff or funds, do

---

* France has created and exported an astounding assembly of visual aids, which I was fortunate to see later in Lisbon.

with two buildings? I was in the odd position of being offered a house to live in without any means of sustenance or earning a livelihood. The problem was to find them so that one day we could afford to inhabit them.

"I knew of two teachers from the special schools in Rome who were giving private instruction to retarded children. I went to them, secured the names and addresses of their pupils' families. Then and there I started what seems to be my life's work. I called each family individually and invited them to a meeting here in my home. We met and I said, 'Let's do something!' Thus in 1958 was founded the Associazione Nationale Famiglie di Fanciulli Sub-Normali. I would like to add that everyone here that night was extraordinarily well educated.

"At first there was no money, no credit, no office. The parents volunteered to organize themselves in circles familiar to them. Thus they were able to propagandize within political, social, and educational groups. My brother-in-law contributed an office, rent-free. The parents began to meet regularly. One of them found an exceptional teacher for her child, so other parents began to bring their children also. Thus we formed our first educational and social setup. The ones who could afford it paid, the rest came tuition-free. The money was raised by benefits and private donations.

"This exceptional teacher, who started with two rooms, now, four years later, has a villa and a hundred pupils. The parents, proselytizing through the newspapers, frequent visits to government offices, and personal pressures, finally obtained the desperately needed funds from the country so that now they pay the tuition for all the students. It is still called a private school because it is not under the Minister of Education.

"Since the government began to set aside funds for the subnormal, new institutions continued to be formed.* In each place where a local association was organized, the parents were able to get schools es-

---

* An Occupation and Education Center for Mentally Handicapped has since been built in Rome, the first school of its kind, since it accepts children whose IQ's are too low to be admitted to special schools. In 1967 the Italian Government granted an appropriation of 1,555,000 liras to build educational centers with sheltered workshops in Cosenza, Cagliari, Trieste, Rome.

tablished. The support of our national group seems to have given them the courage to move."

We spoke of the difficulties that still impede countrywide organization, one of which I mentioned before: the lack of response from certain provinces. Where there is an organization, the circulars sent out by the Minister of Health for proper statistics were answered correctly, where there was none, the information was scant. Again, whether this was because the parents did not want to acknowledge such children, whether they hid them, or whether they did not recognize the signs of such injury, no one knows, but it has made the situation more difficult for the Associazone for obvious reasons.

Mrs. Menegotto had another one of her constructive conversations with her three-way self and began to petition for a teacher-training school for specialized teachers for the mentally retarded and for a day-care center. Three days earlier, in February of 1963, the province of Rome had set aside 5 million lira for a day center,* approximately $8,000 in American money.

There was still no workshop in Italy, but Mrs. Menegotto had high hopes that one would be opened within a year. She was devoting most of her energies toward that end. Actually, the first workshop was opened in 1965 under the auspices of the Associazione Nazionale Famiglie di Faciulli Sub-Normali. Such is the determination of this one mother who had the courage to discharge her futile companion of despair and engage a counselor of hope. She has set a shining example for all the world to see what can be done where there is the will to do it.

I asked if I might visit another family, and she suggested I see the mother of the slightly hyperactive but very friendly boy who had just come in with her son. She said Mrs. Catarazolla had been of inestimable help and was one of the hardest workers and greatest guiding lights in the Associazione Nazionale Famiglie di Faciulli Sub-Normali.

The next day, I found the house and went up in a tiny elevator. From there I was ushered into a marble-floored living room whose mood was modern against a beige background. Large plants were

_____

* The day center that has since been built and is mentioned in the previous footnote.

growing in red and blue containers. The Chinese home furnishings for which I had searched in the Far East had found a home here, and there were a black teakwood sideboard, table, and chairs. Several good water colors and a Chinese scroll adorned the walls. The coffee table in front of me held cigarettes, a lighter, and some of the small articles that make a house a lived-in home.

In a few moments, a freckle-faced beauty came in. She looked so very Irish that for a moment I could not reconcile her with this Italian atmosphere.

Mrs. Catarozzola was gracious enough to tell me a little about herself. She and her husband had met in high school. She had been barred from going to college because it was the time Mussolini had united with Hitler in his nefarious practices against Jews.

During the nine-months' height of the German occupation, a German Catholic professor and his wife sheltered her in their home, risking their own lives, while the Germans and Italians hunted non-Aryans like game for deportation and death. Later this same professor, head of the Archaeological Institute of Rome, was discharged from his job because he was suspected of helping "non-Aryans." It would seem that this was one of the most honorable discharges in history.

Finally, the professor thought it was safe for Mrs. Catarazolla to return home. She did and was promptly arrested with her sister and thrown into jail. Their mother appealed to the head of Police for Foreigners, and since he was secretly a partisan, he ordered them released after two days.

In the interim Mrs. Catarazollo and her schooldays sweetheart had kept closely in touch with each other, and after the war they were married. I asked her if the religious differences had caused any difficulty. This was her reply:

"My husband is a Catholic and our boy was baptized. Formal religion makes no difference to me. Let each believe his own." And then she paused and added something, which to me expressed a deep philosophy. She said slowly. "Let us all believe in one another."

Mrs. Catarazzolo went on to tell me that her pregnancy had been normal except that she had suffered from thyroid disease. The correlation between the thyroid state of the mother and the development of the fetal or baby's brain is not completely or fully understood. Current research on this is being carried on at Johns Hopkins and Brown universities.

Mrs. Catarazollo said that the delivery itself was a nightmare, and lasted forty-eight hours. Special injections were used to force delivery, and finally the baby had to be removed with forceps.

The baby, weighing four pounds at birth, was almost dead on arrival. He did not cry for some time, and they had to work hard to revive him. His body was overly long and his head small as an orange. The doctor said that as a result of his being abnormally long prenatally, his feet were deformed. At fifteen months of age, his feet were put in a plaster cast for six months. He was late in sitting up, he walked late, and his heartbeat was weak.

When he was a year old, Mrs. Catarazollo's mother-in-law suggested that the boy was abnormally apathetic. The parents took him to a doctor, where he was diagnosed as retarded.

Then began a series of experiments with medication. The doctor was unsure of the dosage and could not seem to give accurate directions to the parents. The boy became very excitable. Mrs. Catarazollo, suffering from thyroid difficulties herself, was not able to react as calmly as she would have liked. Until her son was seven, she and her husband lived in torment. They tried everything, including a treatment which consisted of injections from animal cells, but nothing helped.

Mrs. Catarazollo could teach her son nothing. She hired a private tutor, who met with little more success. Finally the parents decided to institutionalize the boy in an effort to train him in some vital areas. He was in Geneva for two years, but they always knew they would bring him back one day. They, like the parents of so many brain-damaged children, were afraid to have any other children for fear of being unable to care for them.

The shock of sending the boy away was very severe for the parents. In addition, the child missed his obviously loving parents desperately. They brought the boy home as soon as he was able to function enough to attend a special school. Heretofore, his behavior had been far too abnormal.

One of the most interesting things Mrs. Catarazollo had noted in her association with retardates is how kind, and generally how willing, they are to help one another.

The boy came home at the age of ten, four years ago. He went to a special school, which unfortunately was not well run, so they changed to another school a year ago and are now pleased with the results. He attends the same school as the Menegotto boy, and they have become close companions. Mrs. Catarazollo is always home when he returns, although she works in the mornings. I had the feeling that the work was imperative in order for her to function as ably as she does.

Both boys measure within two IQ points of each other. However, one should never be impressed or too depressed by IQ scores. First of all, they can be abysmally inaccurate and, secondly, many authorities think that the scores often test what they cannot do rather than what they can do.

It will be interesting to see what these boys accomplish once they enter a workshop. In both cases, there was the feeling of a vast unexplored potential. By this time, the boys have probably been given that opportunity, for the workshops were in the planning stage when I left.

A return to Rome will be worthwhile, if only to assess the results of further training.

11

Switzerland

SWITZERLAND REVIVES MEMORIES OF AN EARLIER TIME IN AMERICA: snow, frosted windowpanes, and blurred light. Inside, seated near red, blue, and white ceramic tiled stoves, heads bent over hands occupied with knitting or other handiwork, members of the family form a strong family circle, the backbone of a civilization. The daughter, at her loom weaving fabric for a party dress, is not indulging in busywork. All manner of handicraft is part of the national tradition and activity.

The Swiss, I was told, are unlike the Americans in that their social life is confined mostly to the home. This type of home compatibility relieves the family and the retardate of many social pressures, one of our most serious problems in the United States.

The USIS had put me in touch with a Swiss authority, Dr. Maria Egg. She was kind enough to come to the hotel in Zurich to meet me. From the moment she walked into the lobby, this famous psychologist of stern mien and warm heart became synonymous in my mind with Switzerland.

Dr. Egg and her twin sister Mrs. Rossier, both married, have spent most of their lives in the field of mental retardation. Dr. Egg has two children. I told her the proposed scope of my project in writing this book, and she shook her head, either at my temerity or courage, probably the former. She said she had been in this field for thirty years and would not have attempted this kind of book*; but she acknowledged the need for readable books about mental retardation, and she thought I might possibly be able to write one. She promised not only to help, but looked forward to reading it.

Dr. Egg confirmed for me that in Switzerland the tradition of a closely knit family life still remains firm. Everyone comes home for the hot midday meal, their dinner, and so the family is together three times a day. She said the divorce rate was not high in Switzerland. In 1961, there were 42,257 marriages and 4,737 divorces, or 11 percent. The same year in the United States, the divorce rate was 25 percent, that is, 393,000 divorces out of 1,580,000 marriages.

Retardates do not have as catastrophic an effect on the family as they do in other countries, Dr. Egg told me. Later, however, I spoke with a Swiss social worker who knew of many families who had lost their friends as a result of having a retarded child, and who disagreed with this opinion. Dr. Egg, in all her years of work, knew of only one mother who had committed suicide because her husband had left her and their mentally handicapped child. This is impressive since Switzerland's suicide rate ranks among the nine highest in the world.

In the opinion of Dr. Egg, Americans feel that life must be pleasant. Europeans sense life as a task that one must master. Perhaps they take

---

* She has published four books on various aspects of retardation.

life and struggle to fashion it so that it best fits their needs. If pleasure is a concomitant, then that is all to the good, a gratifying bonus; if not, the challenge is that much greater for one to meet.

Switzerland has a fine network of detection in mental retardation. The mentally retarded make up about 4 percent of the population. But Switzerland includes the dull normal in that figure (IQ's of 75–90) so the figure is actually less. The letter I received from the Budesamt für Sozialversichering said they had no accurate statistics but they thought their true retardates were somewhat less than 3½ percent.

Switzerland is composed of twenty-six cantons, and procedures vary with each one. In a city like Basel, a canton unto itself, which is urban, detection is easier. In the rural areas it is not as comprehensive.

Figures around the world vary according to the country's assessment of what constitutes retardation. (The late President Kennedy said the United States has two to three times as many retardates as Sweden. The explanation of that figure is that after the Swedish people have completed their program of rehabilitation of their 3½ percent of retarded children, many have returned and function so well in society that they are no longer considered retarded.)

Education in Switzerland is left up to the individual cantons, but it is compulsory countrywide up to fifteen years of age as a minimum.

On June 19, 1959, a federal act put into force a disability insurance scheme that provides for contributions toward the cost of the special education of retarded children and for vocational measures such as vocational guidance, initial training, and placement facilities; it also pays subsidies to institutions and organizations who assist the disabled.

The educable or mildly retarded, trainable moderately retarded children, and even the severely retarded receive contributions toward the cost of their special education, including a school allowance plus a maintenance allowance if the special education prevents them from living or from taking their meals at home.

The nontrainables or the severe and profoundly retarded receive a contribution toward the cost of their maintenance at an institution. Under certain conditions, the insurance will also pay a contribution if these children need such maintenance but are looked after at home or in a family in the same way as in an institution.

Switzerland, which is about one-third the size of New York State, has about 100 special schools providing for the education of the mildly and moderately (educable and trainable) retarded. Their IQ's range from 75 down to 20. The residential schools are run by private non-profit organizations, and their costs are met by Federal Handicapped Insurance; the day schools are mostly community (public) schools.

Every city with a population of from 50,000 to 400,000 has at least one diagnostic clinic, completely staffed with psychologists, physiotherapists, and art, play, and speech therapists. If the clinic is too small to warrant retaining all its own therapists, they are contacted on the outside for every child who needs them.

Individual psychotherapy is offered for the parents and children. There is group therapy for the children, but generally the therapy for the parents is on an individual basis.

Switzerland attempts to train every retardate possible up to professional capacity and to the highest possible level as regards school and profession.

After the special education, the retarded young people attend special training centers if a normal apprenticeship in industry is not possible. They are instructed by very qualified professionals.

Eleven regional offices for vocational rehabilitation of the disabled, supported by the insurance scheme, provide for placement facilities as long as the retardates comply with the legal conditions of the State.

The aim of the rehabilitation of the retarded children is to enable them to conduct a lucrative activity or an activity in a sheltered workshop or at the very least in the household of their family.

Important special schools have their own social services to advise their former pupils on all vital questions.

It is legal for retardates in Switzerland to marry.

Dr. Egg feels there is no limit to how retarded a child can be and still be admitted into school. I found this viewpoint not only refreshing, but the most exciting I had encountered. As she sees it, anyone who can walk can come to her public school. She has worked to have the birth of a retardate reported early to the National Association for the Retarded. She feels that this is the first family crisis. If the Association can learn of it quickly, they have an organized group of experienced parents of retardates who get in touch with the mother of the newborn and help her in its acceptance.

Dr. Bernard Farber stated in his treatises on psychological impact of the retardate on the family, and Dr. Egg affirmed his thesis, that when the marriage is a good one, the problem of the retardate is easier. If the marriage is a shaky one, the problem is that much greater: One can dare to generalize and say that this statement is probably true in all countries all over the world. The difficulty of the situation increases when there are healthy teen-agers at home who are disturbed by one retardate. This also creates a worldwide problem.

Miss Hodell, a former social worker in Switzerland, who now works for the Swedish Benevolent Society in this country, told me how Dr. Egg started on what has turned out to be a lifelong dedication.

Dr. Egg was on a streetcar and, seeing a distressed mother with a retardate, spoke with her. The mother begged Dr. Egg to help her child. The good doctor's husband was (and is) a very successful businessman, and there was no need to work, but her compassion was aroused and she resolved to try. The lady immediately told a friend who also had a brain-damaged child, and in no time at all Dr. Egg had five children in her care. The number continued to grow, and Dr. Egg became convinced that the children could be taught to live useful lives within the confines of the home rather than vegetate in institutions.

For many years in Switzerland there had been special attention and special classes for the very dull normal, but nothing in a public school for any grade of retardate.

For ten years Dr. Egg and her sister, Mrs. Rossier, battled material and moral odds to secure education for retarded children. In an effort to awaken the public she gave lectures about mental retardation to various women's groups and to anyone who would listen.

In 1947, at long last, the school was granted a subsidy by the Zurich educational authorities, and in 1951 it was allowed to move into three classrooms of a school building. When this happened the teachers of that district gathered together to protest, because they felt that the whole school district would be discriminated against by the presence of the retarded children. She lectured them until some of them had tears in their eyes. So she had her victory. But on the way home she stopped her car in a dark street and in her own words "cried like a baby and felt nothing but revolt. How long would her retarded children be treated as social outcasts? Would she have the strength to win the great fight ahead?"

Dr. Egg has proven she had more strength than she ever dreamed of herself. In 1952, when the citizens of Zurich had to vote whether her school should form part of the public educational system, the question was answered with 56,000 votes for and 7,000 against.

The school these two women founded is the Heil Tadagogische Helfschule-Gotthel Schulhaus. This Zurich school for retarded children influenced the development of similar schools in other places. Forty communities have established such schools, and new ones continue to be opened. Every child is accepted regardless of how low his IQ. This, unfortunately, is not true everywhere in Switzerland.

There are considerable differences in terminology between the French- and German-speaking sections. In Geneva they do *not* group the mildly and moderately to severely retarded in one school as they do in Zurich. Dr. Egg calls "mildly retarded" those with IQ's of 70–90. Those children are in special "help" classes in regular schools in Geneva.

Geneva, for example, has about 20 special classes in public schools for mildly retarded (IQ between 50–75), and a special school (Foyer à Pinchot) for the more severely retarded children, vocational training for mildly retarded, and a training workshop for the more severely retarded. Recently a day center for very handicapped retarded adolescents has been set up by the "Service médico-pédagogique" of the canton. The Geneva Association supports a foundation "Peter Camille"—a short-stay home for eleven children and day program for some young children living at home.

The question inevitably arose, as it does all over the world: What will happen to those retardates whose families are no longer able to care for them? In Switzerland the problem was met by either placing them in the hospitals for the mentally ill or in old-age asylums, even though the retardate might be only twenty years of age.

As Dr. Egg so delicately put it, "this is not the right way." So in 1965, she opened a residential home for 30 adolescent and adult retardates of both sexes near Zurich (Bubikon). Half of these residents will find a lifelong home there because their parents are either too old to care for them or are already dead. The other half receive two-year professional training in housekeeping or in farming. Recently a workshop for industrial subcontract work has been added where day trainees from the nearby community are admitted as well as the resident retardates.

This home is run by the Parents' Association of Zurich and is financed partly by federal and local agencies and partly by private fundraising. Their aim is to increase the capacity of the home to 100.

In the summer of 1967, the father of one of Dr. Egg's pupils donated a four-story house in the middle of the city to provide residence for those retarded who work either in a terminal workshop or in the outside community. The funds for running this home come from local public agencies and the Federal Agency for the Handicapped. It is staffed by 12 professionals who supervise living arrangements for the 35 retarded who reside there.

As the Danish had years before them, the city authorities of Zurich opened a short-stay home in 1965. Children ranging in age from four to twenty are eligible for admission if their parents need to be relieved for one reason or another, or if the children are waiting for a place in a residential home. There are 30 places with 4 of them always reserved for emergency cases. The home is in a lovely holiday resort town (Urnäsch) with a well-equipped teaching staff. It is financed entirely by the city of Zurich.

As Dr. Egg discovered on her many journeys to the different parts of the world, including the United States, the tears of parents are as bitter on both sides of the ocean. If they believe in an Almighty, it is just as hard to accept His will if He is called Lord or Allah.

In an effort to help parents meet the challenge of their retarded children, Zurich, urged by Dr. Egg, established a Committee for Parents' Education. By 1957, the parents formed the first Association of Parents of Retarded Children on the initiative of the very active association that had been established in Geneva. In a few years the Swiss Federation was established, which now has member associations in sixteen different cantons and has also been effective in bringing action on the problems of mental retardation on the federal level. Mr. Jean Wahl of Geneva is the Secretary General; Mme. Y. Posternak, 22 Avenue Krieg, Geneva, is International Relations Chairman.

Before I left Switzerland, Dr. Egg arranged for me to visit her school. The first group were what the Swiss call the educables, and whom we refer to as mildly and moderately retarded. In the exhibits on display— all handwoven fabrics—were a large handbag with a wooden handle, large needlepoint scenes for use as chair covers, and the four seasons embroidered on a piece of cloth sewn only with a needle.

The educable or mildly retarded children were working on two-digit numbers, addition and subtraction, and the use of the abacus. I asked Dr. Egg what method she used to accomplish this rather advanced learning achievement for such a group. She said she used the good old indisputable theory of repetition which, incidentally, was made popular in this country by the eminent educator John Dewey. One of the children had been in this class since she was five. She is now ten and doing well.

The slower group next door was made up of trainables or moderately retarded children with IQ's below 50. In the front of the room, a large green felt board, similar to an artist's easel, was propped up. The children had cut out paper bowls and apples. The bowls were pinned to the board. The children were asked to put a paper apple in the bowl and then take it away, which they did, handling the apple in the bowl. They were then taught that if you have one and you take one away, you have zero. This exercise was continued with one, two, three, four, and five apples.

We then visited the slowest group in the school, the severely retarded or, as Dr. Egg calls them, the nontrainables, whose estimated IQ was about 15 or 20. Dr. Egg said of this group that if you call a child by name and he learns to respond, you know you have attained an improvement.

The teacher had spread colored disks on the floor, then held up a can and shook it while a child whose name was called ran around the disks. When the teacher stopped shaking the can, the child had to stop at the red-colored disk that matched the can.

The same technique was used in matching forms on the floor.

A certain number of these children make remarkable progress, Dr. Egg said. A small quota go on to an academic class, others go to the handicraft class.

The fourth class was a severely and profoundly handicapped group, including many cerebral palsy cases. The maximum IQ was 25. The main activities seemed to be cross-stitching and embroidery.

The children were unable to count. In order to make a design feasible on the handlooms, they were supplied with cardboards to measure the stripes instead of trying to count them.

One child had a needle threaded with raffia. She kept sewing raffia over clothesline and ended with a beautiful basket.

We saw one boy pasting the ends of ribbons on cardboard. He then wove them back and forth until he made a cover for a book. The amount of manual dexterity the teachers were able to encourage was very heartening.

Dr. Egg said there was no waiting list for either a diagnosis at a clinic or for a place in a school in Zurich. There is a place for everyone who wants it, if not in the public school, then in a private one, for the Disability Insurance Act covers the tuition.

I recently spoke with a special teacher here in New York City who works at one of our outstanding centers. She said if only there was a school place for every child who was ready for it, much more progress could be made. She often finds, after working with a child and bringing him up to the required level of learning readiness, that there is then no place for him to go. Either the school has no place for a special class or the special class is too crowded.

In the basement of Dr. Egg's school were the workshops.* We visited the one for boys first.

Teachers who wish to specialize in curative pedagogy have a choice of four training colleges and can qualify after two years. The Swiss are eligible to enter after being graduated from high school or a teachers' college. The teacher in charge impressed me as being excellent in his comprehension of the boys' potential. The workshop was neat, well organized, and busy with a variety of projects.

One boy was inserting material into envelopes for a private firm, another was uncovering wire, splicing it, and inserting it into plugs, a third was varnishing, and a fourth was cutting wooden brushes. In a corner another boy was working a machine that put holes into wooden disks.

---

*In 1966 Dr. Egg opened a branch workshop in a suburb (Küssnacht) where 12 more retardates are being trained.

There was a large group working on quartz lamps. White wire cords were being opened, the wires inside were separated, and small metal connectors put on the ends. Others were putting screws and plugs into lamps, using pliers with amazing dexterity.

Paper-cutting and stapling machines belonged to the workshop; some of the others, such as the splicing machine, belonged to the factory that had allocated the work to them. Dr. Egg said they get quite a few contracts for work from the outside.

The young people are paid according to the time they put in and their ability to produce. They earn from $4 to $25 (American equivalent) a month. Despite the small wage return, it is considerably less costly to train the mentally retarded for useful lives than to keep them institutionalized.

For the most part, this group were terminal workers. A few of them, after one and a half years of training, were placed in outside industries.

According to the aforementioned Miss Hodell, the reason more of the mentally retarded are not placed is that, as in other countries, it is difficult to convince private industry that they should employ retardates. Persuading them is probably the most important educational project on every national agenda the world over.

The happy warmth inside the girls' workshop belied the winter season outside, combining the parturition of spring and the unhurried hum of a summer day. I was told that the girls were taught knitting, weaving (there are five wooden looms), painting, and other manual arts. Some of the girls were separating wires and putting plugs together much as the boys were doing.

"Dr. Egg," I asked, "isn't it silly to spend so much time teaching weaving when machine-made textiles can be bought so much more cheaply. Who wants those dish towels that child is making?"

"The city of Zurich. They outlast the machine-made ones. We have a good contract with them. That girl," said Dr. Egg, "is a Mongoloid with an IQ of no more than 20. As you can see, we had to cut various pieces of cardboard to measure the design, for she can neither count on paper nor in her mind."

"It must take forever to train them on the looms."

"Fourteen days to three months. That is not much time taken from a lifetime of nothing to prepare for years of something."

I spoke of the personnel in the shops. She said they were all high school graduates who had had the two-year training program and were specially trained in metal, wood, and paper work. The school tries to select those who have the most special kind of ability to teach slow learners. With patience, so much can be done.

What a difference in Dr. Egg's philosophy—that everyone can learn something—and the hopeless belief, held almost universally, that consigns many mentally retarded children to perish within the walls of indifference and ignorance!

Dr. Egg had to go on to a meeting, and the teacher of the terminal workshop was delegated to get me a taxi. Since her home was located along my way, I suggested she ride along. I mentioned that Dr. Egg felt that the retarded child did not affect the Swiss families as deeply as they affected the families of other countries, and asked her if she felt this to be true.

The teacher smiled sadly. "I cannot give as objective an opinion as Dr. Egg. She does not have a retarded child. I do."

12

Denmark

WE ARRIVED IN COPENHAGEN, CITY OF SPIRES, SILVERSMITHS, FLAT OPEN squares, and winding canals, late Thursday afternoon and discovered that a plebiscite has been taken in this remarkable little country, and the people had voted to close all businesses on Saturday and Sunday. That left me with only one day for shopping and research.

In the eleventh century, Canute the Great, son of the King of Denmark, conquered England and, in 1014, on the death of his father, succeeded to the English throne, bringing England, the whole of Denmark, and Norway as well, under Danish rule. Today, having passed through years of political and class struggles and several wars, the territory of Denmark occupies an area about one third the size of New York State.

If Denmark's physical size has diminished, her socialistic growth has been monumental and has given her such stature as to be a model for the world. Like Sweden (though not in size, for Sweden is about three times larger than New York State), Denmark has a homogeneous population and is relatively small, permitting a "family" type approach to stabilize community affairs. This introduces an element of intimacy and humanitarianism that seems to influence all their personal and governmental relationships.

Provisions in both countries for governmental services in the social field are of long standing, dating from the time of the Reformation in the sixteenth century, before the Pilgrims landed on Plymouth Rock. Denmark and Sweden have been the beneficiaries of time as well as of their present small area and population. Considerable emphasis is placed on programs of prevention and rehabilitation in both countries.

It was during the twentieth century that Denmark was stirred to such overwhelming social reforms as to advance that small democracy beyond almost any other in the world.

In England and the United States through the years, trade unionism grew strong enough to win privileges for the workers, but did not force general social legislation, whereas on the Continent, Marxist Social Democratic political parties were able to advance socialism through workmen elected to the lower houses of parliament. The workingmen, more aware of their problems than professional politicians, initiated legslation to solve them. In 1915, long-continued efforts to revise the fundamental law in Denmark led to the much liberalized constitution of that year, which went into effect in 1920. In addition, World War I had required maximum mobilization of all productive efforts under government control, a form of socialism, much of which outlasted the war.

During World War II, extreme shortages of food and other vital commodities forced rationing by coupon to supersede rationing by ability to pay.

After the war, Denmark and Sweden retained more of this government control with emphasis on the social services. The care of the mentally retarded was one of the areas it sought to serve.

As far back as 1850 a Danish doctor did his first work with retarded children, and by 1855 the beloved Hans Christian Andersen spearheaded a private movement to gain public support for them. An institution was established with the title Asylum for the Cure of Epileptics, Idiots, and Backward Children.

In 1933, the State began to assume responsibility and in 1934, the Act of Provisions for Mental Defectives was put into effect.

It was considered inadequate, and in June, 1959, an Act on the Care of Mental Defectives and Persons of Subnormal Intelligence was passed.

Today, the mentally retarded are under the care of the Danish National Service for the Mentally Retarded, which is supervised by the Director of Social Affairs. The service for the mentally retarded covers more patients than any other branch of special case services.

It is said that, thanks to better registration, diagnosis, and contact between the Mental Retardation Service and local authorities, the number of persons receiving help from this service was doubled in the course of the last generation.

The Mental Retardation Service is required to give the necessary guidance to parents on the care and treatment of their mentally defective children, and on the opportunities for help and assistance.

Children unable to benefit from the instruction provided by the ordinary primary school or its special classes for children of subnormal intelligence are still subject to compulsory education. Training is provided for them in the Mental Deficiency Act.

It is interesting to note that there is no question of there being a school for them to go to. There not only *is,* but they *must.*

Owing to its large size (the Mental Retardation Service has some 8,000 staff members concerned with actual treatment of patients and administration) and difficult clientele, the Service has provided its own training college, where new staff members receive theoretical and practical training for three years with full pay, and where senior staff members attend supplementary courses. In addition, augmented courses are provided for teachers, therapists, social workers, and others who are concerned with the care of mental defectives.

Contrast this program with the United States where, in the year 1964, out of 956 four-year teacher-training colleges, only 195 (about 20 percent of them) have begun to offer courses for the teaching of the retarded.

It is a known fact, however, that once Americans are alerted they can move with incredible speed. Growing awareness will, undoubtedly, result in an accelerated, concerted action.

For children with IQ's of less than 45 in Denmark, who are not eligible for schooling, child care centers have been established which provide for simple self-help and sense training, and for physical and speech therapy, in addition to residential care where needed.

The general trend is for day-center training with the child returning home each night. Out in the country, where daily transportation becomes impossible, Denmark has centers that educate and train children five days a week and send them home for the weekend. A number of prefabricated nonresidential schools are being planned all over the country.

Where the Danes have to use residential centers, they have related "satellite" homes housing 12 to 24 patients under the supervision of a husband-and-wife team.

Denmark is one of the few countries that has a large network of nursery schools for the training of the children and alleviation of the parents. Many of these nurseries are private, but they do receive substantial grants from national and local authorities and are under public supervision. I have the impression that their nursery school age is not as young as ours, since their formal compulsory school training starts later.

The facilities for the retarded, in addition to the child care centers, include 8 sheltered workshops in Copenhagen and 28 in the rest of the country, adult in-resident centers, halfway houses, and hostels.

A halfway house is the planned transitional step from institutional residence to independent living. After the individual has received sufficient training, he moves into this supervised environment from which he goes to work and takes part in some outside activities. If he is able to function without supervision, he then moves either to his home or some other autonomous quarters.

Despite the fact that the Rome school in New York State was one of the innovators of this procedure in the United States many years ago, little has been done to further this progressive plan in this country.

Hostels are supervised living quarters for those able to work, but not equipped to lead independent lives. They live under planned control all their lives.

The impetus for the creation of hostels has not as yet been generated in this country. They are rare in the United States.

One of the truly remarkable projects the Danes have established is a temporary boarding home near Copenhagen with residential care for retarded children in family-care programs. It is provided by the Danish Service for the Mentally Retarded and is limited to temporary placement, the maximum stay being three months. It fills such needs as allowing the family to take a vacation and providing care for the child during a physical or mental illness of the parents or during upsetting conditions at home, such as moving.

There are places available for 20 to 30 children at a time, and they are eagerly sought after by an increasing number of parents who, assisted through an emergency, are then able to keep the family health intact.

The term "family care" covers a wide range of services for the retarded and his family in Denmark. It assures continuing service and at least a semiannual review of the child and the family situation.

The national organization of parents of retarded children is responsible in large part for the comprehensiveness of the family care program. Through indefatigable work, public relations, and intelligent planning, it has created a positive public attitude toward the mentally retarded, and as a result there has been an augmented public demand for increased community workshops, special day schools, and temporary boarding schools.

In the year 1953–1954, Denmark spent 11.1 percent of its national budget on health and welfare services which include full care for the mentally retarded, the United States, 5.4 percent.

Under the Directorate of the Mental Retardation Service, which maintains relations with the Board of Sterilization and Educational Health Service, are 11 regional centers. Each one has a Board of Control with three departments: (1) diagnostic and medical care facilities; (2) custody and care programs; and (3) special schools programs.

Compulsory education for normal children in Denmark is from seven to fifteen years of age, for the mentally retarded it is from seven to twenty-one years of age.

In addition to this comprehensive care, 8 principal Mothers' Aid Centers have branch offices and a traveling staff which hold consultations in 86 towns all over Denmark. This was an outgrowth of a private organization familiarly known as Mothers' Aid. The direct translation of the official Danish title means the "lonely ones." This group's objective is the care of unwed, divorced, widowed, economically deprived, and sick mothers.

It is the Danish theory that the best interest of the mother, newborn infant, and society as a whole is served if proper care and rearing are ensured for normal growth and development.

The United States President's Panel Report stated that it was refreshing to observe the universality of acceptance of the mentally retarded by the people of Denmark and Sweden; that as individuals the mentally retarded in these countries are entitled to all the rights and privileges enjoyed by others; that they are eligible for all the social welfare and economic assistance given others; and that, when and if necessary, additional programs and services are provided to meet their needs.

Unfortunately, there was insufficient time for me to visit a private family with a retarded member, but the national organization, apparently justifiably proud of their accomplishments, which are probably the most complete in the world today, made arrangements for a social worker, Mr. Wibroe, to take me to an adult residential center.

Mr. Wibroe gave up his Saturday of leisure, brought his young daughter along as an interpreter, and we crowded into his tiny Volkswagen and careened off along the Danish countryside.

I have been told that social work is an esteemed and well-paid vocation in Denmark. Mr. Wibroe was a convincing example of the intelligent sense of Danish values.

On the drive, Mr. Wibroe told me their workshops had been in existence for over twenty years, long before we had them in the United States.* The trainees earn from 25 to 225 kroner ($3.50 to about $30) a week. They keep that for themselves and the government pays their traveling expenses.

The family unit is slightly larger than ours, averaging 2½ children.

---

* The United States has had for many years some workshops for the physically handicapped which sometimes included a few retarded.

Mr. Wibroe smiled at my enthusiasm for the intelligent and comprehensive care of retardates in Denmark. He said that, unfortunately, it did not prevent many divorces because of having a retardate in the family.

The residential center we were about to visit was made up of men whose families had rejected them or whose parents had died. Before we got there, he told me of an interesting eighteen-month experiment which had just been concluded. Twelve retardates whose average age was over thirty and with a mean IQ of 30 were assigned to a team of five. After the year and a half of intensive education and training, they were retested. Their average IQ had risen to 45, but it was felt that this was the maximum that could be reached.

The first building we entered was the administration building with very tastefully decorated offices for the personnel who care for the 330 adult inmates. The average age for the in-residents at the institution was fifty-eight, and the IQ's ranged from 30 to 40.

We visited a workshop where some of the activities consisted of assembling parts for safeguarding skates, cutting wooden shoes, repairing leather ones, assembling ballast for neon lights, and making curtain pins. Charts are kept to record the piecework done. The workers match what they are doing with their fingers and when five of anything are completed, they hold up one hand.

We walked through groups of cottages, each of which held 16 adults. Each had a kitchen, large airy recreation room, and small rooms set aside to assure privacy for visiting parents.

Three mentally retarded adults are assigned to each bedroom. The beds were made up as daybeds with bright covers on them. Walls and cabinets were painted orange, lime green, and pink. Live green ivy trailed over brick inside walls. Domino-type containers were hung on the walls, and small green plants were grown in those also. The abundance of greenery gave a feeling of life and vitality to the houses.

For the most part, retardates are gentle people with a great longing for receiving and tendering affection. Everywhere we walked the men patted Mr. Wibroe with awkward gestures of tenderness. He seemed to occupy a singular place in their affections.

Groups of men surrounded the numerous TV sets, but one old man sat apart putting together egg separators and forming boxes. So enchanted was he with his accomplishments that he refused to stop and watch the TV which he normally loves. He called us over time and again to admire his handiwork. Each time Mr. Wibroe came when he was called, and never once did he lose his patience.

An isolation room had been built in each cottage, but none of them has ever been needed.

As Mr. Wibroe drove us back to the hotel, he mentioned that he had a son. I informed him that I had once taught health and physical education and had been avidly interested in sports. I wondered if his son had the same interest. He hesitated a moment, and almost apologetically, as though trying to alleviate any embarrassment for my having asked, told me his son was a permanent invalid, a victim of a very severe paralysis.

Was there something I could get him? I asked. If he reads English, perhaps some American magazines.

"There is something, if it isn't too much trouble. He is a stamp collector. Perhaps on your travels . . ."

"We have been buying them for my daughter. She is also a collector. I will see to it that she shares with your son."

When we returned to the United States, I remembered that promise. How much my daughter has sent of her collection I cannot approximate, but I do know she has not forgotten that Danish boy.

If this chapter seems to have been drowned in facts, it is my earnest hope that at least part of the information will rise to the surface, visible and well within our common grasp.

Denmark is a democracy, a country whose social consciousness has given dignity to all its people.

13

England
___

ENGLAND'S PROVISION FOR THE MENTALLY RETARDED HAS, SINCE THE BEGIN-
ning of the century, developed one of the broadest ranges of services in
the world.

Despite this, before World War II, many retarded children were
hidden away, never to be seen, never to be acknowledged, lonely
shadows concealed in dark corners.

Years ago, I visited an upstate New York private school that had
several English as well as American children as residents. I remember
being overwhelmed by the exquisiteness of a blonde elfin-like child.
She looked vaguely familiar, but it wasn't until she was called by name
that my unconscious mind fused with my conscious realization that
she came from a highly publicized family in England.

I remember the patience with which the child waited to help the
housemother on with her coat, and the open watchfulness for the
slightest sign of affection. I recalled the picture I had seen of her older
sister, whom she closely resembled, poised, smiling, and secure before
the family fireplace: the sister to whom she was congeneric only
outwardly.

Today, education and understanding are so much better in England
that it is no longer unusual for a parent to walk along with a Mongoloid child, one of the most easily identifiable of retardates, without the
child being stigmatized by expressions such as "balmy" or "daft" or
being socially banned.

What wrought this emotional revolution?

The change in attitude is due to several complex reasons. One is a
medical advance in medicine that has led to the survival of organically
damaged children who earlier might have died at birth or in infancy.
Many of these belong to middle-class families who, because of their

social position, education, and resources, have become an important pressure group. A second reason is the attitude toward welfare.

England betters the United States in its services because of the general acceptance of the Welfare State and national health service, which ensures early diagnosis and care. The English do not look on their social services as acts of charity with possible attendant indignities. They understand that their government has assumed responsibility for the health, education, and welfare of its people.

It was with the passing of the Mental Health Act ten years after the formation of the National Society for Mentally Handicapped Children, that people began to "unlock their retarded from their hypothetical closets." Free outside services now became more readily available to help families and communities assimilate the mentally handicapped.

England's Mental Health Act, passed in 1959, has become a prototype for most countries of the world. A copy may be purchased at Her Majesty's Stationery Office, King's Way, London. Part Two, Section 6, outlines the functions of the local health authorities: "Provision, equipment, and maintenance of residential accommodation; the care of person; provision of centers or other facilities for training and occupation—all these are delegated to the local health authorities."

Every large city and a good many towns in England have a workshop for the training of the retarded. One of our own social workers, returning from a trip through England, remarked on the dignity with which the handicapped were accepted by the townspeople. There seems to be a wholesome respect and concern for the individual and his family.

In London, a group of semiprofessionals, similar to our Home Aids, are assigned to alleviate the plight of parents of severely retarded children and the aged and the ill.

To care for a defective child at home has meant not only coping with prolonged infancy, but often continued nursing of a bedfast invalid or constant watching over an overactive child to keep him from danger and destruction. Such duties have kept the mother from giving the proper love and care to the other children. Housework could not be attempted until the retarded child was put to bed for the night. Shopping was done hurriedly and inconveniently when the other members of the family came home from school or work.

In many cases these English-style Home Aids are more effective than doctors or psychologists because they offer practical relief to the mothers.

I was able to secure an appointment with Mr. Riche, then an executive with the National Society for Mentally Handicapped Children in London which is now located at 86 Newman Street, London, W.I.

Mr. Riche, a slim, handsome, and engaging gentleman, told me that the national health service in England has resulted in a very dense network of medical communication and follow-up. Maternal and Child Welfare Clinics are responsible for the care of the mother during pregnancy and the follow-up of the child until school age. An official record is kept of every visit. The child is registered immediately at birth. All tests are made, including blood tests and those for phenylketonuria (the inability to tolerate certain proteins) and for diabetes.

Half of the retarded children identified at birth the world over are Mongoloids, but they comprise only about 10 percent of all retardates.* Thus, except in severe instances, it is very difficult to diagnose retardation in newborn infants. Where it is possible in England, the parents are notified immediately. All children are listed in the local-authority maternal and child welfare service. This is important because it forms an initial register for the retarded—a very controversial issue in the United States but the basic source of early case finding.

We have the same early medical testing as the English but we do not have a compulsory health follow-up. In England, Public Health nurses have a statutory duty to follow up every baby registered within twelve days of birth and have developed a skill of early detection of retardation. As a result many of our retarded children are unrecognized until school age or adolescence so that invaluable early training time is lost that can never be made up.

These Public Health nurses can call on the family every day if necessary, and they continue to call until the child is well established.

Mr. Riche and I discussed the excellent communication of the National Society for Mentally Handicapped with local doctors and clinics. When the Society learns of the diagnosis of a retarded child, it contacts the local affiliated society (there are 380) to get to the family if the

---

* Masland, in *Mental Subnormality,* suggests that approximately 20 percent of all severely handicapped children are affected with Mongolism.

affiliate has not already been notified to do so by the local general practitioner.

Sending well-meaning older parents to comfort new ones, however, has its hazards. The Society found that if a wise parent went, it worked out well. But a well-meaning parent was not always a wise one, and if an hysterical one visited, a great deal of harm might be done.

In order to eliminate this risk, the National Society devised a system whereby mothers would be trained for this particular phase of mutual help. It was suggested to the local societies that no mother go out unless she had been trained to cope properly with such a situation. A full weekend training course was arranged. The Society was flooded with requests to take this course.

A large hotel was requisitioned. Parents had to pay to come, and it was filled to capacity, incontrovertible evidence of how many people wish to give of themselves without thought of the cost. The course was conducted by outside authorities and some members of the staff of the National Society for Mentally Handicapped Children. It started Friday night and finished Sunday evening. It proved so successful and produced such good results that another one was planned for within six months.

In addition to this, special youth clubs have been organized by the National Society, others by outside groups. These clubs train leaders to help the mentally handicapped* and their families, particularly to prepare the retarded to participate in leisure-time activities.

Many churches run their own youth clubs for work with the retarded; Cambridge University runs one in a very poor area: Howard House in London was formed by a private individual in the basement of his home and so the clubs have multiplied.

The boys often pay a little to join, perhaps five shillings a year. A shilling is approximately 12 cents, so the dues would amount to about 60 cents a year.

All such youth clubs are privately sponsored.

---

*I presume that the only eligibility requirements for acceptance of a retarded child in this program is emotional readiness. I have found no indication of having to meet any IQ standard.

In some instances, club leaders get paid for their work, but in the main they do not.

In 1966, during Mental Health Week, the National Society for Mentally Handicapped Children called a conference of representatives of clubs for the mentally handicapped. A national organization (known as.The Federation of Gateway Clubs) to promote the development of leisure-time activities for the mentally handicapped was formed. At that time some fifty clubs with a total registration of over 2,000 members were represented.

The last thing I asked Mr. Riche was the difference between the National Association for Mental Health and the National Society for Mentally Handicapped Children. He said the Association was largely responsible for the education and training of professional personnel, whereas the Society concerned itself primarily with providing service facilities for the retarded.

About three blocks from Park Lane on Curzon Street is the Ministry of Education (now the Department of Education and Science). A delightful English girl, Miss Gans, undertook to brief me.

The first governmental recognition of the needs of the retarded was in the Education (Epileptic and Defective Children) Act of 1899. It gave permissive powers for the provision of special schools and classes for physically and mentally handicapped children. When later an insufficient number of authorities failed to comply with this invitation, the Act was amended, making it obligatory for the local education authorities to provide special schools and classes for the handicapped. This Act was known as the Mental Deficiency Act of 1913.

Education is compulsory in England from the age of five to fifteen. The educationally subnormal are required to remain one year longer. In their last term at school those who appear likely to be employable go to the Youth Employment Office of the Department of Education for placement in appropriate employment. When boys and girls cannot settle into work, they may be sent to an industrial training center run by the local Health Authority for training in work habits before being tried out in employment.

But, said Miss Gans, before the Mental Deficiency Act of 1913 could be implemented, much preliminary spadework was needed. Voluntary Associations working for defectives were now eligible under the Act for grants from the Board of Control and from local authorities to help provide the necessary educational setup.

It was at this stage that the Central Association for the Care of the Mentally Defective (later to be known as the Central Association for Mental Welfare, and ultimately absorbed into the National Association for Mental Health in 1946) entered the field. So quickly and so well did this voluntary group become organized that, in June of 1914, the Association was officially recognized by the Board of Control as eligible for a Treasury grant under Section 48 of the new Act.

The outbreak of World War I, with consequent Treasury restrictions on expenditure, came so soon after the passing of the Act that it inevitably slowed down progress. Public attention was diverted into other channels, and it was impossible for the Board of Control to compel the opening of the mental-deficiency institutions planned. Local authorities were urged to encourage the temporary use of Poor Law Institutions that could be certified under Section 37 of the Act for the reception of defectives.

An example of what this meant was related in the letter of an ex-secretary of a voluntary organization for the mentally handicapped.

> The other day I had to take a little mentally defective boy to the workhouse as a "Place of Safety." He talked gaily all the way down, and you can imagine what it was like to be told to take him down to the "Male Lunatic Ward" and on arriving there to enter through a door unlocked to admit him and immediately locked again, and to catch glimpses of old men shambling up and down and great hulking imbecile youths. The mother (who was with me) shrank back in distress at the thought of leaving Teddy there, but it had to be faced and she departed convulsed with sobs while I, feeling like a criminal, accompanied her. The one alleviating feature is that the Chief Attendant is a particularly kind-hearted man who does his level best to make the children there happy.

After World War I, programs for the retarded continued to be built, but the passage of the Mental Health Act of 1959 solidified the goals and brought retardation into a more humane relationship with other disabilities.

A small example in the Act was to make voluntary admission into an institution or hospital possible. Before that the family had to secure the permission and an order from a magistrate who might or might not be sympathetic to the family's needs.

Classification terminology is different in England. Children with 50–75 IQ are termed "subnormal," below 50 IQ, severely subnormal.

Most severely subnormal children remain at home, and the parents are given guidance about their care by the professional staff of the health department of local authorities. If the family is unable to cope with the child, even with help, he is placed in residential care, which may be provided in an institution or small group home. Some of the patients thus placed may eventually be able to rejoin their families; others will always need qualified assistance, perhaps, in some cases, because the family itself is unable to be constructive. According to the Ministry of Health, if the assessment of the child is made by an assistant medical officer or a psychiatrist at an outpatient clinic and his need is deemed urgent, there is no waiting for that child. He is placed immediately.

Some severely subnormal children are placed in convents and in adolescence are trained for domestic work there. The nuns promise to care for them for the rest of their lives.

A sufficient number of places for the severely and profoundly retarded is a problem the world over. In this area, England is no exception.

Thousands of educationally subnormal whose IQ's are above 50 are in special schools in England. Approval of funds to provide for 15,000 additional places has been given, but until they become available, the children are in regular classes.

The special schools work very closely with the parents. The teachers there have an additional year of special training after securing their regular diplomas.

The teachers in the special schools do get "responsibility allowances," and apparently many of them like the challenge as well as the extra stipend.

In England there are parents, as there are the world over, who are reluctant to place their children in residential care, no matter how severely handicapped they may be. One such child was little Gwyneth—lovable, defenseless, severely brain-damaged Gwyneth who at four and one-half was exceedingly hyperactive and inaccessible to training.

The parents, in their thirties, of a lower-middle-class family, are happily married. They have a younger girl of two and one-half and a new baby boy. With the help of the grandparents who lived in the neighborhood, they managed Gwyneth very well. The grandparents became ill, and when the mother became pregnant with the third child, the stress on the family became unbearable.

Fortunately for this family, a Special Care Unit had been built in their town for the care of children and adults who, because of low level of intelligence or multiple handicaps, are unable to be trained at home. Gwyneth is cared for from 8:00 A.M. to 5:00 P.M. five days a week. The daily activities provide an outlet for her excessive energies. In an emergency, or to give the parents a short total break as for a vacation, Gwyneth can be admitted to the attached residential section. These facilities keep the family intact in its early stage (which is important for Gwyneth) even if the child eventually has to be placed away on a longer-term basis, which is likely in view of her disability. Other children who can respond with sufficient success to the special care unit program are graduated to Junior Training Centers.

The aim in England is to provide one place in a Special Care Unit* for every 3,000 of the population.

Home tuition and home training may be provided by local authorities for ineducable children where there is no Special Care Unit and when the children cannot be received into a Junior Training center.

As has already been mentioned, the subnormal children, IQ from 50–75, are in special schools. If more special teachers are needed quickly, regular teachers are enlisted and guided under the supervision of the trained ones.

There is a schism of thought as to sending retarded children to special schools instead of to special classes in regular schools, but the system of separating the normal, educationally subnormal, and severely subnormal seems to be working out well in England.

The Department of Education and Science wrote me that a considerable number of children in the ordinary primary and secondary schools need special help by reason of their backwardness or limited ability

---

* Galen House at Kingston-upon-Hull, England, is fully described in "Special Care Units for the Severely Subnormal," issued by the International League of Societies for the Mentally Handicapped, 1967.

(origin unidentified), but the precise number of such children is not known.

Junior Training Centers serve the severely subnormal from the age of five. An educationally subnormal who is not ready for work may be referred to the Health Authority and sent to a Senior Training Center. He is then classified as severely subnormal.

These training centers, which contribute so much to the successful functioning of a retardate, were begun in England by a very determined young lady who recognized the need for the training and occupation of the handicapped.

In 1919, Elfrida Rathbone, who had shared the experience of training a mentally defective child, along with her friend Lilian Greg hired a dingy room in the King's Cross district of London, grandly naming it the Lilian Greg Occupation Center. Out of her own funds and those of her personal friends, she hired one helper and opened the center to ten low-grade mentally retarded children.

Two other small centers followed immediately thereafter. Once launched, by 1922, 14 centers were opened, by 1924, 57, and by 1932, 180 centers had been established with midday meals served in 57 of them. Today Training Centers are an integral part of the national program for the retarded and are the responsibility of the local Health Authorities.

In some cases in England, a hostel-type accommodation is provided if a child lives too far away from the center to attend daily.

The National Society for Mentally Handicapped Children's pioneer combined Training Center and Hostel at Slough has already made its mark as one of the most forward-looking ventures of its kind in the world. It serves adults over sixteen years of age.

If more supervision is needed than the occupation and training service can give, arrangements are made for admission to a mental-subnormality hospital.

Supervised living quarters for retardates unable to manage independently is a problem the English began to face back in 1925 and 1927 when the Surrey Association opened the first hostels for boys and girls respectively who were on license from institutions. The hostels not only answered a social and economic need, but for boys like Roy and Alan it became an emotional haven as well.

Roy, aged seventeen, classified as mildly retarded or subnormal, came from a multiproblem family. The parents were separated, and the mother lived with a man who had served two prison terms and who created great tensions in the household. Roy had been a good achiever in school, was placed as an unskilled worker in a neighborhood firm, and had settled well until the mother began to make undue financial demands, which he resented. The boy, feeling unloved and abused by the so-called "stepfather," began staying out late and spending all his money instead of giving any portion of it for his keep. He lost his job and came before the court for minor theft.

The court placed him on probation and secured a job for him in a local Health Authority hostel in another section of the city. He is permitted to visit his home but the hostel warden regulates the time he comes in, supervises his money, and makes sure that the mother does not exploit him. This facility forestalled the need for institutional care, and Roy is a happy, constructive member of the community.

Alan, aged sixteen, was severely subnormal with some motor handicap due to cerebral palsy. He was five years old when his mother remarried following the death of his father. A boy and a girl were born. Alan attended a special center for the doubly handicapped. At first the stepfather had accepted him, but as the years went by, the handicap seemed more pronounced and the prospect of employment remote. The family ran a small seaside hotel supported mainly by tourists and the stepfather resented the presence of such a boy who, in addition, appeared unable to work. Tensions rose in the household, threatening the security of the entire family.

The local chapter of the National Society for Mentally Handicapped Children helped the mother place him in a hostel in a larger town nearby that had an industrial training center and sheltered workshop attached. There Alan was trained to work in the shop and is happy in his own self-realization. He has found a niche for himself. Institutional care was avoided, the tensions reduced for Alan and his family, and the marriage was saved.

In World War II, the urgent demand for manpower led to an increasing recognition of the possibilities of obtaining recruits—especially for agricultural work—from among the higher-grade male defectives in institutions. This situation provided the Association for the Care of Mental Defectives (C.A.M.D.) with the greatest opportunity yet. Labor was available and work was available—all that was needed was the provision of accommodations for workers. Thus Agricultural Hostels were born. (These were closed after the war.)

Fourteen hostels were established with an age range of twenty to thirty-five. Each hostel had a married couple as its directors and usually a second married couple as assistants.

Every effort was made to integrate the hostel community with the village. Men were encouraged to take an active part in local events and activities.

The comments from the County Agricultural Committee were "less trouble than any form of labor" and "most reliable form of labor."

A leaflet published by the National Association of Mental Health summed up the experiment thus:

> It has proved itself to be of the utmost value, and the trans-formation of the men, who, when in institutions are a financial burden to the taxpayer, into self-supporting members of the community, is an undertaking of value to the nation as a whole. The benefit to the men themselves cannot be exaggerated. They improve considerably in self-respect and initiative, and develop both mentally and physically in the comparative freedom of hostel life and in contact with the normal community.

The early sense of fairness and compassion of the English for their less fortunate brothers was nowhere better illustrated than by the Central Association for the Care of Mental Defectives back in 1921. At that time not only the retarded but their families were made to suffer when no place would accept them for any kind of vacation, pathetically short though the time might have been. The Council of the Association discussed the need for Holiday Homes for defectives from institutions and Occupation Centers for whom ordinary holiday facilities were not available. Eleven years were to elapse before definite action could be taken.

In the interim, in face of the fallacy that mentally deficient children do not sufficiently respond to holidays to warrant the energy spent on them, Miss Elfrida Rathbone again rose to the challenge. As a result of her experiments, "school journeys" began to be authorized.

In 1931, forty children from Middlesex County were taken to Seaford for a fortnight's holiday and thereafter every year arrangements were made for both holidays and day outings. Activities included Scout Troops, Girl Guide Companies, Wolf Cubs, and Brownies.

Over thirty years were to elapse before the American people began to conceive of organizing units of Boy and Girl Scouts for the mentally retarded. So far as I know, no Holiday Homes have been established in this country as yet other than summer residential and day camps.

The need for permanent Holiday Homes in England had long been recognized, but it was not until 1932 that a beginning was made with the rental of a house at Littlehampton for the summer months.

By 1937, the Association had four Holiday Homes but again a war provided a setback for the mentally handicapped. One of the Homes was taken over by the military, and the others became emergency homes for mental defectives evacuated from occupation centers.

The year 1966 saw the dramatic increase in the provision the National Society was able to make for holidays for mentally handicapped children. Three of the Society's Holiday Homes now in full operation are Pirates Spring, Kent; Pengwern Hall, North Wales; and Hales House, Norfolk. They are all booked to capacity throughout the year.

England, like the Scandinavian countries, and unlike the United States, has long since recognized the undesirability of mass institutional living. The English have found that when those who are expected to become suitable for discharge are assigned in groups of twenty to thirty to houses owned by the hospitals but separated from their main buildings, it is a tremendous aid to rehabilitation.

These patients can live under conditions more like the ones they will meet in the general community.

Darenth Park Hospital at Dartford, Kent, has returned one-third of their resident population to general society. A substantial number go out to work alongside nonhandicapped workers on housing construction, farms, or in gardens, hotels, and factories.

Two Ways to Independence for the Mentally Subnormal

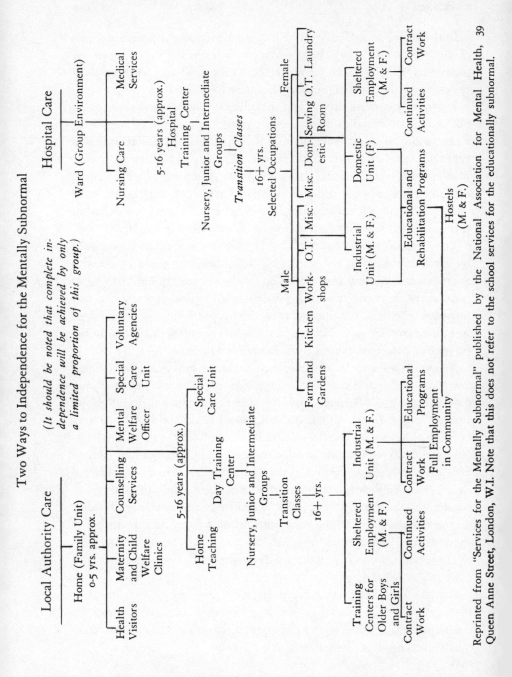

Reprinted from "Services for the Mentally Subnormal" published by the National Association for Mental Health, 39 Queen Anne Street, London, W.1. Note that this does not refer to the school services for the educationally subnormal.

As more individualized residential accommodations develop, it is likely that an increasing number of patients will be able to live in the community after a period of training in a hospital.

My last visit was to the Ministry of Labour.

Retardates are dealt with as disabled persons and are registered under the Disabled Persons Act. They are handled by the Disablement Resettlement Officer. Any retardate up to the standards of open industry applies to the Ministry of Labour. Some of the mildly retarded never come at all. They are able to place themselves.

There is a local employment exchange in each sizable town. Each exchange has a special resettlement officer who has had special training in dealing with disabled persons. People are referred there either by private individuals or social agencies, and are interviewed and assessed for the type of job they can do by this special officer.

The Ministry of Labor had sixteen Industrial Training Centers where people go for assessment and training. Not many retardates enter, but a few do for periods of two to twelve weeks. They are given jobs to do under supervision. A team made up of doctor, psychologist, vocational officer, and disablement resettlement officer make the evaluation. A case conference is held on each one.

Retardates get minimum wages, and they are slow to learn; but surveys have shown that they make very good employees. Those under eighteen who encounter difficulties in their employment are encouraged to seek the help of YEO (Youth Employment Office) by writing or calling after working hours on a regular evening each week. After the age of eighteen they apply to D.R.O. (Disablement Resettlement Officer) of the Ministry of Labor and National Service.

In general, sheltered workshops for the mentally retarded are known as Adult or Senior Centres or Industrial Training Centres. There are comparatively few "mixed" centers for the mentally and physically handicapped. One of the most successful and famous workshops in the world at The Hague in Holland operates as a "mixed" center. There is a great difference of opinion on this score in the United States as well as in other countries.

Remploy is the largest of the organized working and training centers. It is a semi-government agency with a large government grant and has eighty factories throughout the country. They employ only the severely disabled such as epileptics and spastics. Recently they have begun to take mentally retarded. The average wage in these centers is about £8 (approximately $22.40) a week.

Another well-known organization is the Camphill Village Trust* which has two residential establishments with approved workshops. They receive certain grants from the Ministry of Labour under the National Assistance program for the disabled.

Any group in England can come to the Ministry of Labour, and if their plan for rehabilitation is a feasible one, the government will assure the necessary grant. The grant may cover complete costs or only part, depending on the circumstances.

Some private individuals raise funds to build the workshops, but then secure funds from the government to keep it running.

Not all the mentally retarded or disabled secure employment, for many refuse to register under that classification.

As in every other country, the education of employers in industry has been difficult. But they are making strides in England. One factory in London has twenty severely subnormal persons doing assembling under one supervisor. It has worked so well that the firm now wants to set up another group.

I would like to note a final important conclusion I came to as a result of speaking and writing to various people in England.

One of the situations that seem to have disturbed our English friends is that they have received the impression from pediatricians writing for our popular publications that American mothers have been urged to separate themselves from a severely handicapped child. One English correspondent said that they would regard that as sociologically unsound and far too subjective to be scientifically justified. Nevertheless, it is undoubtedly true that some pediatricians and obstetricians in England also urge outside residential care for obviously retarded babies.

My informant went on to say that pediatricians in England generally are not prepared to predict the potential for the development of a Mongoloid baby for example. For the first few years, the responsible medical person would (in most cases) advise the parents to care for the child in the usual way, and to observe his response to their care, before

---

* Camphill Village is discussed in detail in Chapter Twenty-three.

attempting to assess the degree of his impairment or predict the extent of a disability in his particular case.

I am in fairly complete agreement with the English point of view. While it is true that there are some profound retardates who are best cared for in such residential living, institutions are filled with children who have been placed there not so much because of the parents' inability to love and care for them as because of a lack of knowledge of how much can be done for them.

The decision to keep a retarded child at home must depend on the fortitude of the family and the range of supportive services available in the community. Without the maternal and child welfare clinics, health visitors, Community Mental Health Social Services, and training centers, it is often not possible.

Institutions in the United States have been built to stay and, unfortunately, they have. But people's minds are not made of brick and mortar, they are malleable. There is no need for them to remain rigidly in darkness when with patience and education they can be led into the light.

14

Portugal

LISBON WAS THE LAST LAP ON OUR ROUND-THE-WORLD TRIP. WE HAD COME for a brief rest before returning to the United States. Had we stayed on in London we would have had (oddly enough) warmer weather, but then we would not have met the people who have become so well oriented in mental retardation in this slice of a country wedged into the western side of Spain.

Portugal is still being ruled by the dictator, Salazar. While I was visiting there was a certain reserve in everyone I met in discussing politics, down to the taxicab drivers. In New York City, our cab drivers consider themselves competent critics and, with little or no encouragement, will assail city politics as well as presidential policy. Their artlessness can be not only amusing but delightfully refreshing. If any of this spirit existed in Lisbon, I was unaware of it. But the world-renowned psychiatrist, Dr. Victor Fontes, former Director of the Instituto Antonio Aurelio da Costa Ferreira, and the Director, Dr. José Francisco Rodriguez, were far too occupied in trying to help the handicapped to waste time talking politics. They were mainly interested in enlarging the service for the mentally retarded, which still reaches only a small percentage.

My first contact with Portugal's services in behalf of retardates brought me to the Instituto Antonio Aurelio da Costa Ferreira, the only diagnostic clinic in Lisbon, and I can only hope that the people are better acquainted with mental retardation than my taxicab driver was with the location of the Instituto.

Dr. Victor Fontes himself greeted me. He told me that the Instituto functioned as a mental health clinic for children under the auspices of the Minister of Education.

The classification of the retarded is the same as we formerly used in this country, IQ's being the basis for discrimination: 0–25 nontrainable, 25–50 trainable, 50–75 educable, and 75–90 dull normal.

The Instituto Antonio Aurelio da Costa Ferreira has three functions: (1) to observe the children (from a mental point of view) and diagnose their mental impairment in order to classify them and send them to an establishment for reeducation and treatment; (2) to contribute to establishing other institutes of mental health; and (3) to prepare the technical personnel for the assistance and treatment of these children.

The personnel at the Instituto consisted of the director (medical child psychiatrist), 3 assistants, 4 teachers of psychology, a psychologist, 2 social workers, and 8 nurses for the 50 in-resident children.

No day center exists for these children. Classes are held here at the Instituto, but as at several places in the United States, they are solely for observation in order to arrive at a diagnosis and send the child on to a specialized institution when possible. The children are kept here from a few weeks to a few months until the profile is completed.

Speech therapy and individual and group psychotherapy are practiced. (When I wrote to Dr. Fontes and asked him to check certain information, I asked about physiotherapy, play, and art as well. Since he specified only speech, I presume the other services have not been, as yet, offered at the Instituto.)

Dr. Fontes has since retired, but the sessions he inaugurated as a school for parents are being continued.

Dr. Fontes said that there are no exact statistics on retardates, but the impression is that 4 or 5 percent of the population falls within this category.

Education from seven to fourteen years of age is compulsory in Portugal. In Lisbon's public schools there are 53 classes for the educable or mildly retarded. They usually attend up to the fourth grade but are permitted to leave then. If they wish to remain until the age of fourteen, they just repeat the work of the first to fourth grades. So far as I know, there is no public school provision for those who fall below the classification of mildly retarded.

There are 4 Institutes of Social Service in Portugal—one at Lisbon, two at Coimbra, and a fourth at Luanda, Angola, Africa.

These institutes train social workers who are placed in clinics or workshops, in the programs operated under the authority of the Department of Justice (Jurisdictional Service of Minors), and in the general clinics of hospitals.

In the psychiatric clinics for children the social workers belong to the work team which is made up of the child psychiatrist, psychologist, and teacher.

The last letter from Dr. Fontes deplored the lack of sufficiently specialized institutions to receive the children who have been observed and diagnosed at the Instituto Antonio Aurelio da Costa Ferreira. Neither he nor his country is alone in this unhappy situation. Portugal does lag far behind us in the United States, who in turn have a long way to go to equal the Scandinavian services.

Because of the outstanding work at the Instituto, it became part of the first National Congress for the Protection of Children held in 1952 and a member of the 4th International Congress of Psychiatry in 1958, and collaborated with the Portuguese League of Mental Hygiene.

Dr. Fontes and his collaborators have attended many conferences and have published innumerable studies all over the world.

L'Instituto Condessa de Rilvas in Lisbon cares for 60 girls, but I was unable to visit there. Dr. Fontes had suggested that I get in touch with the Provedor da Casa Pia de Lisboa, and the next morning the handsome Dr. José Francisco Rodriguez arrived with his car and chauffeur to drive me out to the Instituto Adolfo Coelero, the school for educables (mildly retarded) and trainables (moderately retarded). They rarely take anyone with less than 40 IQ.

A voice coming over the loudspeaker that is attached to every classroom at the Adolfo Coelho caught my attention. The announcement was being made to the school at large that a visitor had arrived from America.

Within the space of a few minutes, the principal came loping down the hall, grinning broadly. I told him that the director, Dr. Rodriguez, had translated the announcement for me, but that I was not a very important visitor to be worthy of so much attention.

"You are from America and you are interested in our little school. That makes you important to us." He shook his head. "Not many people are interested in such children. In Portugal it is only beginning. In the short time, we have tried very hard. We hope that you will find good progress." He sighed. "We need so much."

"Most people don't know enough about the way retarded children can be helped. When people learn, they will extend their hands. You will see."

Then I smiled to myself. William DuBois, who had reviewed a book of mine in *The New York Times,* had said: "Clearly Mrs. Faber is on the side of the angels." I was furious until I discovered that what he meant was that I was on the side of all mankind. I guess I am.

At the entrance to the building, a room was set aside for the display of visual aids used and the work done by the children. (Some of the teachers for the mentally retarded are enormously ingenious in working out a methodology by which they are able to reach the retardate.)

As I mentioned before, the visual aids here were the most impressive I had seen in one single place, anywhere. Most of them seemed to have come from France, a country I was unfortunately unable to observe.

Picture puzzles with the numbers from 1 to 10 and two disks with number 9 in the center were cut out by the teachers in order to teach arithmetic and subtraction. One smaller disk is on the top and the larger underneath and when they spin the inner disk correctly, the result is on the outside.

The teachers have the children cut out, sew, bend, and handle letters. They feel that a certain amount of learning takes place from touching.

Several complete sets of plastic tools were used, with stars, squares, and triangles for identification.

The handiwork of the students who could neither read nor write was displayed in a room alongside the entrance hall. One child had taken a series of matchboxes and made a doll's dresser of it. Each box had a single brass nail in the center giving each drawer a handle. Another child, completely without guidance, in a free play period had made a doll's bed, mattress, blanket, and pillow. Another had carved a turtle of wood, and a third had dolls with electric bulbs for faces on each of which he had painted eyes, nose, and mouth.

In one room, a teacher had worked out a method of teaching colors through body movements. His arms extended at shoulder height corresponded to the color red. For each basic color, he had a definite body movement.

In another room, colored sticks represented different numbers. The smallest natural-colored one equaled 1, a larger red equaled 2, one slightly larger than that in green equaled 3, etc. The teacher put the natural-colored wood and red ones together to teach that 1 and 2 equaled the green one, 3.

One class was learning letters by using cutout letters as a jigsaw puzzle and putting pieces together to form the letter A, for example.

An art group was doing large chalk drawings. In another corner of the same room, children were cutting colored paper strips and forming pictures from them.

The school accepted only those with IQ's above 45, but I did see a class composed of children with IQ's of 40 to 42 having a lesson on spring. Pictures of a thermometer, nests, animals, grass, kites, and different kinds of clothing adorned the blackboard. The children picked a topic related to one of the pictures and talked about it to enlarge their vocabularies. The teachers then made up songs related to the text of the lesson, and they were sung by the group.

Another ingenious teaching device was a collection of rubber stamps of animals. The children stamped several pictures on a sheet of paper and wrote a sentence about each one directly underneath it.

Everywhere I found a constant use of identification.

When we visited a class devoted entirely to cerebral palsy students, the principal, with obvious pride, called over one particular boy. The boy approached slowly with slightly hesitant gait but quite competently. I was told that when he was brought to the school, he could not rise from his hands and knees. He can now read and write as well as move.

The aim of the school is to have every child ultimately attain the equivalent of a primary school education. To that end, the children are kept until twenty-one years of age when necessary.

The last stop on my tour was to the work-training shop and factory quarters.

The first step in the work-training program was the identification of tools. They were hung on a board, brought down, identified, handled, worked with, and then replaced.

Weaving looms were in constant operation.

The factory quarters had some complicated electrical machinery which had been placed there by private companies for making nails and manufacturing hinges. Electrical planes were used for the construction of wooden hangers, carved wooden chairs, and summer furniture. Some of the boys worked at caning seats and backs for chairs. These were all sold by the Instituto at a good profit.

The shoes of all the in-residents were repaired at their own shoe shop, and all the mattresses used at the Instituto were manufactured in their own factory quarters. In addition, the boys were able to construct mattresses for a 3,000-inmate governmental institution at a handsome profit.

In one of the shops the electrical machines made such a deafening noise that it was impossible for anyone to work there. The problem was solved by a deaf retardate, IQ 70, who took the shop over and ran it with great success.

Former students assist some of the boys in the shops and are paid by the outside employers, who have found that retarded boys in many instances, particularly in repetitive work, do a better job then those not mentally handicapped.

Outside the Instituto, the principal, whose name was Professor Rego, if I remember rightly, motioned to a young girl who curtsied and gave me a sheaf of flowers grown on the grounds. She made a little speech which I was able to grasp without understanding one specific word. At another signal, a long line of boys came marching out proudly, playing their drums, coronets, and trombones to bid me a musical farewell. As I write these words, I can close my eyes and still see their faces before me, and the memory of the poignancy of that moment will never leave me.

The principal had brought out a huge visitors' book, and he urged me to write in it. I did. He read it and nodded. "Yes, good. That is what we need. Not to hide our problems away in the dark, but to face them and bring them into the light."

In addition to the institutes mentioned above, Portugal also has a resident center at Bragana in the northern part of the country.

Most people can survive tragedies so traumatic that they are unable to relate them. And therein lies the greatest tragedy of all, for the problems they are unable to cope with are most often the unspoken ones.

Whether it was the Kennedys' publicized interest in retardation or because the world was beginning to grow up is unimportant. What is important is that mental retardation has begun to be discussed openly, and the spoken word has moved the parents of retarded children not only to face their problems squarely but to do something about it.

Just so, with the moral and technical assistance of the eminent psychiatrist Dr. Alice de Mello Tavares, did the parents in Portugal band together in an effort to help their children. In 1962 the Society of Parents and Friends of the Mentally Handicapped Children (Associacão de Pais e Amigos das Crianças Diminuidas) was formed. Their aim was the same as that of their sister organizations all over the world—the integration of mentally handicapped children into family and social life.

In February, 1964, the Society opened a part-time center for children whose ages varied from four to fourteen years of age. In addition, a training workshop for six female adolescents was opened to prepare them for a sheltered workshop. In the same building is an all-inclusive medical dispensary complete with every type of specialist, including psychological and psychiatric.

With the exception of eleven teachers, 2 bus drivers, and a maidservant, all the nonprofessional work of the center and the dispensary is done by the parents and friends without any monetary compensation. The medical staff and a qualified nurse also donate their work.

The Society is in the process of building a residential training center for 80 children, 40 in residence and 40 from the outside community.

The resources of the Society come from the members' voluntary fees, from the monthly allowance paid by the center's pupils (fixed according to their resources) and from two subsidies.

Since 1964, the Society of Parents and Friends of Mentally Handicapped Children has been an active member of the International League of Societies for Mentally Handicapped Children and of the World Federation of Mental Health.

15

Beginning of a Search

THE ACHILLES' HEEL FOR MOST PARENTS OF RETARDATES IS THE LACK OF acceptance of their child. Retarded children need a great deal of love— more than the so-called normal—in order to achieve emotional security, but most retarded children are isolated. They have no playmates; even young relatives frequently will not play with them. Often the children's movements are awkward and they cannot compete. They are teased because of their funny looks, walk, and speech. Children are not necessarily always cruel, but they are direct and frank.

Socially retarded children are eager to be like other children, but they realize they are not and so are afraid of competition.

There is frequently no place outside the confines of the home into which they can fit with the feeling they are wanted and loved. Thus retardates cling to their parents because they make them feel safe.

To alleviate their child's suffering, the parents take on more and more of a physical burden with the child.

Essentially what the parents of retarded children want for them is what the normal child gets—an education to prepare him for life in the community.

To attain this goal, parents of retardates are dependent on organized public support. Presented in the simplest terms, "public support" means funds allocated publicly and privately to establish and maintain means for the diagnosis, treatment, education, and rehabilitation of the retardate.

This is a solid starting point, but where can such support be obtained in the United States? And supportive action on the part of the community would entail much more than just funds set aside. It was my intention to find out how much people knew about retardation. What degree of responsibility, if any, does the average community assume? I had already seen how the presence of a retardate affected families in different parts of the world. What was the impact on the American family? How could the community and the family begin to understand each other's needs? What kinds of help are available and what more is needed?

Support for the programs for retarded children differs in all states of the Union. In some the responsibility rests either with the Department of Education or with the Departments of Health or Welfare. Government agencies such as the National Institutes of Mental Health contribute money, and sizable sums are raised by local parents' groups to sponsor pilot projects, special classes, and workshops.

The organization chiefly responsible for stimulating and fostering programs for retarded children in the United States is the National Association for Retarded Children, with headquarters at 420 Lexington Avenue, New York City.

Formed in 1950 by a group of parents and professionals in this field, the work of the National Association for Retarded Children is based on the demonstrated fact that "RETARDED CHILDREN CAN BE HELPED." The NARC is chiefly a clearing house, a central information center, and a referral agency. Anyone in any part of the country can write to the National Association for Retarded Children and receive from them referral to a particular person within a specific agency

in his own state. There are now 950 local chapters affiliated with the
NARC in 49 states of the Union. Each state has one state organization
that coordinates the activities of the local chapters.

Historically, the NARC local units have provided services where
none existed before. This included educational programs consisting of
day care centers, workshops, and schools. The NARC also has a listing
of workshops throughout the country. The American Association on
Mental Deficiency, Box 96, Willimantic, Connecticut, publishes a directory of residential facilities.

Today the great need is to assume the role of stimulator in establishing needed services such as recreation programs for the teen-age
retardate, nursery school programs, and in some instances clinical programs. These are demonstration projects set up for one to three years
in the hope that the community agencies or the community itself will
take over the maintenance and perpetuation of these projects.

The NARC publishes a newspaper called *Children Limited,* which
has a circulation of approximately 120,000. It is aimed at all parents of
retarded children—keeping them up to date on new services and
findings.

The NARC is planning to have a community services director who
will be responsible, at the community level, for recreation, vocational
rehabilitation, day care, and religious nurture.

The National Association for Help to Retarded Children is not
limited to the United States. During Dr. Gunnar Dybwad's director-
ship as executive vice-president of NARC, his wife, Rosemary, a Doctor
of Philosophy in her own right, was the unpaid spark who worked on
an international scale to encourage the formation of national associations in other countries. In 1966 parents in 28 nations had succeeded in
establishing national organizations in their lands. No small portion of
the credit is due to Rosemary Dybwad.

I, who had found my way through a labyrinth of organizations
throughout Asia and Europe, now needed direction in where to begin
my search in my own country. It was the patient Rosemary who set me
off on my journey. She suggested that I visit the New York State and
New York City affiliates of the NARC.

Mr. Jerry Weingold, the executive director of New York State's Association for Retarded Children, is himself the father of a retarded

child. Mr. Weingold has done a remarkable job of spearheading legislation to secure state provision for the rehabilitation of the retardate— child and adult. In the past eight years he has had an able ally in State Senator William C. Conklin, who helped effect passage of New York's PKU* bill.

The New York City chapter of NARC, which is called the Association for Help to Retarded Children,† is an active one. It has formed classes in public school buildings for children the New York City Board of Education cannot accept, and has sponsored many experimental projects. Perhaps its most outstanding contributions to date are two workshops the AHRC has established for the training of retarded adolescents and adults. I visited both workshops to see for myself how effectively young retardates could be trained in work that really and truly does contribute to the community—as well as to their own lives.

I was also granted an interview with Dr. William Frankel, director of the New York City AHRC. We discussed the increasing number of magazine and newspaper articles reporting on the possibilities for rehabilitation of the retardate. It seemed to me that there was a great necessity for the public to provide a special kind of education; a departure from the traditional approach toward one that would stimulate physical movement and create opportunities for retarded children to make individual decisions and judgments.

Dr. Frankel observed that the most important thing for the public to understand is that intelligence is not static. It functions on a continuum. In other words, the retardate's mathematical or reading ability might not be enlarged, but his ability to function at a job or socially does, or his ability to form independent judgments grows. Retardates are more than an IQ score, more than recipients of a specialized program or of a

---

* Phenylketonuria, a disorder that damages the brain severely.

† Before 1947, the state association was also called Association for Help to Retarded Children. It was then changed to Association for Retarded Children. The legal terminology for the state is New York State Association for Retarded Children, Inc. The city uses the same and adds, "New York City Chapters," but the city also uses the title Association for Help to Retarded Children (AHRC). This latter is used by many local chapters in the Greater New York Metropolitan Area.

new service; retardates are *people* with limited intellectual functioning who can nevertheless be a *constructive* part of society.

Dr. Frankel concluded by saying, "Do you know we have trained retardates who seem to possess greater potentials, broader interests, and more abilities in certain areas than the so-called normal person?

"People don't know what a concerted community rehabilitation program can accomplish!"

If what Dr. Frankel said was true, and from personal experience I had every reason to agree with him, then it was time to clarify the term "mental retardation."

The NARC offers the following definition of mental retardation: "A condition in which intelligence is prevented from attaining full development, limiting the victim's ability to learn and put learning to use." I reexamined this statement and felt that it was incomplete. What had to be inserted after "full development" was "in some areas, possibly in most, but certainly not in all."

16

What Is Retardation?

RETARDATION ENCOMPASSES A BROAD RANGE OF EFFECTS. AT THE BOTTOM OF the scale, so to speak, is the motionless child, completely out of contact, requiring full lifetime care. At a slightly higher level is the child who is mobile but not coordinated, able to learn little, but who can be toilet-trained. Moving up the ladder we find the child who, with training, is capable of following directions, working with his hands, delivering messages, manning machines, reading and writing to a limited extent. With proper rehabilitative help a trainable retardate can live independently in the community.

"Mild," "moderate," and "severe" retardation describe not only the amount of individual ability but correspondingly also the extent of injury to the brain. Yet the damage to certain parts of the brain may leave other areas open to training and achievement on a more advanced level.

The retardate can learn many things concretely, such as not getting burned, crossing a street safely by watching lights, going on errands to a specific destination with detailed instructions. His difficulty lies in learning abstractly, as in the use of symbols and of fitting bits of information to form a whole and forming independent judgments and decisions.

The extent of accomplishment of some retardates includes painting, designing, needlework, piano playing, knowledge of opera, advanced reading, mastery of complicated addition problems, and empathic social intercourse.

Yamashita, the Japanese artist, referred to as the "Van Gogh of the Far East," whose case was cited in Chapter Three, is the most extreme example of a retardate with exceptional artistic ability.

Gordon Vale in the United States is not only a painter but an excellent designer as well. As of June, 1957, he was twenty-one years old, living at Lakeland Village (an institution for retardates) in the state of Washington. Like Yamashita, Gordon Vale functions on the level of an average eight-year-old in his comprehension, reasoning, judgment, vocabulary, academic knowledge, and social alertness.

Gordon Vale's drawings and paintings show an unusual talent, but his perception of form is most exceptional. He can see something once and then retain an almost indelible memory of its form and shape; can reproduce with astounding accuracy and add certain refinements; can take a blank piece of paper and tear out life-sized silhouettes.

He works for several magazines.

In 1963 and 1964 I visited Camphill Village at Copake, New York. (An explanation of its origin and mode of operation is given in Chapter Twenty-three). While there I met a boy classified as trainable–moderately retarded, who cannot be placed in the outside world. He was an extremely tall, thin boy who sought attention and friendliness. I was told that he could play anything from Bach to the modernists "in toto," reading all notes.

So there we are.

With all the advances made in the field of mental retardation, it still equals *X*, one of the largest unknown factors in science today.

We are assured of two factors. One: there are over 200 attributable causes of mental retardation, most of them lumped under the classification of brain damage. The other is that retardates can learn, perhaps not the same things or in the same way other people do, but indisputably they can be taught to function constructively in many areas and thus to live out full lives.

In our semantically oriented society, the old terminology of "moron" for the IQ range of 50 to 75, "imbecile" for 25 to 50, and "idiot" for 0 to 25 was a cruel impediment to clear thinking. It took years to effect the transition of terminology to *educable, trainable,* and *nontrainable,* respectively. More recently four categories—mild, moderate, severe, and profound—have been widely adopted. The Intelligence Quotient, with its corresponding descriptive term, functions as a grading device at various levels of ability, not as a gauge of potential.

It must be remembered that while categories, much like rungs on a ladder, are fixed, the people thus categorized can, in many cases, occupy various rungs on the ladder. The mildly retarded may be expected to achieve, but not exceed, a fourth- or fifth-grade level of academic competence, and thus can be trained to a satisfactory degree of self-support via occupations not requiring abstract thought.

The moderate to severe retardate may attain an acceptable level of self-care, social adjustment to home and neighborhood, and some degree of economic usefulness via the home, residential facility, or sheltered workshop.

The severe to profound retardate is totally dependent and requires assistance in personal care, makes little response to the environment, and if committed to an institution is apt to remain there.

The greatest number of retardates fall within the mildly retarded group. This means that 75 to 80 percent of retardates can be rehabilitated and returned to the community. This is an incontrovertible fact. An appalling number of people are ignorant of this.

The old terminology undoubtedly played a part not only in society's lack of understanding but in its rejection of any effort to understand.

Some of the erroneous beliefs are, to wit: mental retardates are incapable of love, are sex maniacs, are criminals, are insane.

I knew of the lovableness of many retarded children, particularly the Mongoloids, and the devotion of their parents to them. But one of my most enlightening and moving moments was in the summer of 1965 when two of my friends, parents of a retarded child, drove me to Camp Southills, a camp for retarded children in the Catskill Mountains, on Visitors' Day. The full complement of camp activities was suspended for the rest hour, during which we were directed to Lisa's bunk. Her father and I remained outside while her mother went in to greet her.

Motherhood has been extolled by poets and songwriters, but never had I been moved as I was by that welcoming cry of "Mommie— Mommie—" Drenched by a sudden emotional upsurge, I began to shiver as from an implausible chill on that warm summer day, and I turned away to hide my tears. Two minutes later Lisa ran out into her strong, handsome father's arms. "Daddy—Daddy—" Her father held her, gave her a kiss, and laughed happily. "Hiya, Punky."

In itself this was a minor incident, but within it was a world of wisdom, acceptance, and unstinting love. And love cannot be demanded or manufactured. It has to be earned, and Lisa *herself* had been able to create her own great gift of loving and inspiring love in return.

Lisa is only one example of what does and can happen to an "accepted" retardate. Let us look at the plausibility of other calumnies leveled against retardates.

Official studies have proven that retardates, except in highly unusual cases, have very low sex drives. Mentally retarded people are seldom involved in sexual offenses.

As for being criminals, records show that retardates turn to crime only when someone deliberately leads them into it.

There is a high correlation between emotional disturbance and retardation, but it is a far cry from being what in the vernacular is known as "crazy." Most retardates are conscious of being different and are aware of being set apart from society. How many so-called normal people do we know who can accept such rejection without being in some way affected?

We must remember with vividness that mental retardation is not an illness or a disease. It is a symptom of something that is wrong with a brain that was intended to be whole.

The terms "mentally deficient," "subnormal," and "retarded" are nonspecific and have been used with a certain lack of discrimination.

The Institutes for the Achievement of Human Potential (in Philadelphia, Pennsylvania) take a definite position. They state: "Mentally deficient children are those who from the moment of conception have substandard brains. The brain of such a child does not have the same color or convolutions that characterize a normal brain."

Dr. Glenn Doman theorizes that "at least 70 percent of retarded children are brain-injured—those to whom something has happened during gestation or after birth to damage a potentially normal brain."

I remember the poignancy with which Pearl Buck, in her book *The Child Who Never Grew,* described the physical attributes of her retarded child as she walked toward her, rosy and burned from the sun. I have seen beautiful children whose degree of retardation reached to the depths of severity and very nonbeautiful children who had an exceptionally high degree of achievement.

In my experience, there is one thing that retarded children have all had in common, and that was basically a far-off, lost look.

Brain injury is not always easy to diagnose, but one of the ways in which it can be determined is by certain criteria which are measurable and valid. These measurements gauge brain function in six areas in which man has attained capabilities beyond those of any other living organism. The three motor functions include mobility, language (speaking), and manual competence (writing). The three sensory functions are visual competence (reading), auditory competence (understanding man's spoken language), and tactile competence, which means the ability to identify objects by touch without seeing them.

From the medical data already available there has developed an increasing awareness of need for good care prenatally as well as during delivery. Nonetheless, the number of retarded children born seems to remain constant despite improved obstetrical procedures.

In 1955 there were 5 million retarded persons in the United States of America, which approximates 3½ percent of the population. In 1960 there were 5,400,000 retardates, which reflects a rise consistent with population growth. Unless we find measures to counteract the common causes of brain injury, we can confidently predict that in 1970 there will be 6,400,000 retarded persons in our country.

We Americans should use every means of research, rehabilitation, and experimentation to return those 70 percent, the mildly retarded, to the community.

17

Impact on the Family

LIFE FOR THE AVERAGE AMERICAN HAS BEEN RELATIVELY PLEASANT FOR the last hundred years. Wars have been far away. We have not heard the roar of cannon nor fled before rapacious armies. We have known inconveniences but not horror. As for poverty and grief, they are tucked away in valleys, mountains and city slums, and we have built bypasses. If the circuitous route is longer and more expensive, it is less thought-provoking than driving through misery.

Conscience (about those affected by retardation) does not, in my opinion, make cowards of us; but its promptings do lower our threshhold of emotional pain, and the wounds we sustain do not heal quickly. And, rejected by the community, the hurt can be so deep as to impair the family's ability to function successfully.

Dorothy Murray, a writer and the mother of a retarded child, in a booklet entitled *This Is Stevie's Story,* wrote: "If by some magic formula a serum could be developed which could be administered to the parents of a mentally retarded child for their comfort, do you know what I believe it to be?

"It should be *one which would give them complete immunity to the pressure of public opinion.*"

It would mean being immune to a typical Mrs. Jones who, on seeing a child disobeying for the simple reason that he may not understand what command to follow, offers the authoritative advice: "What your child needs is a good spanking." Or from Mrs. Smith who, ignorant of the fact that sex and delinquent drives are lowest among retardates, urges you to put your child in an institution before he kills somebody.

But there is no serum and no exculpation, self-imposed or otherwise. Time for parents of mental retardates has been packed with silence and swelled with the humiliation of lack of understanding.

Several works by Bernard Farber, a psychologist, were suggested to me by Rosemary Dybwad. Dr. Farber made a survey of the psychological impact of retardation on the American family. In a book reporting his findings he tells us that he found that 70 percent of the mothers felt that their friends were a great consolation and were extremely sympathetic in accepting the retarded child. Ten percent of the families interviewed found that friends and neighbors ostracized them following the birth of the retardate; 20 percent found neither positive nor negative reactions to the existence of their retarded child.

In some communities, Dr. Farber noted, parents report that they couldn't ask for nicer friends and neighbors. When they have to take the child to the clinic friends may offer to drive them or take care of children left at home, so that the parents are able to sit out the long hours in the hospital. Others report neighbors who permit the retarded child to play in their yard and help to keep him occupied so that the mother can get her work done.

One must remember, however, that studies are at best limited in the scope of their findings, for one geographical area can differ enormously from another. But even if Dr. Farber has presented a reasonably reliable picture, let us examine his report.

On the face of it, community reaction does not appear to be horrendous. Aside from the indifferent and belligerent members of the community, how many within the sympathetic category take the trouble to communicate that sympathy to their children? Apparently not enough, for too much heartache continues to come to light.

This story appeared in *Children Limited* of May, 1960.

"My child has been laughed at, made fun of, stoned, beaten up; yet he has influenced me more than anyone in the world.

"Once a group of boys surrounded him and told him to stand against a wall. He did so trustingly. Then the bullies threw stones at him.

"The heartrending part was the boy could not figure out why they did it.

"At the age of ten he joined the YMCA. For the first time there were boys who understood him and made friends with him. He had finally found some understanding and friendship.

"At home he is a blessing in disguise. He has taught the family how to love and understand people unlike us. Taught us how to help others, too.

"Now at fifteen, he is in residence and learning at the state School for Retarded. There he is living with true friends. . . . He is protected from cruelty and ignorance in the neighborhood."

In the summer of 1962 in New Jersey I met a brave and intelligent mother who gave me this account of the family's life in the community.

"My boy is tall and very handsome. He was injured during birth but it did not affect his physical appearance. It is not easy to discern his retardation merely by looking at him.

"The children of a neighboring psychiatrist are the worst offenders. They draw pictures on the sidewalk in front of the house, saying 'This is where the dummy lives.' They hoot at him, jeer, and throw things to annoy him. When they drive past in their car, the mother-psychiatrist at the wheel, they lean from the car and scream 'Rummy-Rummy—there goes the Dummy.'

"Next door our neighbors were having a wienie roast to celebrate the Fourth of July. The man, who is kindly, caught sight of my boy peering longingly at the company and the fun. He called out to my boy to come over and have a frankfurter with them. His wife's sharp scream overruled him. 'Don't you dare ask that dummy here. First thing you know he'll be over here all the time making a pest of himself.'

"My boy shrank away and walked into the house.

"It has so affected my older boy he became an alcoholic."

I asked if that wasn't a singular reaction for an older child.

"He's had some singularly hard knocks," she told me. "All of the time he was in school, the boys would not play with him because of his brother. He longed so desperately to be accepted, but not once— *not once* did anyone hold out a helping hand. Finally my husband was transferred to another town in the Midwest and we moved away. We were happy. We thought things might be different. But it was the same. Only worse, in a way.

"One day some boys came over and invited my elder son to go to a party. He was being accepted at last. His brother was no longer the handicap he had been in the past.

"I'll never forget the day he came home and told me. He could hardly wait. The boys picked him up in the car and they all went out together. He didn't return until three o'clock in the morning. He was so hysterical, we couldn't find out what happened. Finally the story came out.

"The boys drove him out into a strange part of the countryside he had never seen. 'Isn't the party rather far away?' my boy asked. This was a special kind of a party, they assured him. Thirty-five miles out of town, they opened the door and threw him out of the car. They jeered and hooted at him while they drove away and left him stunned and unbelieving in the middle of the road.

"It took him five hours to walk and beg a ride home.

"After that, he never tried to be friends with anyone again. He became very quiet and began to drink. Fortunately, someone interested him in AA. He stopped drinking and is now back at college. He is still too eager to be accepted, but he is able to take disappointments better now."

The story of Herbert Teller at Letchworth Village, a New York State institution, has appeared not only in *Children Limited* but in the *New York Post,* a daily newspaper.

Herbert always loved listening to music. His parents, of modest means, finally bought him an old secondhand piano. He touched the keys and began to play familiar tunes.

The parents tried teaching him but he couldn't read notes and couldn't be taught.

Herbert went through ungraded classes in the New York public schools delighting teachers and children with his piano playing. He ranges from Tchaikovsky's "Piano Concerto" (he can play the melody from the first movement) to boogie-woogie, which he does with a masterful left-handed bass accompaniment.

When he was graduated from the special classes of the public schools, the plight of his difference became more clearly evident. Lonely, ostracized, there was no place for him in the workaday world. The children in the neighborhood made him the butt of their jokes and cruel humor. At that time, no placement in a training center or workshop was available for Herbert, and the parents, unable to watch his misery and complete rejection by the community, placed him in a state training school, Letchworth Village.

A piano was placed in his cottage at Letchworth, and he plays one request after another for the other children. Now when he comes home for vacations, there is a new piano for him in his home.

Herbert has made up a song. He calls it "My Song." It has been tape-recorded, and plans have been made for lyrics and publishing. It is a wistful, memorable melody that says many things for Herbert—things he has been unable to put into words.

In a Southern newspaper, a reporter wrote the story of Eddie, whom he described as "huge, harmless, a pest. He is Lennie from Steinbeck's *Of Mice and Men*."

He is a pest because he wants to be with people and talk about important things. He wants desperately to tell them jokes and to laugh, but nobody wants to laugh when he laughs. Other people laugh at the wrong time.

There is no place for him—no agency. He has an old mother and a sister who is blind. He bought a peanut roaster secondhand and all the peanuts burned. He bought a panel truck and it broke down. He sold it for $10. He tried to mortgage his property, and not knowing how to do it properly, almost went to jail.

Lawnmowers are his obsession. He tried to own one to earn a living but all he ever got were discards that wouldn't work. He cried with frustration. People delighted in promising him a lawnmower for $10 and when he went for it, they always denied having promised it.

On the train back with the reporter, Eddie saw a man running a lawnmower, leaving a great swath of smooth grass behind him.

"That's the park, Eddie. A lot of grass to cut. I'll bet his back is breaking."

Then Eddie said a thing that made him wonder about the things Eddie knows and does not know. Eddie said, "Anyway, his heart ain't." They got off the train and stood on the sidewalk. Eddie's big shaggy head fell to his chest. Tears rolled down his grizzled cheeks and the giant frame shook with sobs. "People promises me. Why do they promise? Why do they want to get me mixed up?"

Why?

How is a man to be judged in his community? By his ability to read and write or by his worth as a human being?

People who indulge in cruel humor and scathing, derogatory remarks about retardates in their presence have no conception as to the understanding and sensitivity of most retardates.

Many of the heartaches retardates and their parents endure from society can be avoided. Communities can be made to understand through proper communication.

On a trip to Puerto Rico I had occasion to interview a taxi driver, a man of humble origin, who was the father of a retarded child. The manner in which he hammered away at the authorities until she was placed in a rehabilitation program is a story in itself, but what impressed me most was the matter-of-fact way in which he ensured the acceptance and support of his child, socially and emotionally.

Upon learning the diagnosis of his child years ago, he went to each and every neighbor in the block and explained what had happened to his daughter. He asked for their forbearance and help.

Understanding what was expected of them, all the neighbors have done their best, not only to accept the child but to extend every consideration to the family.

How many wealthy, bright, and well-educated families have used such a commonsense approach? In these times, we seem to grope for grotesque complications in daily living instead of the symmetry of simplicity.

Clifford MacDonald, former president of the National Association for Retarded Children, has said that the story for understanding retardation must be told to the public over and over again in order that those persons who have not experienced the frustrations of caring for a retarded child may understand the problems faced by those who have. A healthy community reaction can lessen the dismay and the feeling of utter loneliness and helplessness that parents suffer on learning that, because of a birth accident or other cause, their child is retarded.

A most obvious need for parents of retarded children is the time for recreation or some absorbing interest that can be turned to for relief from living and working under an emotional strain. The stress on the family, even more than on the child who has not developed along so-called normal lines, can be further alleviated by understanding from neighbors and friends—not pity, sympathy, or overattention, just understanding.

Lending a sympathetic ear is quite different from pitying the family. Including and encouraging the family's participation in community life is quite different from singling them out to receive an act of charity.

The people most affected by the birth of a retardate are the family: the family, which could be yours or mine, suddenly snatched from the anonymity of everyday living and nakedly subjected to the scrutiny of the public.

What happens to them?

Some people turn to faith and their God. Others pray to another God-savior-miracle man—their doctor. Doctor . . . God . . . help us. Somewhere in those book-lined walls there must be an answer, Doctor. Take a little time. Look. Search. Perhaps in the very fine print. . . . That's not too much to ask for a life. And then what despair the doctor-savior-miracle man engenders when, after examining the child five times, he says, "I'll see you again next year, and then we'll see."

It is not because they won't take the time, it is simply because they don't know what to do about it.

Doctors must be impersonal, humane, businesslike, sympathetic, scientific, Solomon-like; and sometimes in their frustrated helplessness they are compelled to armor themselves against human hurts.

Breaking the news to a family that the child is retarded exacts fortitude from the doctor, for no matter how it is told, the end effect is traumatic. The degree of trauma, however, varies, and a positive approach on the doctor's part can make a considerable difference in the acceptance of the child, particularly by the mother. Until fairly recently, constructive resources for retardates were painfully limited in this country, making the task of telling the family a despairing one and one which led to some indelible experiences.

Oddly enough, the family doctor often feels a sense of guilt that he has in some way been responsible for letting the family down, that in some imponderable way he has failed. In one case, a young mother was kept in the waiting room and the nurse left the child's card on the table where the mother could easily read it. That was how she discovered that her child had been diagnosed as a Mongoloid.

In another case, the doctor requested right after birth that the baby remain in the hospital for reasons of health. The child was found to be retarded. No one wanted to tell the family. Finally, one day six weeks later, one of the doctors called the unsuspecting mother. "Your child is mentally retarded. We recommend that she be institutionalized immediately and we can help you place her. We will be glad to see you as soon as possible." Bang!

It is even more disastrous to hide or gloss over the fact that a child is retarded. Mental retardation is a condition that lends itself to rehabilitation, but it does not disappear.

All this is no reflection on the medical profession. There are probably more coronaries and nervous breakdowns among men of medical science than in any other profession in the world. The pressures are often unendurable. Who has not at some time prayed to him as if to God? And sometimes, in answer to that agonizing prayer, the doctor sheds his coat of objective science and, struggling to remain a supportive human, dons the clothing of false reassurance. After all, he could be wrong. And make no mistake. He could be.

What are some reactions of mothers to the diagnosis of retardation?

This is the story of Mrs. K. The doctor pulled no punches. He told her the child's condition was the result of a disease during pregnancy. "She is a Mongoloid. See the special epicanthal folds in her eyes, her fingers are irregular in length, the small one curves like a fishhook. Her hands are short and stubby." Then, perhaps with a desire to soften this, he added, "She will be a happy one and will probably be double-jointed." He concluded with unctuous wisdom: "But she will never grow mentally beyond the age of six. You may have to decide that it will be best for you and your other children if you place her in an institution."

Mrs. K. did not weep. She said it was as if all her tears were inside of her, and if she let go, her screams would tear the world and never stop. She has since learned a heart can break many times. Death, which had seemed a fearful thing, suddenly became a friendly path. She sat there silently. Her voice was thick. "Why, Doctor?"

He shrugged. "We consider them unfinished during pregnancy. We think, because of endocrine or other deficiency in the mother that we do not know, the unborn child is not completed."

"Not complete." Was that why she did not reach out for things, sit up, gain enough weight, had no teeth as yet. . . .

Mrs. K. wrote: "Some things we share with those we love. Love can be a shield, a banner. But some things, shared or unshared, we still bear alone.

"I had dreams of my child in a room with bars, people beating her, heard her crying against my heart, that suddenly she was in a yellow party dress much too big for her and that she was being torn to shreds.

"I wanted to run away from everyone who knew me, from my friends and neighbors. I didn't for the simple reason that there was no place to hide and so, fortunately, I remained. Everyone has been wonderfully kind. I could not send my child away. I kept her with me —hopelessly, but close to my heart where she could laugh or cry and be comforted."

Another mother, on hearing the diagnosis for her child, related the revolving thoughts that whirled through her mind during night after night of sleeplessness. There was the endless sorting through of terms: retarded, deficient, imbecile, idiot, brain injury. Did it matter whether the retardation was caused by a brain injury or whether the child was born with an incomplete brain? Were imbeciles with IQ's of 20, 30, or 40 any better off than idiots with IQ's of 10 or 20? What did medication like Thorazine, Benzedrine, and Serpasil do? How indicative was the encephalographic record of the brain? Did the terminology "trainable" mean that idiots were any better off with the new name, or were "morons," although called "educables," really able to learn? Did all Mongoloids have broad, flat faces? How to protect her child? An institution . . . over her dead body. But someday she herself would be dead. What then? What then?

To top it off was the doctor's advice: "Change your attitude. Accept your child as he is. Cooperate!"

From Bernard Farber's report on the *Psychological Impact on the Families of Retardates* here are brief glimpses into some parents' reactions.

"I had the feeling that everything in the world had stopped for me. Nothing worse could happen. It would be better if the whole family could be wiped out. I used to dream it wasn't real and didn't happen."

"They explained to me that he would never be normal mentally. It was a complete shock to both of us—the horror was equal. I got hysterical. It is something you just don't ever get over, but now I am feeling better in many ways."

"If you have dreamed all your life of having a child and watching him grow up and go through life, and then having it all smashed at one time, it is pretty rough."

"It was an act of God."

Dr. Ignacy Goldberg of Columbia University, a leading world authority on mental retardation, observes that generally parents of the mentally retarded are continually on the defensive. There is, he says, a tendency for them to seek out the "Why?" and "Who is to blame?" It amounts to digging into seemingly harmless traits and mannerisms in his family, her family: his brother who never went beyond the third grade, her sister who had a maddening habit of drumming her fingers on the table; the uncle who ate the same lunch for thirty-five years; the aunt who was not bright and repeated everything you said to her; the cousin who talked incessantly without ever saying anything. Of course these are interpreted according to the limits of one's own experience, family background, traditions, superstitions, and culture.

And Dr. Goldberg adds: "Parents of the retarded receive the worst kind of counseling every minute of the day—week—year."

Dr. Leo Kanner, a child psychiatrist, states that, broadly speaking, there are three types of emotional reaction by parents to a mentally retarded child in the family:

(1) The child is accepted regardless of his handicap. The parents continue to function in a mature, normal way.

(2) There is evasiveness; the defect is attributed to some specific cause, such as tonsils, glands, laziness, visual disability, and the like. Unless the child is grotesquely deformed, the problem is disguised and the solution is regarded as a simple one as soon as remedial means are taken.

(3) The parents are completely unable to face the facts, and the issue of retardation is completely ignored. The presence of the retarded child in the home creates tension and may disrupt family life.

What philosophy do parents adopt in order to survive?

Mrs. K., whose story was described a few pages back, wrote later of her retarded child: "At the age of two, I watched her, wondering if she would ever walk, and as if in response to my silent prayer, she suddenly stood and walked six steps. I wept because this was a wondrous thing.

"Then she began to say words—a few at a time. She will never be like other children, but she has a special light. No child could love more freely, and if her love is given equally to a kitten, a bird, a pigeon, a neighbor, a shopkeeper, or a doll, it is all part of God's world and of our life."

In August of 1959, a Mrs. G. wrote: "We parents must be teachers. Retarded children learn through imitation. Because it takes so long, what my daughter learns she retains. The danger is in learning wrongly, for then it is difficult to undo. She imitates even a spurt of anger. When she is happy, her face lights up. Her sorrow and frustration are pitiful. But we parents must be strong. We cannot indulge in self-pity and weakness. All day long we use everything at hand to teach. This is a knife. . . . This is a spoon, Cathy. This is a fork . . . over and over again."

Some parents say, "We are no different from other families."

Others have felt the difference: "I used to be ashamed when I went out with my son because of his behavior. I still become embarrassed when he embraces strangers. People who do not have retarded children don't have to worry about this. I steel myself not to mind."

"As parents of a retarded child we must be more lenient. You cannot treat my boy as a normal child. We have greater responsibilities than other parents."

"We have much more tension than other people. We aren't able to get out much because it is impossible to get anyone to take care of him."

"Our life is affected more because I have to work. We can't get people to care for him. He will not stay with strange people. Consequently our life is more restricted."

There is no doubt that the problem of general care for a retarded child is an ominous one, making it practically impossible for a mother to work as long as the retarded child is kept at home. The satisfactions in caring for these children are usually slow in coming, and it is difficult to interest most people in caring for them.

In school the unfavorable comparison between a retardate's abilities and those of normal children is constantly present. If he is placed in a regular class, he has great difficulty reading, and he is soon given different treatment in the classroom. The child is further inhibited by the limits of his social expectancy.

This makes many parents feel uncomfortable about their brain-injured child. If this affects the parents socially, it is logical that the damaged child will have even more conflict in his social adjustment.

The extent to which parents manage to feel comfortable with their retarded child influences the attitudes of others.

In one case, a mother felt tense and depressed because she had delayed investigation of her retarded child when she found him unusually quiet. So overwhelmed with guilt was she that she now appears emotionally detached from any close relationship to the child.

All of the foregoing is just a glimpse into the hearts of these parents. We cannot begin to assess the creative effort and emotional discipline necessary in order to live a fairly normal life along with the acceptance of a retarded child.

Many problems within families purport to originate in sibling rivalry, the normal rivalry along the road of achievement. Competition from the retarded brother or sister is negligible, but other problems arise for siblings of retardates which can affect the entire family.

About twelve years ago, a mother sat staring at her doctor. What was he saying? And she had always thought he was such a good man. Now he didn't seem to know what he was talking about! Poor man, he was working too hard, getting older, no longer able to diagnose properly. What he was saying couldn't be—it just couldn't!

But it was, and then came the inevitable unanswerable question. Why us, oh, God, why us? What did we do wrong to deserve such a fate?

"The child must be sent to an institution." And the age-old fight of all mothers for their children—"No!"

In the agonizing time ahead, the mother asked herself: "Why do I refuse to part with her? Is it shame, or do I pity myself? We have always been religious. Each of our children always attended Sunday school. Was this our reward for observing a strict code of moral and religious conduct?

What would happen to her other three daughters? How would they react to the knowledge that their sister was retarded?

Would the three sisters accept this handicapped child?

What would their life be like? Would they be ashamed to bring friends into their home—this home that was so rich in love and the gift of material things? Would their friends find this child a source of embarrassment and make excuses never to come?

By the time the child was five, the facial characteristics of a retarded child, Mongoloid with the inward slant of the eyes, heavy epicanthal folds of the lids, broad cheekbones, depressed nose, and wide nostrils became more apparent, but oddly enough it merely made their love for her greater. She is a smiling child, loves people, and displays a compassion and understanding that belies her subnormal IQ—below 40.

She was always the subject of her sisters' essays and themes. Each in her own way described the stimulating effect of this child on the family.

"She seemed to give us a greater sense of values and an increased appreciation of the multiple blessings that we all take for granted.

"She made us all realize that human values have far greater significance and produce greater happiness than material values.

"She has instilled in us an overwhelming desire to help others wherever they might be."

The mother recalled: "The day of my eldest daughter's wedding approached. How would this child fit into the picture? Would she have to remain at home under the watchful eye of the maid? I waited and prayed for guidance.

"Then one day the bride-to-be came to us. She said quite simply, 'I want her to be in my wedding procession.'

"In that one sentence were ten years of doubt and anxiety erased—and now there was complete reassurance.

"My retarded child walked down the aisle confidently, head erect and smiling. She performed her part beautifully, and the phone hasn't stopped ringing congratulations yet."

From other families came these reactions.

One young girl said, "The neighbors won't let their children play with my brother. David will always need extra care and be a special problem, but he's a special delight too. He's easy to love because he needs lot of love."

Another sister wrote this story. "Barry breaks, tears, and spills everything. He drools and when his mouth is open he looks stupid.

"He jabbers all the time, and half the time we don't know what he's saying. When we are out, he either wants to hug and kiss everyone or just stands and stares at people.

"He keeps saying the same thing all the time.

"When my friends come over, he has to be right in the way all the time, starting when the front door opens."

One mother said, "My normal children seem to imitate his behavior."

Families' excursions are often limited because the retarded child makes it difficult to go places as a family group. This incurs resentment on the part of the so-called normal children.

There is no doubt that brothers and sisters of retarded children are affected by short-run shifts in their relationships to their friends and family but do overcome these handicaps eventually. It is the parents who are most permanently affected.

Dr. Farber reports that the majority of mothers felt their other children were unaffected, but that was in cases where children were considerably older and understood the child's condition. But the closer a sibling is to being a peer of a retardate, the greater the effect on the normal child.

In 80 percent of the families in Dr. Farber's survey the children were very close to their retarded sibling. The families were close-knit and the mothers say it was because the retarded child himself needed strong family unity.

Grandparents play a supportive role in the family lives of their children as well as of their grandchildren. Yet according to Dr. Farber, only 50 percent of grandparents are able to accept a retarded child, as against 58 percent of aunts and uncles.

I heard the story of one grandmother who constantly bought presents for her granddaughters and never once bought one single toy for her retarded grandson, offering the explanation that she didn't know what to buy for a boy.

Perhaps as one grows older, "difference" is more difficult to accept.

Generally speaking, the husband's mother tends to be less accepting and sympathetic than the mother's mother. Her mother's understanding and sympathy play a large part in the mother's adjustment to her retarded child. It affords the opportunity to talk over her problems and serves as a great relief of tension.

Bernard Farber has written a pamphlet * on the marital integration score of parents with a retarded child. Loosely translated "marital integration" means the ability of two people to get along as a couple and then in a family situation.

The personal adjustment of the parents prior to the birth of a retarded child is important. If they are happy, they work well together toward the child's development.

Dr. Farber makes some interesting assertions. He states that a retardate can be accepted more by lower classes than middle-class families because the middle-class mother often works, divorces are more frequent, and the families are better educated.

Families who attend church regularly score higher in marital in-

---

* *Effects of a Severely Retarded Child on Family Integration.*

tegration than nonchurchgoers. Catholics, he contends, tend to have greater social cohesion than non-Catholics and are more accepting of the retardate. Yet in contradiction to Dr. Farber, the percentage of Catholic children in two large state institutions, Letchworth in New York State and Mansfield State Training School in Connecticut, is disproportionately high. In Letchworth, according to the most recent figures, out of a population of 4,251, 2,183, or 51.7 percent, are Catholics, and at Mansfield State Training School the residents number 1,825 out of which 969, or about 55 percent, are Roman Catholic.

Farber further states that parents have less trouble getting along with a mentally retarded girl than a boy. The normal boy is expected to achieve a status in the community that is at least equal to that of the father. A normal girl is expected to marry and raise a family, help with the housework, and care for her personal appearance. A retarded girl, therefore, can conform more easily to parents' expectations than a boy.

Of all the family of a retardate, the mother is always most permanently affected. The child is part of her. She usually cannot accept the fact of his limitations. But this may bear unexpected fruit in the mother who will continue to try to prove that her child can be taught and thus will seek every means of training and education.

One day Mrs. Rosemary Dybwad and this writer were discussing the supportive role of the Catholic Church, which accepts the feelings and responsibility of its members, whereas the Jewish people, despite the number of Jewish agencies, carry the burden of their feelings themselves. What makes it doubly difficult is that the emphasis among them has always been on achievement, and retarded children will never achieve within an acceptable range.

"But," said Mrs. Dybwad, "it is the stubborn refusal to accept that has made the Jewish families some of the greatest 'doers' in this country."

If this writer has learned anything at all with complete certainty, it is that there are no absolutes anywhere, and retardation is no exception.

18

Diagnosis, Prognosis, and
Services for the
Retarded

OVER TWO HUNDRED CAUSES OF MENTAL RETARDATION HAVE BEEN IDENTI-fied, and yet one of the greatest obstacles in dealing with retardates is the inability of the physician to make an early and positive diagnosis at birth. Only the most profoundly impaired children are identifiable in the very beginning. Of all children diagnosed as mentally defective during the first year of life, those recognized as having Down's syndrome are the easiest to classify because of their unique stigmata.

But not even all Mongoloids are recognized as such at birth since many of their physical characteristics may not be obvious. Mongoloids make up only 10 percent of all institutionalized retardates.

The very low number of infants up to one year of age identified as mentally retarded is, in part at least, due to the fact that their intellectual deficiency is not yet apparent. Sometimes parents do not become aware of retardation until the child enters school, when it may become clinically visible, and often not even then. The largest percentage of children diagnosed as retardates is in the ten- to fourteen-year-old group, where their social difficulties become as apparent as their academic ones.

Except in extreme cases, the symptoms showing impairment vary with the age of the individual. Below school age it is discerned through abnormal difficulty in putting on boots, buttoning clothes, walking, running, eating, and speaking. In school, it is inability to learn or function independently or to meet employment requirements.

A survey done at Flower and Fifth Avenue Hospitals has shown that families go to as many as eight different doctors or hospitals be-

fore they get a definitive diagnosis. Unfortunately most people do not
know that the United States Department of Health, Education, and
Welfare issues a listing of Clinical Programs for the Mentally Retarded.*

There may be one clinic in your entire state or a dozen, depending
on its size and location. But one thing is certain. There will be a
waiting time—three, six, nine months, or a year.

Families have often spent their savings and jeopardized the position
of the entire family for years to come, traveling from doctor to hospital
and back to doctor again before a positive diagnosis is made.

Since the diagnosis of a retarded child is difficult, many doctors
hesitate to make it. Many of them prefer to rest comfortably on the
philosophy that children travel at an individual speed in different
areas of growth. In the end they will all arrive at the same place. Potential rate of learning is one of the most unpredictable factors in the
prognosis of human development. Even with the retarded child, says
Dr. Leo Kanner, experience, contrary to initial theories, has proven that
a child's IQ can and does change, sometimes very markedly, as the
disposition to learn is encouraged or thwarted. So the doctor's diagnosis or prediction can be wrong.

With the factors so variable, few will want to predict how much
learning and utilization of learning will take place.

The best way to estimate a retardate's degree of impairment, with
our present means of measurement, is in a diagnostic clinic; and while
certain potentials cannot be clinically evaluated, the clinic is to date
the only available means of prognosis for rehabilitation.

Diagnostic procedures include a history of the patient's development
and social and medical background; an examination to establish his
present physical development; an examination to ascertain his bone
age (a child with a thyroid deficiency may have a very delayed bone
development and at the age of four appear to be only two); a metabolic evaluation for inborn errors of metabolism (PKU); neurological examination to ascertain impairment in fine motor movement,
isolated reflex abnormalities, and so forth. The observation of physical

---

* This may be secured by writing to the Children's Bureau, Washington,
D.C.

clues to biological abnormalities includes measurement of the cranium and disproportions in the face, eyes, ears, skin, and digits (abnormalities may be associated with identifiable chromosomal disorders such as Down's and Marfan's * syndromes), and requires special laboratory procedures. Last but not least in importance is the evaluation of psycho-sociocultural factors which consists of psychological tests and an evaluation of sociocultural environment.

Over one hundred clinics for the diagnosis of the mentally retarded have been established and are supported by the Children's Bureau, Washington, D.C.† This fills only a fraction of the present need, but some states are more active than others. Cities in Massachusetts, Connecticut, New Jersey, and New York can point with pride to what they have attained, even though it is still insufficient.

I made a personal investigation of diagnostic clinics in the New York City area.

The Morris J. Solomon Clinic for Retarded Children at the Jewish Hospital of Brooklyn, the Mental Retardation Clinic of the Flower and Fifth Avenue Hospitals, and the Developmental Evaluation Clinic of the Albert Einstein College of Medicine are the three medically oriented diagnostic clinics for retardates in New York City.

Medically oriented means that the clinic functions solely under medical administration, with all the interdisciplinary resources available within the walls of the hospital where it is located. If, for example, a child shows signs of a rare endocrine disturbance, he is sent to the Endocrine Department within the hospital. He is not sent to another hospital for evaluation of any medical problem.

The Institute for Retarded Children of the Shield of David on An-

---

* Marfan's Syndrome does not necessarily indicate mental retardation but can accompany it. People suffering from it are sometimes in the genius category. Abraham Lincoln was thought to be one of its victims.

Its physical characteristics include a long thin skeletal structure with long slender fingers. Its most serious concomitant is poor elastic tissue which results in the subluxation of the lens, spinal curvature, and aortic weakness.

† Some retarded children are cared for by psychiatric clinics. Approximately one hundred more clinics have been established independent of the Children's Bureau.

drews Avenue in the Bronx, and the Kennedy Child Study Center on East 67th Street in Manhattan are educationally oriented clinics. The administration is not strictly medical. This means that although the child receives a full medical checkup, the emphasis at these clinics is to prepare the child for entrance into some sort of class within the public school system. The Institute at the Shield of David has some medical facilities, but will refer a child to a hospital when the Institute is unable to complete its picture. The Kennedy Child Study Institute works in close conjunction wilth St. Vincent's Hospital.

Lenox Hill Hospital has a small clinic devoted only to those children under four in whom no minimal or questionable organic cause for retardation has been found. Dr. Katharine Woodward, formerly of their psychiatric staff, writes:

"It is our endeavor by dealing with emotional problems early and intensively to help the children to function at their optimum potential. We have been successful in getting about one-third of the children into normal schools. The others may attend special schools or special classes, but do function better because of the early program. We have very few who have had to be institutionalized. We have thus far selected children with no, or minimal or questionably demonstrable, organic findings. This was largely in an attempt to keep the psychiatric findings as uncomplicated as possible since this is a relatively unexplored area. Eventually I hope that many more types of children may be included."

With the exception of Lenox Hill Hospital and the Albert Einstein Medical Center, I have visited all the aforementioned clinics.

There is one thing that all the clinics have unalterably in common— a list of about 200 waiting for admission, the waiting period being from six months to a year before examinations, diagnosis, and treatment can be started.

In the course of one year, while 1,500 families are on the official rolls of Flower and Fifth Avenue Hospitals, an average of about 250 are under active treatment, and about 5 or 6 new cases are admitted for treatment each week.

The Morris J. Solomon Clinic at the Jewish Hospital of Brooklyn is unable to see as many families since its facilities are more limited.

Despite this, they service from 250 to 300 active cases and admit 2 or 3 new cases a week.

The Developmental Evaluation Clinic of the Albert Einstein College of Medicine in the Bronx, in addition to diagnostic facilities, has experimental accommodations for the study of young retardates in nursery school classes.

At the Morris J. Solomon Clinic for Retarded Children I had occasion to watch Miss Irene Eckstein working with a preschool group to ready them for special classes in the public school system. She was particularly proud of one youngster who only the year before had been completely undisciplined and practically unable to talk. One year's work with the group enabled him to sit in class, raise his hand, and respond to questioning.

All three clinics offer individual and group therapy, but the Evaluation Clinic of the Albert Einstein Clinic has been forced to curtail therapy for parents due to lack of funds. A grant has been made to this clinic and a new $1 million building is being erected for the purpose of research in mental retardation.

The Morris J. Solomon Clinic at the Jewish Hospital in Brooklyn, under the able direction of Dr. Joseph Wortis, one of the leading experts in mental retardation, has long been known for its large research program.

A common problem faced by all the clinics is the difficulty of placing children in schools or programs after a diagnosis is made.

It is at this point that mention must be made of an agency known as Retarded Infants Services established primarily to deal with the problem of retarded children under five.

In 1953, parents who had experienced not only the trauma of institutionalizing their children but the difficulties involved as well, banded together and formed an agency known as Parents with a Purpose to give financial assistance to families for private placement of their children wherever the waiting time to enter a public one was unendurable. It seems inconceivable that families with children so damaged that they attempted to destroy not only themselves but the entire family as well had absolutely no place in the world to go; that they had to take their place on a waiting list even if they became completely wrecked in the interim. This was the vast need the agency attempted to fill.

The parents in the league were fortunate to secure the services of Irene Arnold, a dynamic, driving individual who helped forge the Parents with a Purpose into the Retarded Infants Services now located at 386 Lexington Avenue, New York City. A small budget was secured from the Community Mental Health Board, and a professional staff including a psychologist, psychiatrist, and social worker were added.

In recent years the State has become a little more involved financially, but its assistance is still limited. Struggling with the ever-present handicap of insufficient funds, the agency nevertheless set up a family counseling service for parents of retarded children under five. They also initiated a pilot program of training and placing Home Aids with families in dire situations, as when the disturbed child makes it impossible for the mother adequately to attend to the rest of her family or to overcome complete immobilization.

The agency has worked closely with Flower and Fifth Avenue Hospitals in the training of nonprofessionals to help with the care of the retarded.

The longer-established social service agencies are now beginning to accept families with mentally retarded children. In the past, no city day-care center in New York would accept retarded children. Officially this is no longer true; some now take the mildly retarded. The Albert Einstein Clinic says that in their experience the most cooperative units have been the Department of Welfare day-care centers, the "Y's," and the Bronx House.

The educationally oriented Institute for Retarded Children of the Shield of David and the Kennedy Child Study Center serve as clinics and day schools, are nonsectarian, and take non-toilet-trained children. Their programs are similar, formed with a view toward preparing the children for education in public school classes. There is, however, a nine-month waiting list at the Shield of David, except for children under three years of age.

Several months ago the Institute for Retarded Children at the Shield of David installed a nursery with diagnostic equipment for infant children up to three years of age. Two public health nurses visit these very young children and observe them and the family in the home setting.

The theory behind this procedure is that the earlier rehabilitation of retarded children is started, the greater the strides made. So far as I know, this was the first example of this kind of service to be offered in the United States.

Perhaps a brief rundown of the procedure at one of the educationally oriented clinics would clarify the picture of what is done in New York in order to diagnose, evaluate, and train the retardate.

At the Institute for Retarded Children at the Shield of David, contact starts with the parents being interviewed by a caseworker. (Half the work at the Shield is with the parents.) A series of appointments is then arranged so that the child can be examined by the pediatrician, psychologist, speech pathologist, and child developmentalist. This process takes two months. At the end of that time there are two conferences: one for diagnosis and the other for treatment recommendation.

About 100 children are enrolled in the Shield of David school, and the clinic, via caseworkers, maintains contact with 40 or 50 on the outside. Besides five general meetings with parents each year, the principal of the school has about ten meetings with the parents to tell them what to expect at each step of the way in toilet training and self-care.

Every child who can possibly benefit from speech therapy gets it at the Institute.

Of the 87 discharged in one year, 35 were admitted to regular public schools, 10 were institutionalized, and the remainder were sent to private schools or remained at home.

The service of the Shield costs $2,700 a year for each child. About 8 percent comes from their families,* but most of the funds are raised privately. The Institute now plans to open a similar center in Queens County, not only to provide for additional children but to cut the very long travel time for about 40 children who presently are bussed daily from this borough. It also hopes to raise the maximum age limit for admission from twelve to sixteen.

---

* The average income of parents whose children are at the Institute for Retarded Children at the Shield of David is between $5,000 and $6,000 a year.

Expensive as such programs are, they come to but a fraction of the cost of institutionalizing the retardate for life.

In 1950, when most of the world was at peace, New York Medical College's Flower and Fifth Avenue Hospitals' Department of Pediatrics declared war—a war against the ravages of mental retardation.

Dr. Margaret Joan Giannini, M.D., pediatrician and teaching Professor of the Department of Pediatrics, was unanimously appointed to organize and direct a Mental Retardation Clinic, which she continues to head today. Early experience taught her that the problems of the retardate were not purely medical but encompassed every realm of human existence. A multidisciplined approach to the diagnosis, care, counseling, research, study, and therapy of each retardate was instituted. The family problems were studied by the social worker, the learning problems by the psychologist, the medical and emotional problems by the pediatrician and psychiatrist. Since lack of communication ability is a by-product of retardation, speech analysis, diagnosis, and therapy had to be handled by skilled speech therapists.

When the clinic was founded, three part-time volunteer pediatricians were enlisted to help Dr. Giannini. The staff now numbers a highly trained professional group of about 50.

Of the clinic's population, 35 to 45 percent are retarded cerebral palsied children. The clinic is now a Cerebral Palsy Center recognized by the Department of Health. Because of these children, the clinic maintains a physical therapy unit.

A seven-story Mental Retardation Center, unique in that it will have a dual focus—extensive training of professionals specializing in this field and complete treatment for 500 new patients annually in addition to the 7,000 it already has—is planned as another addition to the growing New York Medical College, Flower and Fifth Avenue Hospitals' Medical Center.

Flower Fifth Avenue was the first to start training physicians, psychologists, teachers, etc., in the multidisciplined approach to the problem of mental retardation, one of our country's greatest needs. Their program will be vastly enlarged in the new quarters. Dr. Robert Lee, Associate Professor of Pediatrics at New York Medical College, Flower and Fifth Avenue Hospitals, an enormously knowledgeable and dedicated physician, will be in charge of the training of pediatricians. The nurses' training program will be contained within the college. Formal application will be made to join university programs in providing graduate and postgraduate training in social work, psychology, psychiatry, etc.

In 1951, Dr. Lawrence Slobody of the New York College of Medicine called Dr. Harold Michal-Smith to ask him to come in and help discuss the future plans for the Retardation Clinic of Flower Fifth Avenue. The talk ended with Dr. Michal-Smith giving up his position as Chief Psychologist for the state of New Jersey and undertaking the challenge of helping to build a multidisciplinary mental retardation clinic which had been so urgently requested by the New York Association for Help to Retarded Children.

It is interesting to note that Dr. Michal-Smith wrote the dissertation for his doctoral thesis on the Predicted Success of the Retarded in Industry back in 1950 when this country had very little interest in or knowledge of the true ability of the retarded.

Today Dr. Michal-Smith is deep in the Flower Fifth Avenue recruitment and training program for professional workers in all services related to the retarded.

I spent a great deal of time at this clinic because of its accessibility and also because it has the most inclusive service of its kind in the world—from the initial interview to the final program for preparation for living in the outside community.

Dr. Margaret Giannini, the attractive and dynamic director, was most sympathetic to the task I had set myself and arranged for me to work with Mr. Lawrence Goodman, the chief psychiatric social worker of the clinic. He heads a large staff, but manages to do a great deal of research in the field of retardation and to share his findings through articles written for professional journals. He feels the most important areas to get into are early identification and prevention, with sufficient emphasis on the culturally deprived. In the sessions he generously granted me I learned a great deal from him.

At Flower Fifth Avenue, parents of a retarded child are assigned to orientation group meetings immediately after the child is admitted. Due to the tremendous influx of Puerto Rican families into the geographic area of the hospital, 25 to 30 percent of the families are Spanish-speaking, and they meet separately; but other than that, parents of diverse social and economic groups meet together. Mental impairment affects families of great wealth and erudition as well as the uneducated and the poverty-stricken.

For parents of brain-damaged infants, individual, not group, appointments are given. Although there may be a waiting period before the infant is admitted for treatment, the parents are interviewed immediately and given the clinical picture of the baby's situation and told what they may reasonably expect. (As of this writing, there are 200 waiting for admission.)

According to Mr. Goodman, the initial impact on the family after learning of the diagnosis is shock and disbelief, followed by feelings of sadness, guilt, and helplessness. They need help even in how to tell friends and relatives that they have a retarded child. To facilitate this, a social worker from the clinic faculty and even a visiting nurse are assigned to the family.

The series of clinical tests include intelligence and achievement, social and functioning quotient, detailed pediatric evaluation, speech and psychiatric assessments, routine X rays, neurological and orthopedic examinations, and an EEG (encephalogram).

When all the testing of a patient is completed, there is a "rounds" conference attended by representatives from each discipline, who decide on the exact diagnosis and on the plan of treatment.

(For children who have achieved a degree of self-help, a liaison officer between the clinic and the New York City Board of Education is able to recommend placements in schools—public, state, and private.)

A plan of action is outlined for the parent. First, the ideal situation; second, the practical attainment within the service limitations of the clinic. The clinic offers medical treatment if needed, individual and group psychotherapy, and art, music, dance and speech therapy.

Part of the clinic service is a two-year program of sessions with the parents. Mr. Goodman assured me that much of the change in the child is the result of the cooperation of the mother.

Miss Esther Griffing, a psychiatric caseworker and assistant to Mr. Goodman, conducts group therapy for retarded adolescent girls. She graciously permitted me to sit in with the group. The girls had made small presents for ward patients in the hospital, and Miss Griffing took them through the wards where they distributed them. Two members of the group were very withdrawn. My attempts at conversation with them elicited either gestures or monosyllables.

We returned to the therapy room and sat down in a circle. Suddenly the most withdrawn child began to speak. She took over almost the entire session. The other girls listened with sympathy and attention; observably their supportive interest helped steer this youngster, seemingly awash in anxieties and problems, to a protected port of verbal release.

Some of the constructive suggestions that emanated from that group of children made me fervently wish that those people who dismiss or reject retardates as "hopeless idiots" could have been there.

I visited some of the therapists briefly. One of them was Mr. Gandor, the art therapist. He was cutting out a dog from a piece of paper for a little red-haired Mongoloid boy. He asked the child to identify it. The child said, "It's a puppy." Mr. Gandor then asked him what he wanted him to cut out next. The answer was, "A girl puppy."

I next visited the speech therapist and was permitted to observe her procedure in her efforts to measure a child's ability.

A very pretty young girl, approximately ten years old with blond bangs and brown eyes, was seated opposite the speech therapist. The therapist handed her a simple book and asked her to read it. One sentence was. "It is wake-up time." The child did not know the word "time." The therapist then asked the child to repeat numbers after her. Next she put her tongue out and had the child move her tongue in the same areas. She then showed her how to make lip sounds and then several vowels.

The girl was eventually dismissed from the room, and her grandmother came in for a report on the girl's progress. The child, who had been attending public school, was overactive and could not concentrate for any length of time.* Her teacher recommended that she be taken to the clinic in order to help the school deal with her.

The child eats and sleeps well and never seems to get tired. There are no bed-wetting problems, and she can dress herself. She is easy to

---

* A standard pattern of behavior for brain-injured children.

take care of, but the grandmother is worried about the girl's indiscriminate friendliness. She cannot be made to understand that she must not go with strangers.

The grandmother's tone was wistful. Her granddaughter is eager to learn to write, but the teacher says her failure is due to her inability to stay with it. "She is lonesome," the grandmother said. "No one wants to play with her. She is alone much of the time. She never complains, but it breaks my heart when I hear her singing sadly to herself."

On the way back to Mr. Goodman's office I encountered two parents. One told me confidentially that her boy was with grownups too much and that was why he was "so slow." The other said, "The way I act is a front. I have tried to keep my feelings on ice because I couldn't bear to look at my suffering. . . ."

I asked if she would consider institutionalization.

"No!" she said. "When the social worker suggested it to my husband, he wanted to hit her. I had all I could do to get her safely out of the house." She sighed. "We have another worker now."

I asked Mr. Goodman if many cases were referred for institutionalization. He said the number was low.

Did the program lack anything important? I asked him.

He said nothing that money could not solve. At that time money was available to the clinic for research but not for services. This was the major problem. The clinic did get some support from the Association for Help to Retarded Children and from the Mental Health Board, but it was insufficient. Their greatest concern was how not to cut the services they have.*

The New York Department of Mental Hygiene has become increasingly concerned with the support of facilities for the retarded.

As I was leaving, I met Miss Esther Griffing. Her voice was eager and excited as she told me of the new projected program. "We hope to have a prevocational training center. The girls in my group will be trained to work in different parts of the hospital and will get paid for it. Isn't it wonderful!"

---

* In 1967 funds were allotted to Flower Fifth Avenue by the Children's Bureau of the Federal Government to expand their services and training activity.

At the New York College of Medicine, Flower and Fifth Avenue Hospitals, exploration into possible areas of employment continue to move cautiously but steadily forward. Mr. Lawrence Goodman, the psychiatric social worker, in addition to his other duties, is in charge of a program where the higher retardates are being trained to work as baby sitters for other retardates, allowing the parent to leave the house for any variety of reasons.

Besides having a highly qualified professional staff at the mental retardation clinic, Dr. Giannini has been ingenious in utilizing the services of many nonprofessional personnel.

In our American way of life, many women of limited background, often indigent, want desperately to contribute constructively to society. In answer to this need, Dr. Giannini and her staff, in collaboration with Retarded Infants Services, evolved a plan of training them to serve as Aids to work with retarded children and their families.

A program was set up for four hours a day for three months. In addition to the practical learning, the emphasis was to help the women look upon the retarded child as a handicapped human being rather than as a freak.

At the end of the training period the women went into various services, first as field placements, then into homes sponsored by private agencies. Some were placed as assistants in the workshops maintained by the Association for Help to Retarded Children.

In some cases the Aids were better able to establish communication with the families of the retarded than fully trained social workers.

Of the trainees resulting from the training program, Flower Fifth Avenue retained two for themselves. They relate so well to retarded children that they literally act as interpreters for them when they visit the clinic.

A second experiment, also utilizing nonprofessional help, was conceived by Dr. Giannini herself. Being the mother of four boys at a private school, she enlisted boys from the school to work with the retarded children for several hours a week at the clinic, playing with them and acting in the general capacity of a buddy. Thus far the program has been one of Flower Fifth Avenue's greatest successes.

Many of us are not aware of the contribution psychiatry can make. Dr. Katherine Woodward, formerly of the staff of Lenox Hill and now with Flower Fifth Avenue Mental Retardation Clinic, has this to say: "Psychiatry for the mentally retarded is still in its infancy but there are reports in literature about individual and group therapy that has enabled some individuals to function more happily and successfully, and in some cases can enable them to function within the normal range."

An article by Stella Chess, M.D., formerly Associate Professor of Psychiatry and Chief of the Division of Child Psychiatry, New York Medical College, published by the *American Journal of Orthopsychiatry,** reports the results of a series of sessions for a group of mentally retarded at Flower Fifth Avenue.

There has been much opposition to psychiatric clinics for the mentally retarded, the article says. The question constantly arises that since there is a desperate need of therapeutic intervention for children of average or high intellectual capacity, why spend the effort on children who will remain functionally inadequate? Biased thinking in terms of psychiatry for the mentally retarded is that it is justifiable only where a combined picture of retarded mental functioning and behavioral aberration is so patterned as to suggest pseudoretardation (functioning as retarded but in actuality not retarded).

Of the 19 children who received treatment under this controlled experiment, one boy's IQ rose from 65 to 92 and another from borderline to 112. But that was only 2 out of 19, so the problem of the pseudoretardate is numerically a relatively small one while the problem of life adjustment of the truly retarded child is a large one. And unless we plan constructively for the mentally retarded's adjustment to his family and community costly institutions could never be built fast enough to meet the demands for placement even if such placement were deemed desirable.

Dr. Chess stated that one of the most important lessons learned from the experiment was that some success, in at least alleviating anxiety and

---

* Reprinted by the U.S. Department of Health, Education, and Welfare from the *Journal of Orthopsychiatry,* Vol. 32, No. 5, October, 1962 (863–869).

fear, might be possible with any child, no matter how limited in intelligence, and that psychotherapy could lead to the inclusion of a defective child in some facsimile of normal life where it had heretofore seemed impossible. "Goals have varied widely from a minimal one of amelioration of fears and of building minimal acceptable social patterns, to a maximal goal of removing the pseudoretardate child from the functioning and improvement of the underlying neurotic mechanisms."

The field of psychiatry lies relatively unplowed. To estimate its potential harvest is not as important at this time as helping the child find a place for himself in society. Whatever furthers that end must surely be worthwhile.

In 1964, Dr. Edward La Crosse, for years the educational consultant for the National Association for Retarded Children, was asked to become director of the newly founded Child Study Center at Newark State College, Union, New Jersey.

For years Newark State Teachers College had importuned the Board of Education for approval of a child study center to train professional personnel in the diagnosis and teaching of retardates. The Board of Education finally gave its approval and the state floated a bond issue. The center was officially opened in October of 1964.

The Child Study Center on the campus of Newark State Teachers College is a low, sleek, modern structure housing eight clinics which test and diagnose impairments in speech, hearing, tongue thrust, stuttering, and basic manual skills. A general diagnosis is made. The clinic is able to provide therapy in all these areas as well as psychological services. It is currently adding an audiological clinic.

Children brought to the center are tested, diagnosed, and referred for proper medical, social, emotional, and educational rehabilitation.

Dr. La Crosse is probably one of the best-informed persons on mental retardation in this country.

It is heartening to know that well-qualified people are being recruited into areas of help so vital to the rehabilitation of retardates.

19

The Early Years

In our American society, it is deemed axiomatic that everyone is a first-class citizen, unless deprived of citizenship by due process of law, and as such he shares the responsibilities and privileges that citizenship entails.

The vast scope of a citizen's responsibility includes paying taxes, part of whose disbursement enables the government to make it mandatory for every child to receive a free public school education.

Families of retardates are citizens like any others. They share the responsibility of paying taxes, but is the privilege of an education available to their children?

It has been proven beyond any doubt that the majority of retarded children can be educated and rehabilitated up to varying levels of ability. The objectives of education for the retarded are similar to those for normal children, though the means of achieving them may vary. These goals should include training for maximum ability academically, for skills in relating, and in social exchange, and for shopping, preparing food, dressing, caring for clothes and makeup; and achieving certain manual skills.

The learning of specific skills is the means by which the individual can be vocationally rehabilitated and this in turn signifies the ability to hold down a job.

Work means financial independence. It is also crucial to the individual's self-concept and to his social status. Proper training and job placement rank among the most important services any community can provide for its retarded members.

The question then arises as to how soon training should begin.

In various parts of the world, theories differ. Some set the date at the age of seven, others much earlier.

Research in the United States has arrived at some of the following conclusions.

Professor S. A. Kirk of the University of Illinois has demonstrated the lasting effect of preschool experience with normal and retarded children. He reported that 43 retarded children who were given preschool training tended to retain the additional growth rate they received, whereas a control group of 38 comparable children without preschool training continued to fall behind in their subsequent years.

Dr. Benjamin Bloom of the University of Chicago believes, on the basis of a survey of extreme environments (very favorable and underprivileged), that these environments in the first four years may affect the differential development of intelligence by about 2.5 points per year (or 10 IQ points over that four-year period), while extreme environments during the period of ages eight to seventeen may have a differential effect of only 0.4 points per year. Dr. Bloom states that the cumulative effect of good environmental influences during the entire seventeen years adds on the average of 20 IQ points, as against no increase in an environment of deprivation.

Dr. Bloom concluded that the loss of development in one period cannot be fully recovered in another.

What, then, is the status of the preschool child today?

From the vantage point of my own home ground, I began my investigation with the Board of Education in New York City.

Since education for retardates is mandatory in New York State, certain regulations are enforceable in New York City.

Mildly retarded children are eligible to attend school from the ages of five to twenty-one.* Classes for the educable (the mildly retarded) in the primary schools are limited to 15 pupils, and for the trainable–moderately retarded to 12 pupils. In the secondary schools, similar classes may be increased to 18 and 15 pupils per class, respectively.

If children at the age of five are included in mandatory education, what provisions, if any, have been made for them?

"Are there any kindergarten classes for retarded children?" I asked a member of the New York City Board of Education.

---

* The so-called normal child may leave public school at seventeen if he desires; if he is a problem he may be requested to do so.

"Yes," he answered. "They are called preprimer, or preprimary." And therein lies the ambiguity.

The gentleman proceeded to explain the matter. While the preprimary class may offer kindergarten work, it actually services children from the six- to nine-year-old group.* As of this writing, there is no public school kindergarten class in New York City for retarded children in the four- to six-year range. There is an experimental group of 6 children at Flower Fifth Avenue run by Dr. Elkin Snyder of the Board of Education, but the only kindergartens for retardates in New York City are run by the city chapter of the AHRC or by private individuals, or are the experimental ones run in the diagnostic clinics.

As for the kindergarten group in state training schools, I visited a New York State training school called Letchworth Village at Thiells, N. Y., near Suffern about 35 miles from New York City. Letchworth, Wassaic, and Willowbrook are the three state schools open to retarded residents of New York City. The minimum age requirement for admission is five years. The maximum, none. Children under the age of five are admitted with special permission. These younger children are kept in the hospital building. At the age of five they are brought downstairs to a special room where a staff member with no special training tries to teach them habits of washing, dressing, eating, and using the toilet. Mrs. Williams, the educational director of Letchworth Village, took me to see them.

In a rather barren room, I found the youngsters to be an unusually good-looking group with the minimum appearance of retardation. One little blond, well-scrubbed boy walked slowly around pulling a mechanical toy. Another child, whose Mongolism gave him a pixyish look, sat by himself banging at a stuffed dog. One child, with the dark good looks of the Mediterranean, sat, mouth hanging open, staring listlessly out the window. Others sat at the table, playing desultorily with toys. A thin Negro child sat at the edge of a bench whimpering. The sound filled the room like the bleating of a little lost lamb. A mildly retarded resident assisted the woman in charge. He held one of the children in his arms.

What will happen to these young charges? Some had been totally

_____
* Many retarded children are not admitted until the age of seven.

abandoned by their families and were never to see or hear from them again. Others had been placed here for training and when sufficiently rehabilitated were to be returned to their families.

Unfortunately, although some abandoned children can be rehabilitated and returned to the community, they cannot, for with no family to assume responsibility for them, there is no community residence to which they can return. And so, for lack of supervised living quarters, they must forever remain within the walls of the institution.*

Local chapters of the New York State Association for Retarded Children have organized kindergartens in certain areas. They may receive up to 50 percent of the cost of maintaining centers from the government for kindergarten schools, or workshops, but the local community must raise the rest.

The chapters of the Association for Retarded Children are in various stages of development, some already well established and others struggling toward formation.

At the recommendation of the NARC, I decided to visit the Special Services School for Nassau County to see what was being done for the young child there.

Mr. Sam La Magna, then the principal of the school, gave me a brief account of its background.

In 1950 a group of determined AHRC parents in Nassau County, Long Island, helped open the first classes for trainable—moderately to severely retarded—children. Today at 280 Duffy Avenue, in Hicksville, 515 of these youngsters are attending a full-day program in a new central school called Special Services School that serves 57 school districts and is now supported out of tax funds. This same AHRC group of parents founded a school in Westbury, Long Island, for mildly retarded children who are also emotionally disturbed.

Before any school legislation for retarded children was even considered, the School for Special Services had a preschool readiness program for the five-year-old child, who attends five days a week for half a day. Other age levels attend a full day.

---

* Supervised living quarters known as hostels have been operating in the Scandinavian countries for over twenty years.

Besides the teachers, the staff has a large roster of specialists who provide psychological counseling, individual therapy, and medical care.

Details of the school's services for the other age levels will be discussed within the section on The School Years, later in this chapter.

Before I left I asked one of the teachers if there was any school which admitted children under five years of age to nursery school classes. "Yes," I was told, "the AHRC school at Brookville, Long Island."

"I suppose Brookville is all the way out here again?"

She smiled sympathetically. "It will be worth the trip."

Dr. Christopher de Prospero, on the staff of the College of the City of New York, is the educational consultant of both the School for Special Services in Nassau County and of the AHRC school at Brookville. He has been fervently active in the field of mental retardation for thirty years. Both the School for Special Services and the AHRC school at Brookville, begun originally by parent groups, have the most complete teaching and training program of any places I have seen.

The AHRC school at Brookville lies at the end of a long, shaded, winding drive through a private estate area that was once the residence of a railway magnate. Its grandeur includes velvet-green fields, two swimming pools, tennis courts, secluded niches for picnics, and greenhouses. It was bought by the AHRC Nassau County Chapter at a cost of a quarter of a million dollars. The estate is free and clear of mortgages.

Twenty-five percent of the parents who work in the Nassau Chapter have retarded children, the remainder do not. Ten percent of the funds needed to run Brookville are donated by the county Mental Health Board. The rest is raised by parents.

My only disappointment of that day was the realization that there were no children younger than four and a half. This is because the law's responsibility for public education does not begin until five years of age. The school is out in the country, and the County Board of Education will not provide bus service for any child below this age even though the school would be more than willing to admit the younger children.

The school, with a capacity for 70 children, has 125 enrolled. The overcrowding problem was solved by holding classes for the less afflicted group three times a week and for the lowest trainables (moderately to severely retarded) twice a week.

There is no IQ barrier for entrance. The school has been established for the more seriously handicapped, but the children have to be ambulatory, because of the stairs.

As we walked into one classroom, I saw a teacher and her assistant take a class of young children to the bathroom. Each one went to the toilet. When he came out, he walked to the basin, washed his hands, and dried them with a paper towel the teacher gave him. He then went back to his seat.

"They didn't learn it in a day," said Dr. de Prospero; "many of these habits take weeks to learn. We couldn't run this program without volunteers. We have a staff of 50, all of whom have no vested interest other than the fulfillment of giving."

Mr. Sansone, the former principal, has written in a report that "teach" is not the precise term. "Often we must be content to condition responses providing the necessary experience without expecting too much awareness on the part of the pupil as to the nature of the experience. In other words, the children may be automatically washing their hands after going to the toilet without realizing why they are doing so. But it is important to bear in mind that the child has taken a positive step toward adaptability to the immediate environment and larger world in which he is obliged to live; it is equally important to realize when certain tasks and activities are beyond him and not to force the child into an activity when he is obviously not ready."

The emphasis in the AHRC school at Brookville is on social competence and adaptive behavior. After a period of training, some of the children go on to the Special Services School at Hicksville.

With Mr. Sansone's permission I have reproduced, at the back of the book, copies of the schedule for the four- to seven-year-old severely and moderately retarded, plus the weekly program for the older group in the hope that some of the material may be of use in setting up programs elsewhere.

The Bureau of Cooperative Educational Services (B.O.C.E.S.) functions under the auspices of the New York State Department of Education. Its purpose is to provide education for children who cannot be serviced within their own school district. The handicapped children are often severely emotionally disturbed or are moderately retarded.

As of January, 1968, 630 students were enrolled in this program in Westchester County. A day-school building at New Castle, New York, is devoted solely to retardates from four and a half years of age and up.

Since education for the retarded is mandatory in New York State, any parent whose child cannot be serviced in the local school district should apply to B.O.C.E.S. for educational placement.

In the summer of 1962 I won a fellowship to the Writers' Conference at Fairleigh Dickinson University in New Jersey.

A long, restful summer respite with less work began to shrink to a very short one, but I couldn't bring myself to refuse.

It became the summer where the motivation to learn about retardation became a determination.

At the conference I discovered a former Pulitzer Prize winner who had a Mongoloid sister; another student attending the conference had a retarded brother. On learning of my interest, this student offered to have his mother drive me to a kindergarten class for retarded children in nearby Morristown, which is close to Short Hills and Bernardsville, all known for years as socially eminent communities.

The kindergarten was privately supported, and the two teachers in charge seemed to have been privately endowed with the special gift of love.

I sat on the side and watched the modish but dedicated mothers arrive with their children. I remember seeing two Mongoloid children, one, lovably dark, pony-tailed Debbie, and a frightened, distracted red-haired boy, Robert. Tow-headed Johnnie might have been beautiful if his eyes had not made such empty dark holes in his head.

Some of the children were under heavy medication, but no sedation had been able to quiet the blond boy whose mother, I learned, kept him tied to a chair at home. Released at the kindergarten, he at once began to run around incessantly, either banging his head into the wall or striking and kicking everyone indiscriminately. I myself received two sharp kicks in the shins. Never once did either teacher lose patience, and eventually he was coaxed into sitting down and putting his head on his arm for a few minutes.

When all the children had their heads down, the teacher played the game "Mary, Mary will you get up?" except that she substituted the child's name instead of Mary, and thus taught the child to respond to his own name.

One of the handsomest boys in the group was Hunter Avis, whose mother, Dorothy Avis, has since become a warm friend of mine and a limitless source of information.

Hunter was born under conditions which undoubtedly caused his brain damage, and early became subject to convulsive seizures which he had up to five times a day. Each incident caused further damage. Hunter has been designated an aphasic child, a category that has myriad classifications but is generally understood as meaning loss of speech.

Mr. and Mrs. Avis are both college graduates, knowledgeable and unusually articulate. Mrs. Avis has become one of the dynamic forces behind the Morristown chapter for Parents of Retarded Children. She reads everything that is written about retardation, digests it and disseminates it when possible, and agitates constantly for legislation to provide adequate care and training for the retarded child.

The law for mandatory education for retarded children was passed in New Jersey in 1955, more than six years prior to that of New York State.

As in New York, education in New Jersey is supposed to start at five years of age but, with the lack of proper facilities, in many cases retarded children who fill minimum requirements do not actually attend school until they are seven.

Individual units of the New Jersey Association for Retarded Children have formed private kindergartens* for groups starting at four and a half years of age. Parents' fees vary according to the district and ability to pay. The average cost per child is $5.00 registration, $2.50 for insurance in case of accident, and $40.00 a month for tuition. In special day-care centers under the New Jersey Association there are charges of $2.50 for insurance, $7.50 for transportation, and $37.50 a month for the training program.

---

* They are located in Bergen, Passaic, Burlington, Cumberland-Salem, Essex, Gloucester, Hunterdon, Mercer, Monmouth counties and in the Raritan Valley.

Many five- to seven-year-old moderately retarded (trainable) children who were excluded from public elementary school have been accepted by the day-care centers. These centers concentrate on toilet-training the child as one of the first necessary steps toward acceptance into the public schools, and are largely successful.

In Connecticut the state must provide educational opportunities for retardates from ages six to twenty-one. There is no provision for the preschool group. To correct this deficiency, the local chapters of the Connecticut Association for Retarded Children have initiated 20 day-care centers, which are now subsidized by the state, much as in New York.

A day-care and residential center at Seaside in New London is an outstanding example of regional planning, which will be discussed later in greater detail. It provides for retarded children who are either too young or too afflicted to attend public schools. As in all such centers specifically for retarded children, the purpose is to relieve the mothers for outside employment and provide specialized training for the child.

Seaside was opened for operation in 1961. I was allowed to review and reproduce some of the case histories and letters in their files to show what this regional center has accomplished for these preschool children who are either residents or daily attendants.

CASE HISTORY NO. 1

Billie—aged five.

Admitted to Seaside in September, 1961, from a private children's hospital.

No records available at time of admission. Comments from owners of the hospital were that he was noisy, whined a great deal, and rocked constantly. He was considered profoundly retarded. (A profound retardate falls within the 0–20 IQ range.)

On admission he was not ambulatory, could not talk, feed himself, dress or undress, and was not toilet-trained.

After one year and a half at Seaside this is his progress:

He is able to occupy himself in a playroom, walks, feeds himself with a spoon, manipulates objects. He is partially toilet-trained.

Billie attends half-day school classes at the center for the young trainable, or moderately retarded, children.

Teacher's report: "Bill has learned some speech, uses words meaningfully, and recently started using short sentences. He mimics others' speech and seems to enjoy talking. Bill can ambulate well, is able to participate in all play activities with the children in his group. His tolerance for group work has increased, and he now enjoys playing and being with other children. He has several friends in the class whom he calls by name. Bill is observant of all that goes on about him. He continues to make progress in all areas of self-help."

Estimated IQ at this time—36.

CASE HISTORY NO. 2

Raymond, known affectionately by the staff as Ray-Ray.

Admitted to first institution in 1956 and stayed until August, 1961, at which time he was admitted to Seaside at the age of six.

Abstract of the case history compiled from the other institution rated him as a profound-severe retardate, estimated IQ of 19. Predicted he would always require institutional care.

At the end of one year and a half of preschool training and care at Seaside, his IQ was 48 to 53, and his behavior was noted as "attentive, quiet, obedient, and generally quite bland."

He is described as a cheerful boy who always has a big smile. His speech is very good, and he is capable of holding a pleasant conversation, which he does often.

In the living unit, Ray is very popular among his peers and also the attendants. He is reported to be completely self-sufficient in all areas of self-care. He can dress, undress, bathe, and feed himself, and is completely toilet-trained.

His teacher in the public school reports: "Ray is very efficient in self-care areas, exceptionally well coordinated in activities involving both large and small muscles, does exceptionally well in arts and crafts, follows relatively difficult directions, takes initiative, asks questions for information, and begins and carries on conversations."

The justification for the early training of retarded children has etched itself into an indelible record.

The following are a few letters picked at random from the files reflecting the parents' reactions to preschool training at a regional center service such as Seaside.

June 9, 1962

Dear Dr. Franklin Foote [Commissioner of Health]:

My son ————, five, has been attending day-care classes at Seaside Regional Center for the Retarded in Waterford since April. I hope in this letter I can let you know how I appreciate what this has done for my child. ———— not only says words now, but also is so much more alert and active, since attending the day-care program at Seaside. He did go to school in Preston last year and part of the previous year, but it never helped him as these few weeks here at Seaside have.

I hope this program will continue, not only for my son's sake, but for the other children who have benefited by it.

Thank you,

Sincerely,
Mrs. A. E.

The next letter was from the parents of a microcephalic child.

Microcephaly is a genetically determined condition in which the head or cranial capacity is abnormally small. The facial features often have a birdlike appearance characterized by a prominent nose and receding forehead and chin.

June 22, 1962

Dear Sir:

We are parents of a daughter who was admitted to Seaside before she was six years old. D. has been at Seaside since October, 1961.

When she first went there she was not toilet-trained, couldn't dress or undress herself. Her temper tantrums were quite frequent and severe. We certainly had no idea she'd be able to learn so much in so short a time, as she is a microcephalic.

Today she goes to school, is toilet-trained, can dress and undress herself, and she can talk a little more clearly than before. She has very few temper tantrums and gets along well with the other children and staff at Seaside.

Since D. has been at Seaside she does not seem to be so aggressive toward her sisters and brother.

The way Seaside is conducted, we are able to have D. home quite often. We appreciate this very much. Since it is our wish as well as Seaside's to have her remain a part of the family.

We think, very sincerely, that Seaside is doing D. a world of good. Also with your support in the years to come there will be more centers for the less fortunate children.

                                          Sincerely,
                                    Mr. and Mrs. E. L.

                                       January 17, 1963
Dear Mr. Schickel [Deputy Commissioner of Health]:

[First two paragraphs full of praise for the Seaside Regional Center omitted here.]

Our three-and-one-half-year-old son, H, has been attending the day-care program at Seaside since its inception in April, 1962. This opportunity has been very beneficial to him because he has been able to associate with children who do not demand of him what he is unable to give. Also, Mrs. Frank Arioli, his teacher, has given him the attention and learning experience which I was unable to provide. I should add that his attendance at Seaside during the day has relieved me of many responsibilities, and this has given me some time for my three other young children.

I am more than aware that this association on which my family has begun with Seaside is only at the beginning stages. I would like to say that the prospects for H.'s future and for that of my family are much brighter than the day that we were told that we had a retarded child. We owe much to the people at Seaside, and for this we are truly grateful.

                                          Sincerely,
                                       Mrs. H. F. C.

The Seaside day-care program is run cooperatively with the local parents' association—the New London County Association for the Retarded. The association pays the teacher, and Seaside provides the facilities as well as the professional supervision of the program. Seaside's social service staff makes all arrangements with the families and other agencies for admitting children to these parent-sponsored programs.

THE SCHOOL YEARS

Education for the mildly (educable) and moderately (trainable) retarded is permissible in all the states of the United States, but mandatory in only ten. Only four states—New Mexico, North Dakota, Oregon, and Vermont—do not provide state funds for the education of the moderately (trainable) retarded.

If the parents of a retardate live in a state where education is not mandatory, the child is apt to receive no formal education. If education for retardates is legally called for but if there is not enough room for a child or he cannot fill minimum standards of a particular school, the formal requirements are meaningless, for there is no place he can go.

Since education for the retarded is mandatory in New York State, does this mean that all moderately and mildly retarded children are in school? Again I turned to my home city and state to find out.

I phoned the New York City Board of Education and was referred to Miss Katherine Lynch, the energetic and well-informed director of the Bureau for Children of Retarded Mental Development (CRMD).

Miss Lynch told me that there are approximately one million school-age children in New York City. The assumption generally accepted throughout the world is that about 3 percent of the population is retarded; then about 30,000 school-age children fall within that category. As of the fall of 1967, 12,800 are attending classes within the New York City school system.

Where then, I asked Miss Lynch, are the other 17,200?

Some are too retarded to attend. Others are in private schools.

All of them?

No, Miss Lynch had admitted honestly, we have a waiting list of about 500 each September. During the year they are absorbed in new classes only to be replaced each year by a new 500.

In actuality, I would venture to make a few guesses. One, there are thousands of retarded children sitting in regular classes, their needs unfulfilled because the Bureau of Child Guidance does not have the staff to test them quickly enough, and even if they were tested, there are not enough special teachers to handle them. Two, no one really knows how many children may be at home because of their parents' ignorance about what is available educationally for their child or because their child is unable to function in a school situation. According to the New York Association for Help to Retarded Children, the situation is not improving with the population explosion.

I asked the Board of Education to advise me which retarded children may not be eligible for placement in special classes. The only reply I received was that "there are no restrictions for admitting other than being obviously handicapped."*

Miss Katherine Lynch told me that the state regulations are that the child must be able to care for his own needs, be ambulatory, be able to make his needs known, respond to teacher direction, and not need the teacher's entire time.

There are three main possible placements for such children in the largest city in the United States: The Shield of David, the Kennedy Child Study Center, and the classes run by the city chapter of the AHRC in Brooklyn, Bronx, and Queens. The New York City AHRC undertakes the training of children who are rejected even by the Shield of David and Kennedy. There are also a few expensive private schools.

In 1966, after the AHRC had struggled to support its classes for twelve years, assistance finally came in the form of state aid.

The people of New York can be justly proud that the first class for children with retarded mental development in New York City was organized as early as 1902 by Miss Elizabeth Farrell at Public School No. 1. Since then, out of 850 schools in New York City, approximately 450 have classes for the retarded. Their jurisdiction, as I said before, lies within the Board of Education's Bureau for Children with Retarded Mental Development. The children are referred to as CRMD. Each

---

* Board of Education Manual of Office Procedures.

year the Bureau of Child Guidance tests thousands of children and recommends placement for about 2,500.

Last year both bureaus began to work at an accelerated pace. The bureau for CRMD opens from 30 to 50 new classes a year. Training personnel is always a problem. Out of 1,021 teachers for the retarded, about one-third are untrained.*

At least 200 new teachers have to be hired annually because of new classes, retirement, promotion, or removal to another city when the husband's employment changes.

In spite of their tireless efforts, the bureau of CRMD is never certain that, come September, all their classes will be covered.

The Bureau of Speech assigns speech therapists to the schools but admits it could use many, many more.

Throughout the city, the bureau for CRMD has organized clusters of classes for the retarded in the schools, rather than having isolated, wide age-range classes. One such centralized grouping is in P.S. No. 146 in Brooklyn. Mrs. Connors, the principal, told me that before she was appointed to No. 146, the district's 20 schools had isolated CRMD classes. Many were subsequently transferred to her school to achieve greater uniformity of instruction. This has helped the school become more flexible and constructive in the CRMD program, because they now have more uniform mental and chronological age groupings.

There is no known teasing of the CRMD's by the so-called normal children, and their parents have learned to be very understanding.

The children are bussed to school. At one time, the retarded child had to live within the district that had clustered classes for CRMD. Now there are no longer district lines. Children are now bussed to a cluster in another district if that is the nearest class that meets the child's needs.

Eleven classes are in the cluster at P.S. No. 146, and since the course of study for both the moderate and the mildly retarded is undergoing revisions, the teachers use initiative with a temporary curriculum provided for them.

---

* As has been discovered all over the world, teachers with no formal training sometimes have greater empathy for and do a better job with the retarded than some trained teachers.

The trainable (moderate to severe) classes are held on the first floor of P.S. No. 146 along with some normal classes. On the second floor are the educable, or mildly retarded, also interspersed with the normal. The retarded children on both the first and second floors are used as floor monitors. They are sent from room to room to collect roll books, office material, etc. This gives them an opportunity to learn more about the school, and the pupils to learn more about them and to accept them.

Children who have the most difficulty in learning are put into vestibule classes. These are composed of severely, moderately, and mildly retarded, for the IQ in itself is no positive barometer as to how the child will accommodate himself to learning.

Unfortunately, in a situation that calls for the utmost cooperation and exchange of information between the school and home, there is a shortage of liaison officers. Social workers are assigned to those children who have been discharged from institutions, workers are assigned from diagnostic clinics and retardation centers, but there is still a large group with whom there is little or no home communication.

When I arrived for a visit at P.S. No. 146, Miss Marilyn Bord, a teacher, was on her way out with her group of children whose IQ's ranged from 23 to 49. Another teacher, Mrs. Rosemary Winke, accompanied her with a class of blind retardates. They were going to the neighborhood grocery store where the children would buy food for the lunch they would cook in school the next day.

Both Miss Bord and Mrs. Winke used their own money for the food they buy for the parties at various holidays of the year.

When Miss Bord returned with her group, I went up to visit her. The chronological age of her group is from seven years and three months to nine years and six months. They stay in the group with her for two years, then move to the next teacher.

The children in this young 23 to 49 IQ group do not have enough intelligence or maturity to learn academic work. The very young lack the patience even to listen to a story read aloud, but they do like to look at the pictures. They all have speech problems, and a great deal of time is spent working on this.

The room is equipped with a stove, cooking utensils, a refrigerator, and an ironing board. The children are taught to set the table and play house, for one goal is to make good citizens in the home. Most of them can put on their own coats. If a child has trouble with the buttons, another child usually helps him. Another goal is good grooming and self-care.

The attention span of the young children is about five minutes. Many of them are spoiled and undisciplined when they enter school. This is often the case with retardates due to the inability of the parents to handle this particular type of child.

Many teaching aids have been devised for this group. Some commercial firms have been expanding the equipment, based more or less on the Montessori approach. This class had zipper and snapper frames, sound boxes and odor kits, a lacing boot, and a picture puzzle with knobs on the pieces for the child with manipulative problems.

Every Thursday morning, there is a movie from 9:45 to 11:00.

The trips for the children include visits to Coney Island, to a zoo, to parks, etc. The teachers at P.S. No. 146 pay the expenses of such outings themselves with voluntary contributions from parents. The goals of the trips are to teach behavior, vocabulary expansion, and better communication. Educational discussions always take place before and after the event.

A teacher of another group was absent, so instead I was given the privilege of looking at her plan book for the day. This group was pre-primary. Only one child had no speech at all, the rest had some.

The school day was divided as follows:

Speech—vowels and sounds.

Language Arts—library visit, read a story, choose children to retell it. See a movie and retell it.

Art—Draw a picture of the sky. Color the picture. Work on Mother's Day cards.

Music—Sing songs.

Social Studies—manners at a party, greeting to friends, courtesy to visitors and to others, wait for others to pass you.

Safety—danger of being near the stove, of things spilling over, and getting on and off the bus.

Health—daily inspection; need of more baths in warm weather and why.

Science—watch Fun at One on TV.

Math—concept of money. Review combinations of 4 and 1 are 5, 1 and 4 are 5, 5 and 1 are 6, 1 and 5 are 6.

Review counting objects.

In the upper classes the program becomes a little more demanding. One class had allotted 20 jobs among 13 youngsters. They included dusting, straightening desks, cleaning the blackboards, watering the plants, sharpening pencils. The date on the calendar was checked every day by the class. The children learned to make a calendar.

In one class where the IQ range was from 50 to 60, only two boys were unable to gain from the instruction. I understand this is unusual rather than the average expectation. One, a boy with an IQ of 52, had repeated toilet accidents. The other boy, whose IQ was in the 60's, was an epileptic and under strong medication. Four hyperactive boys in the class were difficult to work with, since they were not under medication. The latter present a problem in all preprimary classes, so the class count is kept low to help the teachers.*

I visited the lunchroom and observed even the most retarded handling his food with very adequate ability. Most of them had learned this when they came to the school.

One thing that impressed me above all else was the great compassion of the teachers. Having once taught myself, I know that any teacher can plan and display a good classroom lesson for visitors, but none can prepare the impulsive outburst of affection so many of these children lavished on their teachers.

A Puerto Rican Mongoloid clung to his pretty blonde teacher. He had been placed at Willowbrook State School and then withdrawn. He is functioning well in this school situation.

During that lunchroom period I spoke with several of the teachers. They seemed to have great reservations about any further potential of these children and estimated that only one-third would ever be able to move into the community independently, one-third might be able to

---

* The New York City Board of Education might do well to consider hiring teachers' aids as the AHRC does. They are considerably less expensive and often do a fine job of helping to quiet these youngsters.

work in a long-term or terminal workshop, but never anywhere else, and the remaining third would have to be institutionalized. Miss Lynch estimates that 70 percent will move into the community, 20 percent might be able to work in a long-term workshop, and only 10 percent would have to be institutionalized. But all these figures are elastic. So much depends on the educational opportunity for the child.

Before I left I visited the class led by Mrs. Gillen. Her group is classified as trainable (moderately retarded). One little girl, whose name was Maria, had made a mobile of various colors and had done some very impressive artwork.

Maria's IQ measures 48.

Into which third does Maria fit? Miss Lynch says at age seventeen she will attend an Occupational Training Center and may possibly be able to be trained for a routine job. If not, she will join a terminal workshop.

The same situation exists at P.S. No. 146 as with so many other services. There is a waiting list of one year to enter.

The love of a parent for a child is no measure of his ability to train him. Emotional involvement can cause qualified teachers to fail. Sometimes it becomes mandatory to send a child to a live-in state or private school, for a period of one to three years in order to teach, train, discipline him and help him become more mature so that he may return home and function more adequately. Certainly if he needs the entire time of a teacher to the detriment of others in his class, he may be better off in a state school.

Letchworth Village, mentioned before, is one of the 6 New York State schools that try to encompass that function. Mrs. Glenna Williams was, and so far as I know still is, the Educational Director. She is refreshingly honest and gave generously of her time.

In-residents at Letchworth Village number approximately 4,300— 2,296 males and 2,039 females.

Many severely retarded at Letchworth are barely removed from the lowest level—profound retardation—and will need lifelong nursing care. Mrs. Williams said they are considering hiring a teacher to reach these children through toys and whatever means they can contrive.

(Many researchers feel that these profoundly retarded children who appear to be completely out of contact with the rest of the world do perceive and conceive but in a way quite different from the norm. Mr. Francis Kelley of the Mansfield State Training School told me that of the 166 people applying for a grant in 1965 from the National Institutes of Mental Health under their Hospital Improvement Plan two-thirds have requested financing to work in the area of the profound retardate.)

The classroom training program at Letchworth covers a wide range of intelligence quotients. For the severely retarded children whose IQ is under 30, there is a new training program. Since the budget does not allow for a qualified teacher, the person in charge is a training aide. She arrives early in the morning in time to help with breakfast, and stays all day. She has been given a small classroom and 12 children. She teaches them dressing, self-help, self-care (toilet training, dressing, washing, brushing teeth), and games. As these children improve, they advance to the classes for the less severely or moderately retarded.

From the total enrollment at Letchworth there are more than 650 children who are only moderately to mildly retarded. I was gratified to hear Mrs. Williams say that the teachers use their own powers of observation in advancing the children and do not rely completely on the official IQ. In other words, advancement is not a matter of a higher IQ.

I visited the classrooms and was greatly impressed with the caliber of the teaching. Music and choral singing are popular teaching devices. Teachers are recruited and appointed from the Civil Service lists.

There was a positive approach in the instruction, as if each child was slated to reenter the community, and the teachers were making every effort to make that return as fruitful as possible. This attitude seemed to carry over to the more severely retarded even though most of them will never leave Letchworth.

Mrs. Williams said the goal of the school was to make their residents into the best possible citizens no matter to what environment they may be confined.

The school has its own curriculum centered upon the child's living situation. It includes learning about types of clothing for different occasions and seasons, as well as how to sew hems, fix zippers, and launder and iron.

Communication is the area most stressed. There is great need for more speech therapists, but the school attempts to teach students the use of the telephone, making their wants known, elements of safety and shelter, and the customs of various people.

The academic training that takes place is oriented toward job preparation.

In the Special Services School in Hicksville, Long Island, the divisions are primary, young intermediate, older intermediate, general senior departmentalized program, workshop program, advanced workshop, and, for twenty-year-olds, the work study program.

As I walked past the space usually allocated to the lunchroom, I saw boys and girls dancing, some faces emptier than others but all moving to music.

Twice each year each child in the school is evaluated by his teacher according to his productivity. They are then regrouped on the basis of their performance and social behavior, not age alone. Individual differences are greater among the younger children, which makes early detection of their potentials mandatory.

Special Services School in Hicksville, Long Island, is the largest centralized day school for retardates in the United States.

"It does not mean we have reached the ideal working situation," said Mr. Sam La Magna, the principal of the school. "Each day is a continuing fight for more vital services. One of our major problems was the lack of communication between the child's psychologist outside of the school and the school itself. Each was working in his own direction. We have finally succeeded in obtaining one full-time resident psychologist, who works side by side with the teachers."

I understood that a satellite workshop working in close cooperation with the school had been set up in Hempstead.

Mr. La Magna nodded. "It's one of our most advanced work study groups, teaching factory and clerical work, which includes running the mimeograph, collating papers, stapling, and stuffing envelopes. It's all done under close supervision. The years of working with the trainables, the moderately and severely retarded is paying off. They are doing very well."

Before my visit ended, I had a brief chat with the music teacher. The social studies program, she told me, is implemented through music. "One year, we taught the development of the American West through music and choral speaking; the growth of man, through the cantata on the *Little Man;* development of the country and immigration through a unit of study on the Statue of Liberty, which includes the poem by Emma Lazarus set to music by Irving Berlin. The book I used the most is called *Music in Our Times.* One other part of the project is encouraging the children to formulate pertinent sentences which are then used as lyrics and set to music."

This teacher also has 22 moderately retarded students who make up her Glee Club.

I had observed in my trip around the world that no matter how backward or advanced, most countries were using music to advance learning. Music is part of the appeal to ear and eye.

The following incidents at Brookville, the AHRC school for moderately to severely retarded children on Long Island, are, I believe, excellent examples of the use of audiovisual aids to stimulate multiple sense appeal.

When Dr. de Prospero, educational consultant to the AHRC, took me on a tour, one of the classrooms we visited had a group of very young Mongoloid children. They were well dressed, with a scrubbed, clean look. The little girls' dresses were full-skirted and stood out like picture-book clothes.

The teacher had a chart * at the front of the room. On it were pictures of children sitting, walking, jumping, sleeping, and so on. Underneath each picture was one word describing the activity. The teacher called a little boy up to the chart. "Now, Johnny, point to where the little girl is jumping." The boy pointed. "Now you jump, Johnny," the teacher said. Johnny, who had a recorded IQ of 40, jumped up and down with enthusiasm. "Now, Johnny, run out of the front door into the hall to the back door of this room and to your place."

The child responded perfectly, and as he ran back to his place the

---

* There are many manufacturers of visual aids. This particular one was the Ideal School Supply Company, 8312 Berkhoff Avenue, Chicago 20, Illinois. Teaching Resources, an educational service of *The New York Times,* 334 Boylston Street, Boston, Mass. 02116, also has excellent material that I have received.

whole class applauded his speed and accuracy. A little red-haired girl, who sat next to him, jumped up, threw her arms around his neck, and hugged him in delight. The whole class laughed and clapped.

For years Mongoloids were indiscriminately committed to institutions, their physical characteristics giving the mistaken impression of a complete inability to learn. Their appearance is still the greatest handicap to job placement no matter how capable an individual may be.

In another classroom, a teacher was also working with a chart. She was about to speak of various objects on it when one boy stood up, walked to the chart, pointed to an isolated door, and said quite clearly, "This door doesn't have a house to go with it."

The teacher laughed heartily and said, "You are quite right, Clifford, it doesn't."

Dr. de Prospero said he had visited this particular child at his home one year ago. The mother had been frantic. The child could not sit still for five minutes at a time. He had little or no speech and was untrained in many elementary areas of development. Now he is one of the best behaved children in the class.

Did the speech therapists effect this change?

Speech people do come in, but the school has an integrated speech development program. Each individual teacher concentrates on speech. They do not know whether the progress stems from the child's getting a certain discipline or if it is the individual attention that is securing the results.

After I had visited several classrooms, Dr. de Prospero and Mr. Sansone, the principal, took me on a tour of the girls' craft shop. The President's Committee in Washington on Employment of the Handicapped has judged this program as the most outstanding one in the country.

The teacher was a lively, attractive young blonde who had an exuberant enthusiasm for her work. She had conceived some of the displayed items herself, but most of them were created by the students. One approach to getting ideas for this class was through encouraging students to go to the stores and see what items they could reasonably expect to duplicate, and perhaps note additional specialties that the stores didn't have and could use.

The craft shop's counters had a large, attractive display of ceramic trays, fancy covers for commercial deodorants and toilet tissues, fancy packing of stationery, and other novelty items.

The teacher said the projects did a great deal to remove tensions and relax the girls. It has become a valuable part of the program.

The last stop of the day was at the school's greenhouses. The young man in charge is a graduate of the Farmingdale Agricultural School and is presently working toward his Bachelor of Arts degree.

The boys under his direction have planted forsythia bushes, pachysandra, and tomato plants within frames. They have been taught to get rid of poison ivy and to identify trees and shrubs. They are also taught how to use a lawnmower and keep landscapes in order.

The greenhouse group is taken on expeditions which include the International Flower Show at the Coliseum, the Brooklyn Botanical Gardens, and nearby estates which have been opened for them to visit.

Ladies on these estates and from other areas have contributed cuttings, which the greenhouse nurtured into a thousand dollars' worth of plants by the end of their first year in business. With a supervisor in attendance, the boys do the selling.

Only three hundred dollars have been spent on the program in all this time. The teacher and his crew have accomplished most of their production by dint of hard physical labor.

Fifteen young men, ages eighteen to thirty-seven, are enrolled in this program. The goal is to place each one in a job after they have been trained. Three have been placed thus far.

As I walked to my car, Dr. de Prospero greeted with great affection a lady who had just driven up.

"Helen," he said, turning to explain to me, "in a meeting with seven or eight parents in her living room, only a few years ago, became the driving force which ended in"—he waved his hand widely—"*this!*"

Helen, who turned out to be Mrs. Helen Kaplan, the mother of a retarded child who died a few years ago, beamed. "I have great news. We have just secured a forty-five-thousand-dollar donation, which will enable us to build a new one-story building." She motioned over to a lovely field. "We will have twelve new classrooms, which means we could begin to take nonambulatory cases, for we would no longer have the problem of the stairs. We also will be able to fulfill one of my dreams—to accept children from the age of three instead of waiting until they are five."

"The waiting to be helped," I murmured, "it must be the hardest to bear."

Dr. de Prospero intervened. "We hate waiting lists here. As soon as a family applies, even if we cannot accept the child immediately, we meet with the parents once a month. It seems to help them. Just meeting with other parents and talking over their problems with us. They seem to be revived."

I found the ride home not so long after all.

Mr. Sansone and I have been in correspondence. What was his prognosis for the mentally retarded?

"With proper help and special schooling, 25 out of 30 retarded children can be educated in the basic skills of reading, writing, and arithmetic and can be gainfully employed as adults in unskilled and semi-skilled work. Four more of every 30 can be trained to take care of personal needs, and many of them can go on to do simple tasks at home, work in long-term, or sheltered, workshops and be partially independent. One out of 30 individuals will require round-the-clock care throughout his life.

"A small percentage of children now attending Brookville will achieve educable status and go on to receive special schooling. The greater majority, however, constitute the 4 out of 30 who will be trained here at Brookville and elsewhere in areas of self-help, care of personal needs, and semi-independent work so that as adults they will be able to lead happy and useful lives at home and in the community. Such children are considered as trainable—the moderately to severely retarded—and for the most part, it is a 'trainable' program that we present at Brookville."

I think time, educational experts, and experimental schools like Brookville will demonstrate that there should be special schools for trainables, the moderately to severely retarded. They are desperately in need of these individualized programs, and they are worthy of receiving them.

20

Workshops and Training Centers

Workshops can mean basement rooms or sunny sheds outfitted with power tools and such, used for recreation and repair work. Workshops can be collections of people involved in "learning how" and gaining experience in various endeavors—from drama to photography. The term is a generic one because it suggests many projects, but it most strongly connotes "occupation" and implies "training." For the retardates in the past ten years this may have meant learning to lace toys, stuff envelopes, make egg boxes, or cook. Simple tasks indeed, but for them a new meaning of life.

Years ago centers for training young adult retardates were improvised affairs—of necessity. Groups of parents organized and often, when necessary, staffed whatever training programs they could assemble for their afflicted children. With the growth in public acceptance of the *legal* obligation to educate the mentally retarded, there came a measure of understanding that even severe retardates can be trained to perform useful work. Also the question arose: What is to be done for those who have attended special classes in public schools and been "graduated" at the required age limit? And from the anguished parent came the cry, "Where do I go now?"

One response was the creation of nonresidential training centers for mentally retarded adults—in brief, workshops.

In some states the idea has scarcely taken hold; in others, such as California and Pennsylvania, there is a respectable number. Although a detailed roundup of the types of workshops for retardates is beyond the scope of this book, there are some overall comments and a few close-ups that might help to orient the reader to the aims and problems of such workshops.

First of all, the terminology used to describe workshops for the mentally retarded is not yet standardized, but there are two general classifications: "transitional" and "long-term." Transitional workshops are for training those who will be able to enter competitive industry, and long-term workshops are for those who can absorb enough training to work constructively but who will need a sheltered working environment indefinitely. The latter have been called "terminal workshops," but the term has fallen into disfavor because of its unpleasant connotations.

An extreme example of a retardate being trained in a workshop to enter competitive industry is that of a deaf and dumb lad who has become expert in disassembling machines so as to preserve intact their tiny precision parts, thereby saving a great deal of money in the rebuilding and reconditioning of machines.

A typical case of a retardate who can profit from employment within the long-term workshop is that of a Mongoloid boy I talked with. He was approximately twenty years of age and quite verbal. He realized his plight but said that at least he was happy working and at being treated as an adult. He added with a wistful smile, "Who knows, maybe someday someone will want me to work for them."

For the most part the supervisors or foremen in the workshops have a background in the specific skills they teach at workshops, but they seldom have specialized training in teaching retardates. As for the "bench" section, which generally refers to the unskilled work of sorting, stapling, and loading, the workshop looks for an instructor with personal qualifications such as patience, tolerance, and some exposure to production techniques.

However, all professionally classified workshops have a full complement of trained people—psychologists, social workers, and rehabilitation, vocational, and placement counselors.

The problem of getting trained personnel who are able to carry forward the workshop programs has to be met. One of the first steps was taken in New York.

About ten years ago, the late Dr. Abraham Jacobs of Columbia University applied for, and received, a grant from the federal Vocational

Rehabilitation Administration to hold a two-week seminar to acquaint professional personnel with the nature and processes of workshop training. Dr. Jacobs together with Jerry Weingold (Executive Director of the New York State Association for Retarded Children) and Dr. Max Dubrow (Director of the AHRC workshop at 380 Second Avenue, New York City) were the seminar's leaders. From that time on the course has been held each summer at the AHRC workshop and is attended by people from all parts of the United States as well as from Canada. Those who attend are reimbursed for all traveling and living expenses by the VRA.

Despite the death of Dr. Jacobs, Columbia University has continued to sponsor the seminar. As of 1966, it was condensed to one week.

The course has been so successful that similar seminars have been set up in other states.

The federal Vocational Rehabilitation Administration (VRA) is basically responsible for subsidizing all demonstration and research programs in vocational rehabilitation undertaken by public agencies, and extends grants to private ones. In order to qualify, a workshop must present research programs, professional staff, and a history of reliability.

These federal funds are available for establishment, construction, expansion, and improvements, but not for operating expenses. There is no provision by federal legislation for ongoing operations. When the federal grant (VRA funds) expired at the conclusion of the demonstration phase, it placed the New York City chapter of the Association for Retarded Children in a financial hole. They operate 3 workshops in Brooklyn, Queens, and Manhattan. Less than one-third of the money for running them comes from the Division of Vocational Rehabilitation. Private funds from philanthropic and donor groups, as well as small tuition fees, make up the rest. Occasionally some help comes from the Community Health Board.

Originally the mentally retarded were included in the workshops for the physically handicapped. This relationship was gradually dissolved as workshops in many communities were allocated to either the physically handicapped or to the mentally handicapped. The trend in small communities is now back toward combined workshops for the disabled no matter what the cause. The chief argument advanced for this fusion is that workshops in small communities service 15 or fewer mentally retarded and thus are economically unsound.

New York City does not have the problem of too few candidates in any area for a workshop program. Indeed, the reverse is true: there is always far too much of a backlog of applicants who have to wait for years to be accommodated in existing workshops in New York City.

Within the jurisdiction of the New York City Board of Education, Children with Retarded Mental Development (CRMD) whose IQ's range from 50 to 75, and whose achievement level in reading and arithmetic is at the third-grade elementary school level, may be admitted to the New York City high schools after they have fulfilled CRMD requirements in the elementary and junior high school levels. Nineteen academic and two vocational high schools have classes for the mildly retarded. If a child whose IQ is under 50 can attain the required level of academic achievement, he is eligible for admission also, but this is a rare occurrence.

It is not, however, rare for mildly retarded youngsters of high school age not to measure up to the requirements for admittance to public high schools. To accommodate these students the New York City Board of Education set up an Occupational Training Center at 250 West Houston Street for students between the ages of seventeen and twenty-one who fail to qualify for CRMD high school classes.

The only bar to admission to the Occupational Training Center is emotional disturbance that results in uncontrollable behavior and inability to follow directions.

The program offered by the center is based on available opportunities that exist in New York City places of business and on the trainees' abilities. The teachers at the center have assessed the range of skills they feel their students can acquire and based the program on this. In conjunction with this, a placement counselor goes out to interview potential employers two to three days a week, in an effort to line up jobs.

For most of the trainees at the center, the first class period of the day is an academic one, oriented toward practical matters. For example, the students learn to read and fill out application blanks, and learn about tax deductions and fringe benefits. Along with this there is a greater effort to instill helpful attitudes toward working—and this is quite a challenge considering the problems one is apt to meet in the business world of New York City.

Training courses include messenger service, mail room procedures, shipping, wrapping, sorting items according to shape and color, punching holes in strips, putting rings and nuts together, running mimeograph and addressograph machines, and various other light factory work the center can cope with.

For the girls there is emphasis on domestic science. They are also taught to cut, measure, and sew fabrics, and to use power machines under supervision. Since no one donates material in bulk to the center, the sewing must be done on odds and ends of cloth. The girls make their own uniforms, potholders, aprons, and at times dresses.

In training courses in a food workshop, the boys are taught to be busboys and waiters, the girls to make sandwiches and coffee. There cannot be any further elaboration of restaurant training due to the center's limitations in equipment and space.

Every student is given a course in good grooming.

After a trainee has been placed, he is not discharged from the center until his employer confirms the fact that the trainee is able to handle his job successfully. This is a very important part of the program, since adjustment to a new situation can be especially difficult for the handicapped.

The waiting list for entrance to this Occupation Training Center stays at about 250, since only 50 are discharged from the Center into jobs each fall, and new applications are constantly piling up.

In an old building, donated by the Daughters of Israel, the New York City AHRC, in cooperation with the State Association, has set up an Occupation Day Center at 222 East fifth Street, New York City, for the moderately to severely retarded. The IQ range is from 15 to 40. In the main the IQ's are below 30.

The Center is primarily for the purpose of training young adult retardates in self-care and a measure of independent activity, although one-fourth of them do go on to long-term or sheltered work situations. Sixty people are accommodated in the programs, the minimum age being seventeen and the average running in the early twenties.

It was to this Center that Stephen came. A retarded boy, IQ 40, unable to handle the simplest of chores, he had nevertheless occupied a space in school until the legal age of discharge—seventeen. For the next three years he sat literally motionless at home. A radio or television set was turned on for him. Whether he absorbed anything from those long hours will never be known. As in so many cases, the parents became increasingly concerned for his welfare—for the time when they would no longer be alive to care for him. They began to think in terms of lifetime institutionalization.

One day his mother heard of the Occupation Day Training Center for the severely retarded. Scarcely daring to hope or dream, she called. The dream became reality when Stephen was granted an interview, given a battery of tests, and accepted for training.

Living skills are stressed at this Center. Young men and women are taught to plan and prepare meals, set the table, and clean up the kitchen. They repeatedly practice lighting a match, turning on a gas stove, using a can opener, pouring milk and hot liquids, and cutting and preparing sandwiches and wrapping them in wax paper. They take turns washing the dishes and silverware; scrubbing tables, sinks, and stoves; sweeping floors; emptying garbage; making beds; and washing and ironing clothes.

Stephen learned all this and more. Upon acceptance to the Center he was unable to cross a street alone. Here he learned to travel independently on public transportation. A position was found for him as a messenger that would make him self-supporting. The picture taken of him as he boarded the Third Avenue bus alone, the first day on his job, shows a face lighted with happiness. The boy who was headed toward lifetime institutionalization had joined the world.

This Center has been made possible by a grant from the National Institutes of Mental Health. The cost of maintaining it is $61,000 a year. Since the National Institutes of Mental Health can distribute funds only for demonstration and experimental purposes, the support they are giving is decreasing every year; and unless the state or the city helps support it, this Occupation Day Center, one of the few in the United States admitting retardates with IQ's as low as 15, will have to close.

The maximum tuition is $35 a month* plus a fee for those who are

---

* The actual cost of the average training period at any of the New York City workshops is $1,800 a year.

transported back and forth by bus to the center. Inability to pay tuition is, however, no barrier to acceptance in the program. About one-third pay less than 15 percent of the tuition.

Since the majority of these young people are unable to be trained even to function in a sheltered workshop, very few people leave. The waiting list at the Occupation Day Center has a list of applicants dating back to its inception six years ago.

During a visit at the center I had the good fortune to run into an old acquaintance, Dr. Jack Tobias, a leading research psychologist and an indefatigable champion of the retarded. He has since been named Director of the New York City Association for Help of Retarded Children. He volunteered to walk through the center with me.

Dr. Tobias told me that many of these people have managed to communicate all their lives with gestures instead of words. One of the most energetic parts of the program is activity to encourage speech.

The center has much more complete kitchen equipment than the Board of Education Occupation Training Center has. When the group meets for the day, there is group discussion on what to eat. Some are assigned to go out of the building and shop; the others cook, set tables, and serve.

One of the difficulties encountered by the Center is convincing parents that their children are now capable of making beds, doing dishes, and so forth, and that they, the parents, must forego their habit of doing for the child and must expect him to do for himself.

At the time I visited the Center, 24 of the trainees were being brought in by station wagon each day because they were as yet unable to travel alone. The other 36 made the trip each day on their own. Dr. Tobias said that training the retardate to travel alone took less time than it took to reassure parents that their children would not be lost, led astray, or run over.

A boy with a 30 IQ travels from Queens daily. He is a stocky young man, dark and quite good-looking. Dr. Tobias called him over and asked, "How did you get here this morning?"

"By train. By myself. Nobody helped me. Nobody at all." The young man's smile deepened and widened like a ripple in a pool. "I fix my own room before I leave. I make my bed. All by myself. No one helps me." He shook my hand happily and left to go about his duties.

One young man who had been classified as a profound retardate, below 20 IQ, had in twenty-two months attained full ability to travel independently; had progressed in eleven months from having his father shave him daily to shaving himself; and in nine months he learned to tie his shoelaces without help from his mother.

Had these three young men not been placed in such a center, they would be wasting away either at home or in an institution under twenty-four-hour care and supervision.

How many like these three are on that six-year waiting list?

How many will never be admitted?

I was told that New York State has set up community mental health boards. They are staffed with psychiatrists and medical people to service alcoholics, emotionally disturbed adults and children, along with the mentally retarded. In some counties nothing was allocated to the mentally retarded; in others it remained less than 2 percent. As recently as January 1, 1966, the New York City AHRC secured its first funds from the New York City Community Mental Health Board for services. In order to secure this, the AHRC had to agree to hire two more social workers for their own staff for greater communication with the families, and start a preschool program in Queens.

Dr. Tobias himself is working on a project to care for children in the three- to six-year-old range. Fewer than one hundred retarded children under the age of seven are in any kind of city school in New York. The need to start earlier, the knowledge that the retarded require more training, not less, is acknowledged the world over.

As I was leaving, Dr. Tobias informed me that a new program will probably be set up in conjunction with Metropolitan Hospital to detect pregnant women who are either mentally retarded themselves or have already given birth to a retardate. This will help identify high-risk mothers and help them. The earlier a retarded child is identified, the more chance there will be of training him to function independently.

Years ago, when I began my pilgrimage on behalf of the retardate, one of the first places I visited was the AHRC Training Center and Workshop on East 22nd Street and Second Avenue in New York City. Here the IQ range is from 30 to 60. The majority of these people are placed in outside jobs.

I had the opportunity of attending a meeting of some parents whose sons and daughters were in the lower IQ group, who would always remain in a long-term workshop situation. The discussion was led by Dr. Max Dubrow. In complete empathy with the group, he so managed to reassure them about their children that when they left they seemed buoyant over the fact that, unlike parents of the higher IQ's, they would not have to worry about their children encountering hazards of placement in the "outside" world but could depend on their safety within the confines of the workshop until such time as the family wanted to make a change, if ever.

Some trainees travel alone, others are accompanied by someone.

One day a distraught mother arrived with her son, whose IQ was 25. They lived in the Bronx. She had been unable to find anyone who could bring him in daily. Please, could they help? "You will be giving two people a reason for going on living," she said, "my son and me."

One of the psychologists attached to the workshop, deeply moved, went home and told the story to his wife and thirteen-year-old boy. Although the AHRC was planning to provide personnel to train retardates to travel independently, this child on the borderline between severe and profound affliction might never be able to learn. It seemed unlikely that the AHRC could spare anyone for what might be an endless task. If there were only someone . . .

"I'm someone. I mean I could. At least I could try," the psychologist's son said, his face aglow. "If he doesn't learn, it'll only be my time instead of someone who is needed. If I succeed, it'll be great."

The boy's father looked at him. Perhaps he saw something great also, and they agreed to try.

It took a hundred round trips before a young boy's vision produced the hoped-for results—and the young retardate whose 25 IQ had doomed him to vegetation became an independent commuter and thus a functioning trainee at the workshop.

The faith in success with which the staff itself is imbued is well illustrated by William, age twenty-nine.

The first notations of his appearance read:

> Short, squat, somewhat stooped, phlegmatic. From time to time he broke out in noiseless laughter, especially over incongruities. Rather shabby in dress. Nails bitten down. Strong

mouth odor. Slow, hesitant, defective speech. Quite timid and uncommunicative at first. Impression of him improved as he allowed himself to speak more freely. He left an impression of wanting to have positive relationships but needing encouragement to respond. In later stages of interview, he seemed friendlier, more relaxed, and much more secure with his interviewer than at first.

The results of his psychological tests were as follows:

Mentally retarded young man, overprotected. Cannot travel alone or handle even small sums of money. While he is neat, polite, and friendly, he does not have abilities that would be trainable except in a very sheltered situation. The overall evaluation indicates that the chances are poor that this person will make a favorable rehabilitation risk.

At the end of the year's course, which generally sees trainees on their way to competitive industry, he could not make out in the training center. In October, 1961, his report read:

Extremely slow and uncoordinated on benchwork [assembling, packaging, and sorting]. Cannot earn ten cents per hour to meet even minimum sheltered or long-range workshop standards. On messages, he takes twice as long as other messengers. He is never absent. Is more at ease with himself and others. Is now able to travel. Likes the workshop and says he hates to go home. Said he will "die again" if terminated.

The staff found that William really liked messenger work the best and he really could do nothing else with any degree of efficiency. They decided to keep him and continued training him as a messenger. Now, after five years, he has become so proficient that the expectancy is great that he will be placed with an outside business firm.

The Training Center and Workshop activities are extraordinarily diversified, allowing the staff to vary workshop projects in accord with the season and with changes in placement opportunities.

There is great emphasis on socializing. The age range is from eighteen to somewhere in the thirties. Activities for the younger group include training as Boy Scouts, arts and crafts, camping, and other community-sponsored programs. The older group, which includes the alumni of the Training Center and Workshop, meets every Friday night. They have dances, dinner at a Chinese restaurant, and go bowling or to the movies.

Social workers are on the alert to locate social activities within the trainees' home area so that they can eliminate travel for them and give them neighborhood companionship. They are receiving increasing cooperation from the YMCA, YMHA, churches, synagogues, and temples.

I think all parents should be encouraged to visit workshops. They are a source of understanding and inspiration.

The efficiency and scope of workshops are being increased in state institutions such as Letchworth Village, Willowbrook State School, Mansfield State Training School, and Seaside because the administrators know that the emotional and intellectual stimulation of gainful employment is the greatest spur toward self-realization and where possible returning to society.

Work projects in some cases are inaugurated by the residents themselves. At Mansfield, a group of 14 boys, IQ's ranging from 50 to 70, who were not yet of age or ability to leave Mansfield, organized a car-washing service which has proved a successful venture. The boys run it under supervision but arrange their schedules and buy their own materials such as simonizing wax and cloths. The first three weeks, they earned a total of $50, with the salaries earned individually ranging from $1.75 to $37 a week.

Another unit sold night crawlers to fishermen and made $67 in one week.

The work programs of the schools heretofore discussed have led to off-campus placement on a daily basis in the surrounding communities, plus, of course, the permanent return of a number of trainees to their own communities.

These work training programs are becoming so successful that Hospital Improvement Plan funds have made it possible for Mansfield State Training School, for example, to establish long-range workshops for the training of 100 of the older moderately and severely retarded residents who are paid for a 30-hour work week. All monies are received in subcontract work from local industries. With time this should eliminate a great deal of institutional inactivity.

The transitional workshop program at Mansfield has enabled 47 trainees to leave and work independently at Iona Appliance factory, earning between $85 to $90 a week.

The work training program has so proven itself that Mansfield's director, Mr. Francis Kelley, told me in December, 1965, that the institution has received a half million dollars from the United States Department of Labor to train 300 retardates from the outside community and 100 in residence for job placement.

It should be borne in mind, however, that some of the state schools discussed here are among the most enlightened in the country. In some states the picture is a dark one indeed.

One of the greatest difficulties facing all schools is the dearth of job opportunities for their trainees. The next most logical project is the education of businessmen to the valuable work potential of this large group of trained retardates.

21

Within the Walls

IN PREVIOUS ACCOUNTS OF INSTITUTIONS FOR THE MENTALLY RETARDED, OR state schools as they are now named, I have presented constructive aspects of their programs. It is true that some retardates confined to institutions are being rehabilitated and returned to their families. It is also true that a dishearteningly large percentage, never having been given an opportunity to lead useful lives, now completely out of contact with human relationships, are vegetating purposelessly.

Out of fifty states only Nevada and Alaska lack at least one state institution for retardates. Nevada sends their retardates to hospitals for the mentally ill, and Alaska pays for their care outside the state.

It has been estimated that in the United States 40,000 mentally retarded are mistakenly placed in hospitals for the mentally ill.

Washington, South Dakota, and Louisiana do not charge for state institutionalization but there are those who advocate a change in this policy.

The state of California has passed a law making it illegal to charge for the commitment of the mentally retarded in state institutions.

Mr. Allen Menefee, a former executive of the NARC, said that in his opinion the states of Connecticut and Washington offer the very best residential care in the country. As for specialized work with severely and multiply handicapped, he thought Plymouth in Michigan, Monson in Massachusetts, and Colatral Colony in Wisconsin were the best examples of accomplishments. They are taking bed cases and making them mobile and ambulatory.

Unfortunately the foregoing few are not representative. Some institutions have horrendous histories of brutality and abusive care.

Institutions for the retarded vary from state to state but share communally two tragic characteristics: they are oversized and overcrowded. Some institutions accommodate over 6,000 patients—adults and children. The average waiting time is three years.

In 1960, there were 160,000 in state institutions for the retarded; 40,000 in hospitals for the mentally ill, where they should never have been committed; and 10,000 in private institutions, a number accounting for possibly 4 percent of our 5,400,000 retardates as of that date.*

The average waiting list for all institutions is growing, and the quality of the institutions' care diminishes due to limited budgets, with consequent low salary and personnel shortages.

There never have been, and perhaps never will be enough institutions to care for retardates in this country. Accommodations are not only

---

* The NARC has a record of 245,000 institutionalized retardates as of 1965.

expensive to build but costly for the state to maintain. Most institutions have shown a damaging effect on the children committed to them because of inadequate stimulation via activity, both physical and mental, and the often squalid living conditions. For one reason or another the average institution cannot take a look at the total needs of the child.

The remoteness of institutions was planned to remove the retardate from society and thus they have successfully protected society from the sight of them. Many of us, therefore, have little chance to become acquainted with the realities of the problem because the retardates are physically and psychologically removed from us.

As soon as children are placed in an institution, the parents are told there is a quarantine period, usually of three months' duration. Parents are given various reasons for this, but its true purpose is to make real the break between parents and child. The cold truth is that the child adjusts to no longer being a part of the family.

There is always a secondary reason why retarded children come to an institution, such as illness, inability to be trained, the family's incapability to cope with the problem, and so forth; but apart from such factors, no residence in an institution can give a child what a family can.

It has been said that institutions were built to stay, and unfortunately they have. The buildings, though expensive to maintain, can be put to good use for education and rehabilitation.

A small percentage of retardates who need constant nursing care will always have to be institutionalized, but for most of the inmates there is a place in the outside world. State schools must not be used as dumping grounds. Indeed, it is at such places that intensive training programs could be efficiently provided and a concentrated area devoted to rehabilitation services so that young or old could be returned to the community where they could serve useful lives and give some comfort to their families as well as receive it.

Unfortunately, for decades state budgets have not allotted the necessary funds to provide a proper program of education and rehabilitation for the retarded. As a result many retardates have been defrauded of opportunities to learn to function on the level of their untapped potential. They represent a tremendous number of wasted manpower hours that could be channeled into constructive work.

There are now 10 state schools (publicly supported institutions) for the retarded in New York State. I visited Letchworth Village near Spring Valley, New York, and Willowbrook on Staten Island, New York.

A retardate admitted to Letchworth is first given a battery of tests, which include IQ, projective, physical, psychological, and psychiatric. A tally of the results determines to which unit the patient will be assigned.

It is claimed that 50 to 75 percent of the 4,250 residents at Letchworth are being rehabilitated and returned to the community. These figures may decrease, due to the state legislation passed in 1961, which made education mandatory for retardates in New York State's public school system. This means that many mildly retarded (a few years ago, 90 percent of the inmates at Letchworth were termed "mildly retarded") hitherto committed because there was no other educational opportunity available to them, are now remaining at home and going to school in their own communities. This leaves openings at Letchworth for those with moderate to severe mental retardation.

The state schools, Letchworth among them, must now accept more court cases and delinquent retardates, many of whom formerly were sent to reform schools.

The staff of Letchworth, aware of the changing makeup of its residents and the problems they will present in the future, cite the real tragedy at institutions such as theirs, namely, the older group of people who either have been abandoned or are unable to function outside the institutional walls. Many could have profited by rehabilitative measures earlier, had there been funds and personnel to provide training.

I visited some of the wards. Platoons of beds stretched before me, 60 to a ward. One of the wards had just been reduced from 66 beds to 30. Mrs. Williams, the educational director, said one of her prime objectives was to reduce the 60-bed wards insofar as possible.

It was a sparkling spring day. The ward was being cleaned, and its occupants, men of indeterminate age, were outside in the courtyard. I saw wave upon wave of apathy vegetating in sitting or standing position, a sea of human wreckage.

Willowbrook State School on Staten Island admits patients from all five boroughs in New York City, including those from Long Island.

The wind was blowing briskly as I waited for the ferry that plies between Manhattan and St. George on Staten Island. It almost filled me with a spirit of adventure; for I knew this island borough of New York City only slightly.

I drove a long way after I left the ferry but I didn't mind. The leaves jigged in the breeze and the sun held the warm promise of beauty to come.

Willowbrook has the familiar complex of buildings and large grounds that I was beginning to dread. I passed a children's playground which featured a carousel that had been donated, I learned later, by the parents' league after many years of work and benefits.

The young woman in charge permitted me to be part of a conducted tour for parents who were considering placement of their children. We sat together in a small room waiting for the social worker.

Three of the sets of parents were young. The fourth set, an older couple, were the first to speak and volunteered the information that their boy was quite grown up and that they had been told to "put him away" six years ago.

One of the couples asked hesitantly, "Why didn't you?"

The mother shrugged. Her voice was empty of expression. "I guess we wanted to prolong the agony."

"What made you decide now?"

"He is getting too strong. He's so powerful—"

Her answer was a silence heavy with hopelessness.

A beautiful young mother spoke up. "I didn't know until my boy was two."

Someone asked, "Can he speak?"

"Some words. But he prefers to communicate with a punch or a squeeze. He likes to fight and wrestle all the time. He is so strong—I don't know what to do."

"How old is he?"

"Five. But he is so strong. I don't know. I have one daughter who is physically able to subdue him, but I don't know—"

But she did know. Barren and cold as Willowbrook was, she kept reiterating, "It's so clean, isn't it?" This applicant had been sold before she came. But who knows what any one of us, driven to distraction by a child we could not train, would do? Ignorant as to the amount of potential for education a retardate might have, what could one look forward to? Perhaps any number of us would also have found consolation in the fact that Willowbrook was "very clean."

Children are admitted to Willowbrook at the age of six weeks. At one time the acceptance age was indiscriminate, and as a result the mortality rate was abnormally high. Now the state has authorized referrals of children under five years of age to come through Dr. James Russell, 270 Broadway, New York City. Parents are sent an application upon request, and when it is returned an appointment is made to determine if the child qualifies for admittance.

We passed through the nurseries. Attendants were changing diapers. There were 39 infants in this unit, but the staff expected it to be filled to the usual 50 very shortly. I watched one of the attendants. Mechanically she pulled a child forward by holding on to both legs, flipped him over, put on fresh overalls, flipped him on his back, pulled him forward, and went on to the next, without a smile, pat, or even a touch. The children's eyes seemed dead; had nothing ever stirred them to life? But no one seemed to have the time to find out. Perhaps it was because there were so many to be cared for by so few.

In the next unit, a prison-like line of gray overalled figures waited in wheelchairs. This group was from four to nine years of age. They were waiting to be wheeled out of doors, but they appeared to be suspended in eternity.

We were then led to a small ward of sick toddlers. There are never more than 15 in this group at one time. The illnesses here were minor afflictions.

The next stop was the children's unit of 70 youth beds. The urinal odor so filled my lungs that I seemed to be breathing it for days afterward. The children were all out of doors in a large grassy meadow. There wasn't a sign of a plaything or a cuddly toy. Inside, a barren cement area was set apart from the bed area where the children play in bad weather.

We were told that if a child showed potential he was given classroom instruction. The facilities are so limited that a very small percentage of the children are afforded this opportunity. Classes were held for two hours at a time. Another group of children has recreational activity. The largest number are left in the general care of attendants with little or no planned activity.

We passed through a large TV room where some young boys sat

alone. The doors are locked as you pass from one area to the other. I was told it was to prevent the children from wandering away.

For an hour and a half a day, paper craft, needlcraft, and ceramics are taught by occupational therapists. The more advanced occupational training shops make articles for hospitals or for sale to the public.

As a part of Willowbrook's effort to restore its young adults to the community, a prevocational training program has been set up which includes laundry, cafeteria, and domestic work. The day program has 20 girls going out as domestics. They return to Willowbrook at night.

The older, more capable boys have a recreation program which includes baseball and football matches. Their work program includes training in janitorial work, laundry, and being porters and office boys. They are sometimes used to help other patients.

In July of 1964, a new director, Dr. Jack Hammond,* was appointed head of the Willowbrook State School. As part of a new philosophy in the proper placement and restoration of the mentally retarded, a diagnostic and counseling clinic has been set up to screen applicants. It is staffed by a psychiatrist, a psychologist, and two psychiatric social workers, who determine whether the child could profit by admission to Willowbrook or whether there are sufficient opportunities at home for him to get as much as, if not more than, at Willowbrook. In the latter case it is recommended that the child be kept with his family and not be subjected to the traumatic experience of having to leave his home.

Willowbrook is seriously overcrowded, and Dr. Hammond has announced that no new retardate will be admitted until there is a vacancy. Exceptions will be made only in dire emergencies.

Governor Rockefeller, apprised of the lack of personnel and facilities, gave his pledge to ask the Legislature to provide funds in the budget for 200 more staff positions for Willowbrook.†

---

* Conditions at Willowbrook have been improving steadily since his appointment, but because of the size of the institution an enormous amount remains to be done.

† In September, 1965, Senator Kennedy presented long testimony to the desperate conditions at Willowbrook and Rome state schools. Both the Governor and Senator Kennedy claim credit for unearthing the shocking need of the state schools.

The state of Connecticut is unique in that it was the first to formulate what is called regional planning.

The idea behind regional planning is to have a centrally located training center which works with social service agencies and boards of education within a feasible area. The training center educates and rehabilitates the child, and works with the family when necessary. The purpose of this kind of program is to make it possible for the child to live at home.

On a blustery July day, which was more like a March one, I drove up to New London to visit the first regional center established in Connecticut—Seaside. Mr. Fred Finn is the superintendent of Seaside.

Seaside, he told me, provides directly and indirectly for all retardates referred from the southeastern portion of Connecticut. There are 185 persons from the age of two to sixty-four in residence. About 400 more are cared for daily, who return to their homes at night.

In essence, Seaside is an attempt to prevent the institutionalization of the mentally retarded in an effort to keep them in their own home environments, and to train the young child, where possible, to be admitted to the public schools. Diagnostic and psychotherapy services are available at Seaside for residents and nonresidents alike. The staff at the time I visited included 5 social workers plus 2 visiting social workers, a clinical psychologist, and 6 psychologists in training.

The state of Connecticut supports 6 diagnostic clinics but is aiming for 11.

Mr. Finn told me that Connecticut College for Women, which is close by, furnished 50 volunteers a week. He keeps a station wagon going constantly between the college and Seaside. The students come for two to six hours at a time, and he feels it is a small investment for so rich a return.

Mrs. Doone was assigned to take me through the buildings. The size of the units and number of staff attendants were impressive. Some units did have 24 beds, but Seaside is striving to keep them down to 12-bed units. The attendants seemed to know their charges very well and showed a personal attitude toward each child. One little boy who could not walk was put in a playpen. Given support, he learned to pull himself up to a standing position and tried to walk around holding on.

In one room I saw an attendant holding a child in her lap. The little boy's arms were around her neck and she held him close. After a while, she put him down and went over to a rather forlorn-looking youngster, picked him up, and held him lovingly. The recognition of the importance of feeling loved and wanted was being put into practice. Research has proven that the impersonality of institutional living coupled with lack of expressions of love not only impedes progress in the mentally retarded but leads to further deterioration.

The individual and community cooperation at Seaside is reflected in letters sent to Seaside from parents.

June 8, 1962

Dear Dr. Foote [Commissioner of Health]:

I would like to take this time to tell you how pleased I am with the care that my daughter is receiving at Seaside.

At _____ she had stopped walking, didn't know me, and looked so bad that I expected a call any time that Gloria was no longer with us.

In the eleven months she has been at Seaside, she has gained weight, is walking better, always knows me, and her overall appearance has improved so very much.

I know at the former institution they are overcrowded and cannot give individual care. That is why Seaside has been such a blessing.

My only other child is five and also is on the waiting list at Seaside.

I would like to thank you doctors who opened Seaside and also the people who work there.

May God bless you all.

Sincerely yours,
Mrs. V. T.

June 12, 1962

Dear Dr. Schmickel [Deputy Commissioner of Health]:

My husband has asked me to write to you. We are guests of our son and his wife. Their firstborn has been a resident of Seaside, Waterford. He is now six years old.

As a grandfather and a physician who watched the lad grow, I found it very difficult to pinpoint the baby's trouble (first trouble with walking), then a rolling gait, his inability, so far, to talk. Specialists were of little help. Several said the lad was deaf with an 80 percent decibel loss—"How could you talk if you couldn't hear?" Other specialists, after the parents had bought a Zenith hearing aid at the suggestion of a supposedly qualified doctor, said, "Throw it away—he can hear!" (Opinion at Massachusetts General Hospital). Finally an opinion—"Mentally Retarded. Cause Unknown."

F____ was entered at the Seaside Regional Center on medical recommendation. He has two sisters, and expert opinion said Seaside was best for him as he was affecting the other children. We have visited him at Seaside, and taken him for a drive since our arrival. He is improving. Not so much "out of this world." He is a handsome boy, and we know the need for places like Seaside with specialized aid for children like F____. A child to be saved—Ours—

Devoted grandparents,
C. and F. P. ____

[Undated]

Dear Sir:

We, as parents of a son now presently at Seaside Regional Center, wish to express our appreciation and thanks to you and the state of Connecticut for providing such a place for the care of the mentally retarded. We also feel that this new concept in the care of the mentally retarded is *the* answer to getting these children rehabilitated so that they may enjoy the rights and privileges that they have been so denied in other and outdated institutions.

As our son was fortunate enough to be one of the first to go to Seaside Regional Center, we can see and honestly say that a year has done our son a world of good and it almost seems like his rebirth. Formerly at [typical institution] he was unable to walk or speak, having suffered from a paralysis, coupled with a brain injury and epilepsy. Today he is the picture of health and walking and running with the other children and is also attempting to regain some speech. This we say has been accomplished at Seaside Regional Center and therefore again say, thanks to you and the state of Connecticut for your efforts in promoting such a facility in the state, and hope that more such places will be made available so that other children so afflicted can be helped and brought back to life that are not so fortunate at this time.

Most sincerely yours,
Mr. and Mrs. C. R. W.

When I finished reading, Mr. Finn said he thought the case studies spoke for themselves. Many retarded persons are sitting in overcrowded institutions today, unable to care for themselves, denied an opportunity to live as human beings. Institutions, when faced with overcrowded thousands, find individual reconstruction a physical impossibility.

Individual rehabilitation, such as is attempted at Seaside, has demonstrated that the price of returning a retardate to the community is a fraction of the cost of lifetime commitment to an institution. The promotion of similar programs would substantially decrease the expense to the national budget, not increase it.

One of the tenets on which Seaside was founded is rehabilitation. When it was opened, they decided to add to their program for young retardates, and admit 35 for work training who had long institutional placement records, whose prognosis for community living had been judged poor, and try to reintroduce them to community living. The ages of this group ranged from eighteen to sixty-three. The IQ range was from 40 to almost normal.

At Seaside they were given a chance to develop a sense of responsibility and control in managing their own affairs, each according to his latent abilities. For their work they were given a salary of ten dollars a week. They live in the employees' buildings, eat in their own dining room, manage their own bank accounts, and go into the nearby towns for recreation, to attend religious services, to buy their own clothes and items of decoration for their own rooms. The 35 are now leading a semblance of a normal life with great emotional satisfactions from at least semi-independent living.

The day I heard that the Mansfield State Training School's band from Mansfield Depot near Storrs, Connecticut, was to appear on Ed Sullivan's TV show, I wrote to Mr. Sullivan requesting permission to meet with them.

Mr. Harris, a publicity aide of Mr. Sullivan's, arranged for me to meet with the superintendent of the school, Mr. Francis Kelley, and to attend a dress rehearsal of the show, which takes place before a live audience at the studio.

I cut short my weekend and drove back into New York on a very hot Sunday morning. I waited for Mr. Kelley in the lobby of the Warwick Hotel. He arrived, wearing a blue blazer, looking like a health education instructor on a college faculty, which he formerly was. He told me the band was having lunch in a nearby restaurant and suggested we join them. Between bites on a steak sandwich, I spoke with several of the boys. My note-taking continued for the rest of the afternoon in the dark basement and the stuffy stairs of the TV studio.

Standing alongside such celebrities as Paul Anka, Tiny Little, and the Maguire Sisters, I met with Mr. Bert Schmickel, Commissioner of Mental Retardation in Connecticut.

Mr. Schmickel told me that the Commissioners in Connecticut, usually public health officials, are career men, not political appointees.

One of the greatest difficulties in dealing with retardation, he has found, has been the lack of public awareness. Members of Mr. Kelley's staff at Mansfield State Training School go out to speak to Rotary, Kiwanis, and Lions clubs, and at the high schools, where they try to attract the students' interest and help, on the assumption that if the parents won't listen, the children will. They are also making a determined effort to remove the doors between the institution and the community by having nonpartisan advisory councils whose members come from all walks of life in the surrounding communities.

While waiting for the boys to go on, I spoke with two of the three music teachers, Mr. Nemerov and Mr. Romeo. I never did get to meet the third, Mr. Tate, formerly the arranger for the Les Brown orchestra. They told me that one of the spastic boys I had spoken to, IQ around 50 or less, was one of the most talented members of the band. He has nearly perfect pitch and outstanding rhythmical sense.

The boys and the one girl in the band waited around, bearing the heat patiently. They did not appear nervous and were extremely well behaved. When their turn came to go on, I walked out to the auditorium and stood in the back so that I could see the group perform onstage. As the first brave strains of "When the Saints Come Marching In" trumpeted over the footlights, an excitation shot through me and tears came to my eyes.

After moving among retardates and their teachers for three years, I knew what patience, fortitude, and faith lay behind this performance.

After the rehearsal, I spoke with Mr. Ed Sullivan and complimented him on allowing the band to appear.

"Why shouldn't I?" he demanded. "They're a darned good band."

Before I parted from Mr. Kelley he said he felt a personal visit to the school was necessary in order for me to understand the school's program—its implications and ramifications. I promised him I would make the trip.

Several months later, in July, I was able to keep that promise. That morning a furious flight of rain dashed tumultuously against the motel windows and a chill wind blew.

The ride to Mansfield would be a long one, the road unfamiliar. I had visited Southbury, the handsomest state training school in Connecticut. It was then summer, so no classes or workshops had been in progress. So far as I could tell, as state schools go it had been impressive. Would I find anything at Mansfield different enough to justify my journey?

Perhaps unheralded, they were accomplishing something as yet unknown to me. I decided to chance the trip.

I drove off Route 15 too soon, had to make an agonizing decision at a fork in the road, and moved blindly ahead.

I was undoubtedly lost and becoming very frightened. I prayed for a sign or semblance of civilization. If only there were someone to ask!

At the end of the road I came upon a young man fixing a car in the rain. I did manage to get back on the highway and saw a sign which said East Hartford, and knowing Mansfield Depot lay to the east resolved to exit once more.

An automobile service agency had its doors open and I drove in out of the rain. He also gave me succinct directions and I left with the fortified feeling that I was on the right road at last. I followed directions minutely and was about to go to Willimantic when I saw a tiny sign at the fork saying Mansfield State Training School. I backed up, gratified that while I had followed directions, I had also tried to be on the alert, in case there was another and a better way.

How similar a journey how many parents of retarded children must have made! How lost and frightened, how confusing the directions, the signs and suggestions. How agonizing the decisions as to the right road to travel.

I entered vast grounds with many buildings (I later learned the exact number was 27). There was one important difference in this state school. Its rolling acres form the backyard to the University of Connecticut, which has proven to be a boon to both. A cooperative program has been worked out between Mansfield State Training School and the University of Connecticut, involving the latter's departments of psychology, home economics, physical therapy, physical education, speech, education, political science, and agriculture, plus a university research program. In addition, 250 volunteers from the University annually donate their services to Mansfield State Training School.

The University's Dr. David Zeaman has had a research laboratory for years and has been endowed by the government's National Institutes of Mental Health with a lifetime grant to study learning discriminations of the mentally retarded.

In accordance with the plan for dividing Connecticut into 11 regions to encompass education and aid for all their retarded, Mansfield is working away from institutionalization and toward becoming a regional center.

With this objective in mind, Mr. Kelley encourages the parents to take their children home from school as often as is practicable and most especially for weekends and holidays. Their last survey reported that 85 percent of noncustodial-case parents visit their children at Mansfield.

As at Seaside and Southbury, there is a large waiting list to enter Mansfield. People pay according to a scale. Those families whose income is less than $4,000 in taxable income per year pay nothing. New legislation has been passed in Connecticut reducing fees so that no family ever pays more than $94 a month. The average cost of maintenance per patient is $54 per week.

When a family applies to Mansfield they are required to visit the school. Mansfield appraises the child and outlines what it can offer. They tell the parents what the program will consist of, and if they want it the child is accepted when his turn comes.

In addition to the classic services rendered at other state schools, a consultant in pediatrics visits the children's wards daily and provides medical guidance and leadership in the programming for the young severely retarded. However, there is a definite need to increase the medical staff to the full complement necessary to care adequately for all its approximately 1,900 charges. Mr. Kelley mentioned that he hoped one day to have this figure reduced to 1,500, for it is very difficult to do "an individual constructive job" with any more than this number in any one place at one time.

For those uninitiated into the complexities of institutions, there is generally an education department that oversees the classroom programs. At Mansfield, 700 residents are in the school program, whose achievements I cannot vouch for since I visited Mansfield in the summer when no classes were in session. The Department of Education and Training is responsible for providing a formal educational program for all the mildly, moderately, and severely retarded who can profit by it. This is in accordance with state regulations regarding the retarded between the ages of six and twenty-one who reside at state schools. They also supervise all work-training programs at the Training School for those who are beyond school age. Included in this program are the off-campus work placements on a daily basis in the surrounding communities.

In the school year 35 classes are in session. Of the 700 students, some attend school for only a few hours a day, some for half a day, and the rest for the entire day. The program includes recreational and religious instruction.

Mr. Kelley said he would like to enlarge the program for a full day's schooling for everyone, but it would require doubling his teaching staff, and the funds are insufficient for such a move.

The educational quality of the teaching staff is high. And in Miss De Leo, sightless herself, who teaches music to the blind, there must be a quality that transcends education. I visited her class the day I was at Mansfield, and perhaps her regrettable absence made the experience even more memorable.

In her group the pupils' IQ's ranged from 35 to 53. As I stepped into the classroom my first impression was that of a jumble of deformity, of an oversized head, stumpy arms and legs, a hunched back, a dwarfed body, and universal blindness. A young, vibrant colored girl, an old

man, and a sparsely gray-haired lady were all rocking violently in rocking chairs. They had been told of the teacher's absence and apparently
had been trained in how to conduct themselves without her.

A large group of nuns from St. Joseph's in Hartford was visiting
that day and the room was quite crowded.

The old lady in the rocker was called Vivian. She started the group
by pressing her finger to her nose and singing the first word of a song.
When she repeated this procedure the entire group came in. I also
learned afterward that not only does Vivian play the clarinet but she
has perfect pitch.

When the first true notes of the young colored girl's soprano rose
surely into the air, it crowded out deformity, and a breathless excite-
ment stole into the room. The harmonizing was astounding. The
group sang their own parts, came in without a single cue, waited, and
came in again. It was a most remarkable feat of training.

One of the songs they pertinently sang was, "If we all said a prayer
for each other every day, what a wonderful world it would be."

Two-thirds of the teaching staff at Mansfield are wives of professors
at the University of Connecticut. One-third have their master's degrees
in special education. Mr. Kelley himself is the recreational consultant
for the National Association for Retarded Children. That may account
for the fact that Mansfield is the only institution which has a football
team playing an eight-game schedule with junior varsities of other
schools. Mansfield also boasts a $15,000 swimming pool donated by the
parents.

In nearby Manchester, a summer camp for retardates was made
possible by a grant from the Kennedy family. Mrs. Eunice Shriver,
sister of the late President, takes an active interest in it. Ten retardates
are admitted from Mansfield State Training School and 30 others come
from the surrounding communities. The camp is run with 4 full-time
workers and 65 volunteers.

During the school year, Mansfield holds classes for 25 trainable
(moderately to severely retarded) children from the surrounding communities that have too few retarded children in their particular village
to justify forming such a class. The Board of Education provides for
their transportation.

Mansfield's staff includes 6 social workers, 4 psychologists, and 2 psychology interns. Recently the school has received a grant to train a psychologist for one year. Peabody was the first institution to receive such a grant, and Mansfield is the second.

The diagnostic outpatient clinic is held every Monday. Two children are scheduled each week. There is a complete work-up on the child and recommendation. The schools can get their preevaluation and then ask for psychological evaluation.

The services at Mansfield are becoming so comprehensive in scope that a family whose son had been at the most expensive private school in another state moved to this distant part of Connecticut in order to have their son eligible for admission.

I asked Mr. Kelley if I might interview the three young people who had interested me when I spent the afternoon with them while they rehearsed for the Ed Sullivan show in New York. He kindly arranged it for me.

Flora, about eighteen, had an IQ of 67.

She was a remarkably pretty girl, pink and white, slender, with very even teeth and long-lashed blue eyes. She was strikingly interested in music and said she could recognize a chord just from hearing it played. I said I was impressed because I couldn't tell the difference between a B flat and an A sharp. She smiled and said agreeably that perhaps it was because they are the same. It was a moment in which I wondered who should be on which side of the desk.

I inquired about the education Flora had received at Mansfield. She said she thought it had been very poor but she had learned to read and write. She attended school on a full-day session until she was fifteen and then half a day till she was sixteen. She has been trained to work in the dining rooms and kitchen, washing tables, dishes, etc. She has a day and a half off a week in which to take care of her own clothes.

The dormitory in which she lives houses 18. When I asked her how she liked it, she answered that it was not so bad. You got used to learning not to expose too much of yourself while getting dressed.

She goes to church every Sunday. Confession seems to make her feel better. Then she smiled and said confidentially, "But it doesn't seem to make any real difference because you smoke and do the same wrong things all over again. You only feel good when you walk out."

Flora remembers nothing of her family and in fact doesn't know if there is one. She has been at Mansfield for thirteen years and came there from a foster home.

I discovered later from reading the records at Mansfield that the reason she knows of no family is that they do not know of her. Her mother, who was unmarried, had come down from Canada to give birth and had never told her family of the child's existence.

As Flora rose to leave me, she said that Mr. Kelley planned to place her in the outside community within six to eight months. She smiled and said wistfully, "I want so much to go. Do you think it will really happen?"

My next interview was with the colored lad, IQ in the 60's, who was the drummer of the band. He told me he had gone to school until the eighth grade and left to go to work to try to care for his aunt, who had brought him up. His mother was "somewhere around" and his father was dead. He has a twin brother, whom he hasn't seen since he was nineteen (he is now twenty-eight), and some distant cousins in Hartford, but has no desire to live in that city. He has played the drums since he was seven and wants desperately to become a professional entertainer.

He was certainly very articulate, but whether he had sufficient talent to succeed in the music world I had no way of knowing.

Later I spoke with Mr. Kelley about him. He smiled and told me the boy had been out in the community twice and seems to have a few little weaknesses he cannot control. He has a passion for taxicabs and likes to drink. As soon as he is permitted to leave the school he manages to get hold of a bottle of liquor—brand or quality makes no difference—and thus fortified satisfies his other weakness by the simple expedient of stealing the nearest taxi and going for a drive.

This practice understandably causes great difficulties. In fact, it probably led to his first commitment at Mansfield.

Mr. Kelley said the school had been working with the lad for some time now and were prepared to make another effort to return him to community life by placing him in a semiskilled job at the university which adjoins the school. The music staff did not feel he had sufficient talent to compete in the musical world but thought he might get some odd jobs singing or playing on the side.

Before our interview ended, the boy said, "I'm going to show Mr. Kelley and all of them. I had a fine musical education here. I'm going to make good. You'll see."

My last interview was with a boy who had one of the lowest IQ's in the band but was, nevertheless, its mainstay. He is put in the center of the group and rhythmically helps carry the other band members around him. In appearance he has the look of an apple with thick glasses. He is a spastic with little use of one arm.

He spoke of a family in New York who did not want him. He stated he had two brothers, a sister who is a nurse, and parents who both work. If they would only see him, he would apologize for anything he ever did, though he doesn't know what he could possibly have done to offend them. But they refuse to see him or have anything to do with him.

I checked on his record in the files. His half-brothers and half-sister do not know he exists. The mother bore him illegitimately and hid the knowledge from her family. The father had wanted to marry her, but her response had been to try to provoke an abortion which resulted in brain injury to the boy. After a few tries at foster homes with the help of the social service, she committed the child to Mansfield.

The boy said his most difficult moments were when parents came to the school and took their children home for weekends, holidays, and summers. For him there was never anyone for a day or even one hour.

Later Mr. Kelley told me that when the boy was sixteen the miracle he had prayed for had come to pass. His parents had come and were outside in the car waiting to see him. The attendants helped him dress in his best and down he came. He was invited to sit in the car.

Apparently the mother and the man she married had come to check on his earning capacity. When the boy appeared, slightly dragging his foot and with little or no use of his arm, they had seen enough. They sent him back to his room on some pretext, and when he came down they had driven off. He never saw them again, and in all likelihood he never will.

Before our interview ended, I asked him if he could read. He said his faith was very important to him and he read only religious books and carried one with him always. He pulled a paperback out of his pocket and showed it to me. The title was *Jesus and I* by Father Kleeg.

I asked him whether, if he could be placed, he would like to work in or around a monastery.

"What's that?" he asked.

This startled me, as he had been quite verbose. Then I remembered a conference in which Dr. Goldberg of Columbia University had spoken of being fooled by the verbalization of some retardates. Dr. Jack Tobias of the Sheltered Workshop made a survey in which he concluded that there is little correlation between a retardate's ability to speak and his intelligence. Often the words they say have little or no meaning to them. They just repeat what they have heard without any conception of its meaning.

I explained as lucidly as I could about monks and monasteries. The boy nodded and said, yes, he would like that very much.

The monastery idea turned out not to be feasible, but Mr. Kelley said he certainly might to able to place him in a rectory with one of the nearby priests. He promised he would take it up with the Child Study Group which met every Tuesday morning. He did not think the boy could function on much of a paying level, if at all, but certainly such a job would fulfill some of his emotional needs.

As at Letchworth and other state schools, years of neglect have resulted in large idle groups. Mr. Kelley has been trying desperately to create sufficient work programs for them but admits he is far short of reaching his objective. The latest of Mr. Kelley's projects involves the placement of some of his residents who are sixty-five or older. He wants to settle them in the community before it is too late. Often when retardates are released from an institution to make their own way in the community they find that they are lonely, and request placement back into their familiar surroundings where companionship is not a problem.

Mr. Kelley wants to settle them in the community in groups of four and have them work in such places as convalescent homes, nursery work, farming, etc. He feels that the danger of loneliness would be averted and that many of them should be given this chance to live within the community before it is too late. Settling them in groups of four would give them social independence and reassure them.

22

The Outside
World

In September, 1965, Senator Robert Kennedy of New York visited two state schools for the retarded and made public his findings. It resulted in a rash of publicity, of charges and countercharges, and included a human-interest article on the front page of the *World-Telegram*. A parent's voice echoed the cry of the centuries. "But if I don't place my child in a state residential school, what will happen to him after I die?"

There is an answer, and social security can be assured through the establishment of halfway houses and hostels, long since set up in Scandinavian countries but barely beginning to make their appearance in the United States.

Hostels are controlled residences for life for those retardates who have been sufficiently rehabilitated to go out and work but are not equipped to live independently. For example, their cleanliness and change of clothes are checked, and assistance is given in shopping and management of money.

A man who had worked in special education established a hostel in Madison, Wisconsin. The residents contribute what they can toward their own support, and the parents supplement the difference.

Mrs. Williams, Director of Education at Letchworth Village in New York State, told me they are experimenting with this type of hostel in Suffern, New York, in the private home of a woman who is intensely interested although not specially trained.

When I spoke with Mr. Allen Menefee, formerly of the NARC, he said schools are undoubtedly beginning to be aware of the value of this semi-independent form of living but he did not know of any other hostels established at that time. Even if a few have since been set up, we obviously have not even begun to provide for the retardates who fall within this category.

A halfway house is a temporary home in which retarded residents make the transition from institutional living to placement in the community, including independent living.

One of Mansfield State Training School's most constructive moves has been the establishment of what they choose to call a "hostel" in Hartford but which is in actuality a halfway house.

This residence for young retarded women was established by the school in May, 1963, under the supervision of the Office of Mental Retardation in the Connecticut State Department of Health. It is a modern three-story house, attractively furnished, located in a quiet residential area, convenient to a bus line and a variety of community facilities, shopping center, theatres, restaurants, banks, churches, swimming pool, and so forth. The program has received the full support of the Hartford Association for Retarded Children.

The housemother, who owns the building, supervises the cook and housekeeper. She derives her income from the girls' payment of room and board. Girls whose salaries are insufficient to pay the full rate are subsidized by funds from Mansfield State Training School. The housemother is not on salary. She operates the residence as a private enterprise.

The housekeeper and cook are girls from the school hired at the standard rate of pay by the owner, and under her guidance have done very well.

A social worker from the training school has an office in the residence and is available one day each week for scheduled counseling as well as for emergency matters. In addition to this, a house meeting is held monthly during which time the young women have an opportunity to discuss any problems regarding the general operation of the residence.

Although there have been a few young women who have had a difficult time adjusting to living in the community residence, the majority did not find it too overwhelming. A girl can move along quickly in this program; on the other hand, it might take two years before she is able to move on and out into the community.

As of this writing, 24 young women are living in the community residence, all are employed, and all but one are self-supporting. Each has established a savings account. They do not want to identify with the local association for the retarded. All they ask is to be accepted by the community.

Perhaps without realizing it, they may have already partially obtained this goal, for recently an inquisitive young man who lives nearby inquired of the housemother, "How is the group of attractive nurses who are rooming at your residence doing?" The housemother informed him that the girls were not nurses but were working in convalescent homes and restaurants.

"Well, maybe they are not nurses," he replied, "but they sure do a lot to dress up the street."

The project has been so successful that the school is now planning to open a similar residence for men.

Friends of the Kennedy Center,* Bridgeport, Connecticut (no relation to the late President Kennedy's family or endowments), purchased a home for young men and established a halfway house.

Eleven young men from institutions come for short-term placement. They are lightly or moderately supervised according to their disability. Temporary jobs are secured for them with friends and families for a period of two to six months. They are then placed on a permanent job in the area where they have had the most success. A telephone number is available to them twenty-four hours a day where someone can be reached if necessary. Highly selected individuals have an apartment in the house and serve as supervisors and parent figures. A cook and college graduate make up the staff, which is augmented by daily visits from a social worker.

Rome State School in New York State, which was probably the first in the country to inaugurate a halfway house, abandoned it, but recently reestablished one.

---

* Mr. Stanley Meyers, who developed the first community programs for the retarded in New England was the first Director. He is now the Special Assistant in Mental Retardation for the New York City Community Mental Health Board.

Today's Health of January, 1965, offered an article on "Halfway Houses for the Mentally Ill," stressing the approach of the Dixon State School in Illinois.

> Before admission to a halfway house the patient goes through a retraining period in a resident self-government unit within the state school. Here an effort is made in socialization and even greater emphasis is placed on the individual developing skills and self-care.
>
> Once the patient shows he is ready to step out with a minimum dependence on the institution, he is ready to seek his first community job and moves into the halfway house.
>
> The patient works in the community for an employer, the same as any other employee. He travels from his home—the halfway house—to his place of employment and back again after his day's work is completed. He has his own bank account, provides and takes care of his own clothing, and engages in conferences with a professional staff.
>
> It usually takes a male one year for his training period and graduation from Hill Top, which is the halfway house for males, and eighteen months from Pine Acres, the residence for females.
>
> The average age and I.Q. of the men is 30.4 years and 71 IQ. For the women at Pine Acres the average age is 26 and IQ is 63.1.*

Merbridge House in Houston, Texas, is a large home for 20 people. As in Hartford, it was selected with an eye toward ease of transportation, churches, and community facilities. House parents plus a cook supervise and run the home. The housefather finds the residents jobs in hotels, country club kitchens, plumbing supply shops, and as busboys, housemen, and messengers. Some of the funds come from the Vocational Rehabilitation Department and some from the families. Ninety percent of the men pay their own way.

Encouragingly, many state institutions are beginning to plan for halfway houses in their training program.

---

* From "Halfway Houses for the Mentally Ill" by Howard Earl, reprinted by permission of *Today's Health,* published by the American Medical Association.

THE RESIDENCE IN THE COMMUNITY OR HOSTEL LIVING

The mildly retarded can learn to live as independent adults in their own apartments and enjoy many facets of a so-called normal life. Practically, this has already been established.

That is why when on March 14, 1965, a small headline in the Sunday edition of *The New York Times* caught my eye: "Housing Is Planned for Mentally Retarded," I felt a surge of hope.

One of the major problems confronting the country today is how to provide housing for the thousands of employable mentally retarded adults.

Most of the mildly retarded live sheltered lives with parents or relatives. When their guardians die or are no longer capable of supporting them, they usually end up in an institution, even though they have the ability to make nearly normal adjustments to everyday life.

This is what happened to Steve. When he was sixteen years old, his parents died. What they had feared all their lives happened. There was no one who wanted to assume responsibility for him. He was placed at Letchworth Village. He remained there, what was for him five long, lonely years until one day an aunt decided to invite the boy to visit her for a holiday. The family were impressed with his good behavior and truly touched at the boy's unhappiness at having to return to the institution.

The aunt called the New York City Association for Help of Retarded Children (AHRC). The AHRC contacted the Department of Welfare, which arranged for his support outside the institution, a battery of tests, and a scholarship at the workshop. In three months he was sufficiently trained to be placed on a job and become self-supporting. And thus a life was saved. From last reports, Steve has a girl friend, is ecstatically happy, and plans to get married.

The Educational Guidance Center, a privately sponsored group, feels that, even as a normal young man or woman, the "bright" retarded adult needs an arrangement that offers him a chance to live independently with a job of his own, a home of his own, and a social life of his own. This group is capable of enjoying a social life and of self-support; most can earn from $40 to $70 a week.

The problem was to find a way to give them the ingredients of independent adult living in a context that also provides the "bolstering" they need over a lifetime.

In the summer of 1965 the Guidance Center purchased 20,000 square feet of land between 47th and 48th streets and Ninth and Tenth avenues for the purpose of constructing an Educational Guidance Center and pilot residence.

The Guidance Center, now known as The Rehabilitation and Research Center at 441 West 47th Street was completed in October, 1967, and is now servicing retardates of all ages in both counseling and training programs.

Unfortunately the living plan has not fared as well. The concept had been to build cooperative apartments which parents would purchase for their children so that they could live independently. Since the inception of the idea, the cost of building the apartments has soared, and whether the plan will prove feasible from this point onward remains to be seen.

Hope for hostels arose most unexpectedly.

During the New York State legislative session of 1967, of the many proposals considered, the most exciting one adopted was the law making it permissible to secure hostels or supervised community residences for mentally retarded adults.

This was the realization of the dream of all those tireless ones who had labored all their lives to succor the retarded. All agencies were invited by the state to explain what they would do if funds were made available. The first grants were awarded to the AHRC in New York City, Nassau County, and Rochester, New York.

The state Department of Hygiene plans to purchase and equip these residences. Either the state itself or an approved voluntary nonprofit organization will run them.

The New York City AHRC under the aegis of Dr. Tobias has already selected a site that the state is negotiating to purchase. The personnel will include a director (a specialist in the field of mental retardation), house parents (whose minimal requirements will be high school graduation), a relief staff, and maintenance people. Thirty to 40 adult retardates will be accommodated.

A prime requisite for admission will be that the adult retardate be able to participate full time in an outside program. This will mean paid employment for many and workshops for others.

Fifty percent of the cost will be guaranteed by the State and the other 50 percent will be from contributions of those able to pay either from their salaries, the social security benefits of their parents, legacies, or Department of Welfare relief.

How much will this hostel actually cost the government?

A realistic estimate is about $3,000 per person a year. Institutional cost, as at Letchworth, has now risen to about $4,000. Even if there were no monetary advantage in hostel living, think of the saving in terms of the family's health and sanity.

The New York City AHRC under the aegis of Dr. Tobias has al-service this hostel, for the site being considered is a short distance from their offices. This means that a complete complement of professional people will always be available to service the residents.

The leisure-time program within the hostel will include TV, puzzles and other table games, ping-pong, and an attractive lounge. The staff in charge of recreation at AHRC plan to take the young people bowling, to choral groups, and to various other activities outside the building.

Similar constructive plans are under way for Nassau County and Rochester hostels. Three small hostels! What a cause for joy! What a small cost for such a large upward step in the face of billions going for destruction.

23

New Approaches

ONE DAY AT FLOWER FIFTH AVENUE MENTAL CLINIC, THE CHIEF PSY-chiatric caseworker, Mr. Lawrence Goodman, handed me a flyer on his desk. "You might want to look into this. Our staff is planning a visit there." And that was the first time I heard about Camphill Village, U.S.A.

Several years ago, the late Dr. Karl Koenig, an Austrian-born physician living in Great Britain, came to this country to lecture on the teachings of Rudolf Steiner, founder of the Anthroposophical Society with headquarters at the Goetheanum in Dornach, near Basel, Switzerland.

A lady in the audience, impressed with the spiritual philosophy and educational principles of the movement, donated a 210-acre tract of land at Copake, New York, to start a village comparable to the spectacularly successful Botton Village for the mentally retarded in England.

Camphill Village, U.S.A., was opened in 1961. Two days later adjoining tracts became available, and with borrowed funds Camphill became a 500-acre community.

I was cognizant of the fact that there were Rudolf Steiner schools in many parts of the world but beyond that I knew very little about the movement.

I visited Camphill twice, read what I could, but unfortunately I can do no more at this time than touch on the philosophy of this very exceptional man.

Rudolf Steiner was born in Austria in 1861. He developed a conviction that became his unswerving philosophy of life. He called it Anthroposophy, and has described it in these terms: "It is a knowledge produced by the higher self in man," and he added that in traveling this way of knowledge, the spiritual in man is moving toward a comprehending communion with the spirit in the universe. It calls on man, in the highest degree, to face himself: unless man is willing to grow *beyond* himself, he cannot grow beyond his circumstances, and it is these same circumstances that concern our children so closely. Full tribute is paid to the marvelous faculties of imitation and wonder that young children possess and their natural powers of fantasy.

When studying in Vienna, Rudolf Steiner tutored a boy who, he was told, was retarded. Steiner had such remarkable success with him that the boy ultimately went on to the study of medicine. Presumably Steiner's great interest in the handicapped had some of its basis in that experience. But his work with the handicapped was only a part of his constructiveness. His greatest work was with the normal.

There is a three-year training period in Scotland for the teachers of the Camphill movement. Neither teachers nor other workers in the school and community are paid, nor are they required to take any courses. They have chosen to work within Anthroposophy as a way of life.

The Anthroposophists' patience and strength engaged in helping the handicapped should not be misunderstood as pity or as self-effacing devotion to a chosen duty. The enthusiasm and love they bring to the task stems in the first place from a deep concern for the destiny of each human soul. They believe in a spiritual entity in all men, whether they are handicapped, average, or exceptional. They unite in striving toward a community that will reflect their spiritual aims in all aspects of life: the working of the land, the building of houses, education, human relationships.

Rudolf Steiner died in 1925 in Switzerland but during his lifetime he lectured at length and wrote many books on his theory of education.

According to Henry Barnes, Chairman of the Faculty at the Rudolf Steiner School in New York, the original Waldorf School was founded by Rudolf Steiner in 1919 in Stuttgart, Germany, at the request of Emil Molt, a farsighted industrialist who realized that the social problems of our times required men and women who could think more realistically than the generations which had led Europe into World War I and who were then seeking utopias in Bolshevism and other theoretical solutions which were to open the doors to Fascism and to World War II. Mr. Barnes writes:

These ideas included the view that every child passes through three phases of development on his way to manhood. In the earliest years he is predominantly a will being, learning through imitation. In the second phase, the feelings are especially active and the imagination is the key to learning. And, in the final phase of childhood, in the adolescent years, logical, individualized thought awakes to a degree which it has never done before, and learning emerges as a new ability to grasp concepts in the abstract.

It was in connection with the elementary years that Rudolf Steiner pointed out the crucial importance of the teacher's authority, rooted in the relationship of a class teacher who continues from year to year with the same group of children. This beneficent authority, based on mutual respect and affection, carries the learning process in the formative early elementary years. The teaching method at the same time is artistic—working with movement, color, drama, and music to convey the subject matter in a manner that engages the child's fantasy and active interest as well as his ability to absorb and to retain facts. Behind the various practical aspects of method and curriculum stands a spiritual conception of man which sees in each child a potential for individual freedom as an adult if he can gain the necessary, inner strength and direction.

Waldorf schools vary from country to country and from place to place. They have proved themselves adaptable to widely different conditions, yet they share common goals and have many characteristics which unite them. Each is administratively autonomous and very many are conducted by their faculties. In Germany they were early singled out by the Hitler regime as obstacles to the achievement of a centralized totalitarian state, and all were closed. Since the war they have been pioneers in the development of modern education in every important European country as well as in the United States, Brazil, Argentina, Australia, New Zealand, South Africa, and, most recently, Canada as well.

In Vienna, Dr. Koenig, caught up with the enthusiasm and conviction of Steiner's theory of spiritual fulfillment, held study groups for some students. But anything that freed man to function as a vital, thinking individual was anathema to Hitler and the Nazis. Since the Rudolf Steiner schools were immediately closed by Hitler, its leaders were driven either into hiding or out of the country.

Dr. Koenig, pediatrician, respecter of mankind, was no exception. Seven of his followers decided to leave with him, and these eight people, with eight shillings among them, left Vienna for Scotland, where a friend of Dr. Koenig's kindly lent them a house at Aberdeen.

In 1939 he and his young friends started a small residential school named Camphill House for children in need of special care—psychotic, mentally retarded, multiply handicapped, and children tending toward delinquency.

The school (nonprofit) was soon followed by many others. Special treatments to help the individually handicapped child were developed by Dr. Koenig and his co-workers in patient effort, continuous study, and critical evaluation of their results. The mentally retarded provided a great area of interest in the schools.

Soon a new problem had to be faced, calling with urgency for a solution. What will happen to the mentally retarded leaving special schools when they are no longer children—when perhaps their parents are dead?

Stemming from the Camphill movement, a great experiment began in 1955—a community for mentally handicapped young men and women—at Botton Village in England.

Botton has proven itself—so much so that the British Government now contributes partially to its support. Botton is now 76 percent self-supporting.

In 1959 the Camphill movement came to America. Miss Janet McGavin, director of one of the Camphill schools in England, became director of a school for retarded children in Downingtown, Pennsylvania. It had formerly been run by Mr. and Mrs. W. Hahn, on principles akin to those guiding the Camphill schools abroad.

The Downingtown school for retarded children grew appreciably and had to be relocated at Glenmoore, Pennsylvania. The school is now known as Beaver Run.

In 1961, Mr. Carlo Pietzner, one of Dr. Koenig's first collaborators, came over and helped start a second school, Donegal Springs House, at Mt. Joy, Pennsylvania.* Paralleling this project, with the assistance of American friends, he began the organization of Camphill Village, U.S.A. at Copake, New York, based on its counterpart of Botton in England.

I spent many fruitful hours with Mr. Pietzner on my first visit to Camphill. It was founded in an effort to establish a community for those retarded adults who can function at some constructive level but do not have the capacity to work or live independently in the outside world.

He said that the idea of absorbing the mentally retarded into the normal community is fine, but at best this can only work for the mentally retarded in urban areas where they can get back and forth from home, whereas in rural areas this is well-nigh impossible, particularly when the family is gone.

"I am not saying that every retardate should come to a special community like Camphill. If there is a so-called normal community that is willing to accept him, fine. But mostly they neither can nor will."

Is Camphill Village a hospital, school, workshop, or institution?

The lack of an accurate answer has been one of the greatest difficulties in Camphill's survival. They have no category, which has serious disadvantages when it comes to government help of any kind. In order to be able to function legally, they are registered as a mental institution, although they do not consider themselves that at all.

Camphill has to accept contributions from the parents of retardates —$200 a month. But it is their dream to dispense with this fee as soon as possible, just as their English model does.

"We have certain criteria for acceptance here," Mr. Pietzner said, and motioned toward the rough terrain. "Everyone must be ambulatory. There must be a capacity for self-help. If they can be taught, we

---

* Both schools have since been consolidated into what is now known as Children's Village at Beaver Run.

take them. We do not accept anyone who can work on a job and live independently in the outside community." *

At Camphill no fences or walls limit the physical freedom of the Villagers, no regulations beyond those guiding any normal family household reduce the dignity of their human freedom. The staff strives to enable the handicapped person to enfold his maximum potential with self-respect, in an atmosphere of dignity, confidence, and cheer. He is offered the benefit of a sheltered community built entirely around him, his needs, and his capacity.

In 1963 there were 22 villagers, 11 staff, 8 staff children, and 4 trainees totaling a village population of 45. The village itself consisted of 3 family units, 2 unlicensed houses for staff accommodations, what they called the White Barn, which contained an enamel shop and assembly room, barns, and sheds.

As of 1967, there were 8 family units and 2 more under construction, and a weave shed and greenhouse had been added. The Villagers had increased to 52 and the staff had grown proportionately. To quote Mr. Pietzner, "The seemingly high proportion of staff to retarded Villagers reflects the true 'village' character of our population; namely the presence of staff children as well as trainees in our training course for workers in mental retardation, and also short-term students who are doing their fieldwork in the framework of their college courses with Camphill."

The dream of reducing the family units has begun to come true. There are now no more than 8 in each private home, and in some cases the dedicated administration has succeeded in having only 6.

"We do not ever want more than 200 in the village," Mr. Pietzner told me.

I commented that dedicated recruits to work in such a village without pay must be difficult to find.

---

* Since Camphill stipulates self-care and ability to be trained, Mr. Pietzner's argument would seem to be open to some debate. If an individual is rehabilitated so that he can help himself and contribute in some measure, there would seem to be no reason why he could not remain with his family in his own community even if he is unable to work independently at a job in the outside world.

Mr. Pietzner said it was not as difficult as one would expect. Most of their staff is from abroad but they do have American families joining them.

As new buildings are put up, the goal is to have enough to reduce the family-unit size from 8 to 6, to approximate a more natural situation and to increase the emotional support of family life. Each family does its own cooking, cleaning, washing, and ironing, and it seems to be working out very well indeed.

On a later visit I talked with one of Camphill's staff, Miss Helen Murray, a young, lively, blue-eyed lady with a sparkling sense of humor and a gift of easy conversation. She told me that the woman who had taught weaving was no longer with them but the bread-baking, farming, gardening, enamelware, doll-making, and dressing industries were proceeding enthusiastically onward. (The bread they bake is sold to outside communities as are the dolls and other dispensable wares for sorely needed cash.)

Each family unit is given a set sum a month to care for their needs. They pay for the food, gas, electricity, heat, repairs, expeditions, and so on. When a medical expense or expedition is of major financial proportions, an exception is made.

Heads of households manage to eke out extra furnishings from their funds.

Miss Murray waved toward the houses and volunteered the information that they have all been saving together and have just about managed to wangle a new freezer.

I asked Miss Murray what they did in the evening. I had noticed that there were no television sets and knew that movies were not encouraged. She said they have choir meetings, lectures, slide shows, and study groups.

"You see," she said with a twinkle in her eyes, "we do not believe *people* are backward, nor are they human wreckage." Then she added soberly: "We believe every human being is a human spirit." She walked me back to my car.

I slid behind the wheel of my ancient vehicle. "By the way, which one of the houses is going to get the new freezer?"

She opened her Holland-blue eyes in astonishment. "Why the one that needs it the most, of course!"

24

Institutes for
the Achievement
of Human Potential

I ARRIVED AT THE CONTROVERSIAL INSTITUTES FOR THE ACHIEVEMENT OF Human Potential in Philadelphia for the first time in September of 1963. I use the term "controversial" because a number of prominent physicians in neurology and rehabilitation have criticized the Institutes' treatment for physical and mental defects on both theoretical and practical grounds. There are some who deplore the abandonment of braces and muscular exercises. Others declare that the new treatment cannot be properly judged until controlled experiments make possible an accurate comparison between the Institutes' patterning procedure and more orthodox rehabilitation methods. And still other professional people denounce it completely.*

There are several large divisions that make up the Institutes. For example, at the Institute for Neurological Organization, 1,400 children with injured brains are being treated. In another division, the Institute for Language Disability, 1,000 youngsters with speech and reading problems are being helped. These two centers are the largest of their kind in the world.

Under the Institutes' program, parents do almost all of the work in treating their brain-injured child. The child and the parents come to the Institutes for an initial three-day evaluation, orientation, and pro-

---

* The controversy has become more acute since a University of Pennsylvania research team, under a government grant, was refused cooperation by the Institutes in conducting a survey aiming for an objective evaluation of the validity of its procedures because they and the Institutes could not agree on the criteria for measurement.

gramming period. The children's evaluation takes an entire twelve-hour first day. Parents listen to the why for twelve full hours the next day. The third day is spent teaching the parents how. The latter is done at the Children's Evaluation Institute.

Parents and child report back every sixty to ninety days for reevaluation and reprogramming.

The Institutes are located within a small walled estate area. I was directed to a low building to the right of the entrance gate. Waiting along one wall was a long, uneven line of parents with their retarded children. Some, eyes half closed, lolled to one side in their parents' arms; others sat blankly upright in wheelchairs, or were tied in their chairs to help them sit up; still others sat quite still alongside their parents; one or two moved restlessly back and forth, and one little boy ran around incessantly in circles.

I was ushered into Dr. Glenn Doman's office for a preliminary briefing.

"Europeans," he said, "have much more respect for a retarded person than we have. They regard him as handicapped but believe that work is an essential right of people and if it takes more time to train the handicapped, then they say, 'Let's take that time.'

"The days and weeks of our lifetime are for care, not for storage. There is a stigma attached to retardation among the lesser educated. It is less among more enlightened people.

"This institution has a waiting list for months.

"The Institutes, in order to determine who is brain-injured, have established criteria which they feel are reputable and valid. These criteria measure brain function in six areas in which man has attained capabilities beyond those of any other living organism. The three expressive, or motor, functions include mobility, language, and manual competence (writing). The three receptive, or sensory, functions are visual competence (reading), auditory competence (understanding man's spoken language), and tactile competence (stereognosis)—the ability to distinguish the quality of an object without seeing it.

"We regard the IQ as a measure of disability. Our interest is in the neurological age. We feel that is a better indication of the child's potential."

The neurological approach can be exemplified by a case history such as Jimmy's.

In 1961 Jimmy, aged seven, had been diagnosed as mentally retarded. His IQ tested out at 70, and the family doctor said the boy would never be able to go to public school.

Jimmy's basic problem was poor neurological organization. Somewhere, somehow, during the early months of Jimmy's life, his nervous system had not developed fully and properly in the necessary sequences. Because of this, he could not learn normally.

To solve Jimmy's learning problems, the parents were told at the Institutes that it would be necessary to find ways to stimulate and develop the areas of the brain that had not developed when and as they should have.

First, Jimmy was tested to pinpoint the stages of neurological development that were incomplete. He was asked to throw an imaginary baseball, to kick an imaginary football, to sight with each eye through a tube of paper at a dot. To creep on hands and knees across the room. To sight the examiner through a pinhole in a board. To step forward, backward, upward. To pretend to brush his teeth and to eat imaginary food. To use scissors. To try to write his name. To attempt to read a list of words at his grade level. More technical tests of vision were given.

Jimmy's mother was asked for a complete prenatal history. Details of Jimmy's birth and his condition immediately after he was born were noted to determine the possibility of oxygen deprivation or birth injury, both of which would affect his brain.

After exhaustive questioning about Jimmy's infancy and early childhood, he was programmed. That is, a schedule of patterning was prescribed in an effort to supply information to the brain which would make it possible for the child to develop the necessary sensory pathways. Patterning is a precise, repetitious placement of the subject's arms and legs in order to simulate normal movement as closely as possible.

The idea behind this is the artificial implantation of a movement pattern on undamaged brain cells. This should eventually enable the child to have a normal neurological organization, so contend the Institutes.

The programming of each child differs according to the stage of brain development believed to be incomplete. But this is a reasonably typical program:

(1) Cross-pattern creeping. This is a way of creeping in which the left leg and right arm move forward simultaneously, as the head and neck turn slightly toward the right, or forward hand. At the next step, the left hand and right leg move forward, as the head and neck turn toward the left hand.

Creeping helps the two separate sides of the brain to work together in a smooth operation of both sides of the body.

(2) Cross-pattern walking. For ten minutes daily, Jimmy was to walk precisely and rhythmically in bare or stockinged feet in this manner: as each foot moved forward, he was to point to its toes with the opposite hand.

(3) Sleep position. Jimmy, being left-handed, was taught a sleeping position. He was to lie on his stomach facing right. His right arm was to be bent so that his right hand rested about 12 inches from his face, palm down. His right leg was to be flexed, with the knee opposite his right hip. Jimmy's left arm was to be placed down by his side, palm up, and his left leg stretched straight down. A right-handed child is taught to sleep in precisely the reverse pattern.

(Basically Jimmy was meant to be a left-sided child, but he did some things with his right hand and some with his left.)

Of course no sleeping child retains a position very long. Jimmy's parents were told to place him in this pattern once again every night just before they went to bed.

(4) Visual pursuit. For two minutes each day, Jimmy was to hold a pencil in his hand one to two feet in front of his face and move it horizontally and vertically while he followed it with his eyes.

The human brain has two distinct halves. Each controls the opposite side of the body. But language abilities are controlled by the dominant half of the brain. And unless one half of the brain is clearly dominant, the individual has difficulty with written or spoken language or both.

Children who are unable to become completely one-sided need much environmental help to aid in the establishment of dominance.

Exercises in reading and writing to develop left-sided dominance were added to Jimmy's program.

In less than one year Jimmy tested at third-grade level although he had completed only the first grade.

Jimmy's case was a spectacular success, but many of the children applying to the Institutes are much more severely handicapped.

Dr. Doman invited me to sit in on the next interview.

A good-looking couple in their late thirties came in. Mr. and Mrs. Bougher graciously gave permission for the use of their name. Their daughter Lynn was a blonde child, nine years and eleven months old. Her neurological age tested nine months and fifteen days. A severe cerebral palsy case, she was unable to sit up and was tied in a wheelchair to keep her upright. She had a language ability of about 18 months—about ten recognizable words. Her creation of meaningful sounds was inadequate.

The prehensile grasp of her right hand was poor, and she was even more handicapped on the left. It was at about the 9-month level. Her visual competence was on the two-year level, she had strabismus, which is common with retardates, and her auditory level seemed to be at about the four-year level, although it could not be tested; the startle reflex was moderately severe, tactile sense was at the one-year level, and her perception of vital sensation was sluggish.

Lynn had a severe midbrain injury. She is the second child born to her parents, the first having been stillborn. Two younger children are normal.

The mother was Rh positive and had spotting that began in the fourth month and continued until the Caesarian section after a gestation period of seven months. The birth had not been preceded by any real labor. Lynn's weight was 3 pounds 10 ounces.

The child became jaundiced the third day. For three weeks there was a day-to-day fight for her life. She was placed in an incubator.

At the age of six months the pediatrician decided there was a definite possibility of cerebral palsy. The child had the typical history of brain damage—of little movement to reach, grasp, etc. (This is a difficult diagnosis to make since many children may be slow in these areas without being retarded at all.) At six months of age she had a fever that reached 105 degrees.

The following are notes from Dr. Doman's address to the two parents. He began:

There are three purposes of today's meeting. Is your child one of our children or not? If so, do you want to work with the Institutes? To help you understand about retardation the following facts are basic.

Three kinds of children are mixed together under the label of retardation. Some children are born with undersized heads, the microcephalics. These we cannot help.

A second type is a psychotic brain, which appears to be normal, but which we do not know enough about to help.

The third type is the child whose brain developed normally but sustained damage either before, during, or after birth.

The first two types we cannot help. The third we have answers for. Those we can help.

We have three ways of telling these children apart: by each child's history, neurological findings, and by the profile, which is our chart.

"Mental retardation" is not in the medical dictionary. In Webster's it means, "held back." It is a symptom, not a disease.

Your child has had a complete checkup today. Tomorrow you will return with her. A nurse will care for her while you attend the lectures on brain function, which take a total of 12 hours. You will then have an opportunity to ask whatever questions you like.

Your decision to work with the Institute for your child must be made while you are away from here. We do not want to influence you. If there is one thing we have plenty of here, it is children.

We have spent years learning to make brain-injured children well. We are adamant that parents follow instructions. If they do not do what they are supposed to do, the Institutes will drop them.

In sixty days from the time you have begun to follow our program you will return with your child and she will be retested and remeasured. The blue line on her chart is for the first measurement, the red is for the second. If the red line isn't higher, then there is something wrong. As the red line goes higher, a new program is devised periodically. When it reaches the top of the page, the child is discharged.

We expect those of you who decide to work with us to bring your child back to us for a checkup about 12 times, that is, every 60 days. The cost to you will be approximately $500 for the entire program covering the two-year span.

Every time you come, a letter will be sent to your family doctor. If you have absolutely no success with the children, the Institutes will take them for in-residence and try once more.

Glenn Doman rose and held out his hand. "If we're smart enough and you're brave enough, we'll win."

The parents left and Dr. Doman held up the next record. "Want to sit in on the next one?" he asked me.

I stared at it. It couldn't be. I glanced down the record rapidly. Far from here I had known these parents well. They were bright, handsome, well-educated, with a dewy radiance. I had not seen either of them since they were married.

What had happened? The record noted one hydrocephalic son who had died, two bright girls, and now this retarded boy.

Why?

There is no answer. It just could happen. To you, to me, to anyone.

But there must be some answers. And someday we will have them. In the interim we must explore and utilize every means of rehabilitation for those children who have been hurt. The United States has not been as far behind in research as it has been in a practical approach to helping the retarded. We have accumulated theories, but have not put enough of them to use.

That is my reason for including the Institutes for the Achievement of Human Potential. I am no expert—medical or otherwise. I do not know whether the Institutes have found the answers; whether their success is commensurate with their efforts or with that of the parents.

But the Institutes are trying. And there is ample evidence to support the fact that in some cases they have been successful.

I explained to Dr. Doman why it was best for me to leave before this next interview. He suggested I walk around with a child who was still in the process of being tested.

I was introduced to the child's mother and to an attractive friend who had accompanied her, and we spent the next few hours together.

The boy was seven years old, weighed 40 pounds, was right-handed and very active, and had the good-looking freckled face of a lively Irish boy.

The father, a college graduate, has an important executive job. The mother had five children, but was still as slim as a girl. She had had one miscarriage after her normal firstborn, then two more normal children and then this boy who was brain-damaged.

The mother had had a good pregnancy, with induced labor and three hours under anaesthesia. The child had a high forceps delivery and showed marks on his head when born but was not blue or jaundiced and was believed to be completely normal at birth.

When the boy was three, the nursery teacher suggested that he be examined for brain damage because of his hyperactivity.

Brain damage!

The parents could not believe it. The boy had sat up, stood alone when he was a year, and seemed to do everything at the normal time except walk. He walked when he was seventeen months.

After two EEG's when the child was a little over four, the physician reported no brain damage. Caught in a mesh of dubiety, the parents sought further help. They were recommended to a woman doctor in Buffalo, who diagnosed it as positive brain damage.

The child has been under medication for hyperactivity and last April he became cross-eyed. The parents said it was due to the medication. He has a speech impediment, but has had no speech or physical therapy.

He was in a public kindergarten class but was taken out and put in school with smaller classes, but still made no progress. The parents searched for private school facilities, but there were none to be had for a child with these disabilities other than boarding schools.

The boy's symptoms are hyperactivity, short attention span, lisp, tenseness without medication, and unwillingness to go to bed. He is toilet-trained, does not care for liquids, will drink little milk, no soup, no water except perhaps a soda once or twice a week, likes vegetables, and will eat meat only in a sandwich. He gets along well with children of his own age except that he is unable to compete with them in reading and writing.

While I was with him, his hearing was tested with a watch. The tester then showed him several objects, put them in a bag, and told him to feel for each one and withdraw it, which he did. He had an abnormal dislike of being tickled for reactions. Blindfolded he counted words from a printer's block by touching. In the mobility room he crawled on a mat. He did this with the same hand and foot instead of the normal cross-patterning. He was able to open and close doors, throw and kick a ball.

At the end of the testing procedure, I asked the mother if I could contact her after a year or more to check on the results of her work with the patterning procedures. She consented to my doing so.

The next day I was invited to hear the lectures given to the parents on *why* the Institutes have formulated the procedures they practice. I recorded as many salient facts as possible.

Dr. Doman estimated that 70 percent of retarded children suffer from some injury to the brain—a brain that at conception was meant to be normal. These are the ones they feel they can help.

The following section is transcribed from the notes taken at the second day's lectures.

In this Institute we have had many varied cases: an eight-year-old cardiac arrest, which means a sudden emergency caused by an actual standstill of the heart with no ventrical or electrical excitation; a twenty-year-old who had a bullet through his head; a young mother who had a clot that traveled to the brain; a thirty-year-old who went through the windshield of a car; and a sixty-year-old who had considerable damage due to Parkinson's disease.

Seven out of every ten children born suffer some brain injury at birth, but not all these result in mental retardation.

Any concussion would be a brain injury.

There is no relationship between brain injury and intelligence.

There is a high relationship between brain injury and ability to express oneself.

Twenty years ago we at the Institutes were interested only in severely brain-injured children who were immobile and made no sounds, the kind it takes three hours to feed. Then we moved to those brain-injured who were unable to walk or talk but could move and make sounds. We found that there was no large gap between the moderately brain-injured and the mildly brain-injured child.

Most of us know we have two brains, the right which controls activity on the left side of the body, and the left which functions conversely. Was it possible for the uninjured brain to take over the functions of the injured one?

The Institutes spent twenty years on research. With a rehabilitation team made up of a brain surgeon, psychiatrist, psychologist, nurse, physiotherapist, speech therapist, and educator they decided to try treating the brain.* At that time we had never heard of a brain-injured child who had got well.

The years spent with massage, exercise, whirlpool baths, braces, and crutches had shown discouraging results. At the Institutes our patients were divided into three groups: one group had improved slightly, another showed no improvement, and a third was actually worse. Ignorance is not so much not knowing as knowing all the wrong things.

Dr. Doman advanced some of the theories under which the Institutes operate. Thus far they have been unsubstantiated by the medical profession. (This does not mean that all doctors disagree with the Institutes' procedure.) There are countless brain cells, estimated to be in the billions. If one hundred or even a hundred thousand were dead as a result of brain injury, you might not even notice any difference in the person's behavior. If, on the other hand, the damage was a handicap, why couldn't the undamaged brain cells be utilized to take over the functions of the cells that had been destroyed?

At the Institutes they demonstrate how the human patterns of locomotion are impressed on the brain by a patterning team at the various developmental levels at which the brain functions. Ultimately the pattern of the highest level of human locomotion, that of cross-pattern ("tandem") movement is impressed on the brain. The kinesthetic and proprioceptive stimuli provided by this means are repeated many times a day.

---

* The Institutes claim their procedure consists of 6 surgical and 7 nonsurgical ways.

The warmth and pressure of the hands of the patterning team, the sounds of their voices in conversation, the visual sense of movement as the head is turned from side to side provide numerous and varied additional sensory stimuli. By means of such patterning, the brain, the most remarkable computer the world has ever known, is patterned through its sensory pathways.

Techniques in brain surgery through operations for Parkinson's disease and other ailments have been developed on a wide scale. Why couldn't some of these surgical techniques be further refined, adapted, and used for some of the younger brain-injured?

Athetoids may have a very high intelligence but they look gruesome. (Athetoids have slow, repeated, involuntary, purposeless muscular distortion involving part of a limb, toes, and fingers or almost the entire body.) They drag their legs, hold their arms in abnormal positions, and often have blurred speech. Ten years ago there was nothing to do for athetoids. Now some athetoids can be surgically helped.

In concluding the morning session, Dr. Doman said the most electrifying experience he ever had was five or six years ago, when a little girl of five came in, climbed his lap, talked to him, sang him a song, and did a little dance for him.

Inside that child's head half of the brain was missing. It was in a jar at Children's Hospital. Such heroic procedures are used when there is absolute certainty that the injury has occurred to only one side of the brain, the other side being unharmed. It is extremely dangerous and utilized only *in extremis*.

There are certain conditions that must exist before a hemispherectomy can take place. The child must be paralyzed on one side, have wild aberrational behavior, and be subject to constant interactional convulsive seizures.

Out of 70 recorded cases 40 had to remain hospitalized after surgery for treatment; the other 30 were able to be returned to their homes right away.

After the lecture, several parents came to ask my opinion of the Institutes' methods. I explained that I was a novice just as they were, was doing a reportorial job, and without a thorough investigation could verify neither failure nor success.

Eight months later I returned to the Institutes. Everyone was very busy, but a Mrs. Le Winn took me in hand.

Mrs. Le Winn's husband, Dr. Edward Le Winn, is the former chief attending physician at the Albert Einstein Medical Center in Philadelphia. He had heard of the Institutes from some friends who had called and asked him to look in on their mother who had been brought there in a wheelchair. She had made a tremendous recovery.

Mrs. Le Winn said her husband was so amazed he began to return for further investigations. He returned so often that he acquired a permanent office and a secretary there. He is now the Director of Research with the Institutes.

I told Mrs. Le Winn that I would like very much to interview a parent whose child had been treated. She took me back to look through the files for a parent who would be available in the vicinity. She directed me to one who happened to drop in that day to do volunteer work for the Institute.

Michael's mother agreed to tell me her story and to have it published as she told it to me.

Michael was an adopted child. Two weeks before his birth, the natural mother had a heart attack. This was her fifth child.

The adoptive parents had a girl and they desperately wanted another child. It was ten years before this boy became available. The boy was premature, born during the eighth month of pregnancy. At birth, he weighed 4 pounds 11 ounces and was jaundiced. The child developed thrush and colic, but his reflexes appeared normal and the doctor assured them he reacted perfectly.

The adoptive mother said she cried when she first saw him. The baby looked so ill, she knew something was wrong, but the pediatrician who had examined him at birth reassured her and she took him home anyway.

The boy began to thrive and gain weight. There was no abnormal crying, but at three months he could not hold his head up. He was a beautiful child. At six months he said "Mama" but still could not hold up his head. Nor could he sit up as late as ten months of age. His left hand was open but his right remained clenched in a fist. Finally the mother took him to Children's Hospital for an examination. He was given a series of tests. The diagnosis: cerebral palsy, mildly brain damaged, IQ about 85.

The mother was told to put him on the floor and let him develop on his own. By the time he was two and a half the mother noticed that something was wrong with his foot. She took him to an orthopedist who put his foot in a cast. At the end of three months the foot came out of the cast exactly the same way it went in. The boy could not walk but could creep, and he was still unable to keep his head upright.

A neighbor, who later refused to help with the patterning, created some of the mother's most agonizing moments with such questions as "Where did the boy come from? How could you accept a child like him? Why do you keep him?"

How about her husband and family, I asked her. Had she suffered any recriminations there?

Michael's mother looked surprised. "Why should I? He is our child."

Her introduction to the Institutes came one day when she went to the beauty parlor. A woman arrived in a wheelchair for a shampoo and set. She was so cheerful that the mother became interested and began to talk to her. She learned that the woman was being successfully treated at the Institutes.

She went home, discussed it with her husband, and they decided to take the boy in on the very next appointment day, which was a Thursday. She brought him back home at eleven o'clock on a Friday night, and on Saturday she made one phone call to her temple. Eight patternings were immediately set up for Saturday and Sunday. By Monday morning the women in her temple had set up a schedule where each in turn came to help her pattern the boy eight times a day. Each patterning session takes five minutes—three people at a time for a baby, five for an older child.

A total of sixty-five women became involved in this program.

The minimum patterning must be done at least four times a day. Michael was patterned eight times a day for nearly ten months. The first two weeks he screamed and cried. He was not frightened by the patterning, merely annoyed and angry. The mother learned to divert him with songs and games.

The mother said soberly, "Sitting around helplessly doing nothing is hard. Having something to do is easier."

Michael's hand was spastic and he dragged one leg. Actually his ankle lay on the floor. He had hemiplegia, a paralysis of half of the body.

At the end of eight months of patterning, he was permitted to walk half a day. At the end of ten months he could walk as much as he wished. He was then taken off patterning.

She showed me a picture of Michael snapped while he was walking in the park. As I recall the picture, he still lacked the full use of one hand but he looked extraordinarily handsome and was pointing to something in a tree.

"He certainly is a lovely-looking boy," I said.

"And smart," his mother added, and beamed. "He is not yet four and can read over 100 words and some selected sentences. We all adore him, so that I sometimes am concerned that we might not be paying enough attention to our daughter. But she seems to love him so much I am sure it is all right."

I had observed the freckle-faced, mildly retarded boy in September, 1963, on my first visit to the Institutes. In May, 1965, I called the mother and asked for a report on his progress.

The mother was most cooperative. She said she regretted having to tell me that her boy had not profited from his experience with the Institutes.

The family had tried to follow the course prescribed by Dr. Doman for six months, from September to March, but the boy had rebelled furiously. He had always been on good terms with his older brothers but with the attempt to pattern him, he became resentful of them. His mother said it was as if he were saying, "Why can you walk around and do as you please, while I have to submit to being put on a table and have people move my arms and legs?" He became so obstreperous that the mother felt she was exchanging one problem for another, and the family finally gave up.

That summer the family put in a pool, and the boy, having something active to do that he really enjoyed, became quieter. Back in school in the fall he became hyperactive again. He must remain on medication.

At the age of nine he is in a special class for the mildly retarded in the local public school. There are only eight children to a class. The boy is doing limited reading, writing, and simple sums.

Since the mother now feeds this boy and his younger sibling with the rest of the family when her husband comes home at eight o'clock, the boy drinks and eats everything. He is no longer anxious to leave the table and now wants to stay and partake of the family conversation.

He is still cross-eyed and retains the speech impediment but has begun speech therapy.

When he was an infant, the pediatrician had said: "When he grows up, put him on a farm and forget about him." The present-day alternative (hopefully a growing sentiment) is to expect that with available opportunities for education and rehabilitation, at about eighteen years of age he will slip back into everyday society and will no longer be statistically counted as a retardate.

On my second visit to the Institutes, when I had interviewed Michael's mother concerning her son, I asked to see the record of the little blonde Lynn, the severely handicapped cerebral palsy child, to note if there was any improvement within the first eight months of treatment.

The records stated that after eight months of patterning there was some improvement.

In May of 1965 I called the parents long-distance. Mrs. Bougher gave me a detailed description of Lynn's progress.

Had the patterning helped? Not only Lynn, she answered, but those who were part of the patterning group. One lady, recently widowed, was asked to stay for a second patterning session. Afterward she had said with barely contained emotion, "You don't know what it's done for me to help Lynn—to be needed."

The family has followed the patterning procedure religiously. One of the first results was the loss of her strabismus. Before she couldn't look you in the face, now she can, and her eyes are almost aligned. She has gained the use of her arms. Before this, if she tried to move them, the arms would get taut.

Since Lynn's whole left side is more severely damaged than her right, improvement came first with the right hand. She can pick up a penny with two fingers. When lying on her stomach, she can now raise her head, and her eyes travel in normal focus about the room. She is able to push herself down the therapeutic slide with arms and legs in perfect position and remain perfectly still if need be.

Lynn is now crawling but still cannot sit up. The Institutes feel she is not ready, and she is permitted to sit in a chair only for her meals. She is trying to identify all objects and can identify words flashed on cards.

Mrs. Bougher said she knows the work is going slowly with Lynn because she is so severely handicapped.

In the closing moments of our conversation, Mrs. Bougher said: "Before the patterning, when Lynn lay down, she had to kick her leg and try to throw her whole body to move any part, including her head. The other night she was lying on the couch in the living room and I suddenly saw her turn her head, look up at the ceiling, and turn back to look at me. It was beautiful."

These were my experiences in Philadelphia at the Institutes. I cannot state with firmness the specific diagnosis treated. I do know that results have been attained. I leave the relationship of cause and effect to the medical hierarchy to argue.

I would suggest that if a visit to the Institutes is planned, contact should be made on recommendation by the family physician.

25

The Talking
Typewriter

INTELLIGENCE IS MORE SUSCEPTIBLE TO DEVELOPMENT THAN HAS BEEN commonly believed—if one begins early, according to the report of the President's Educational Testing Services' annual report of 1963.

The recently created and widely publicized Head Start program throughout the United States, through which New York City received $4,600,000, the largest grant in the nation, was the result of professional surveys concluding that all children, and particularly those who are economically and culturally deprived, and the retarded and siblings of retardates, often fall far short of developing to their utmost potential due to lack of educational experience in the preschool years. It is undeniable that the human mind is extraordinarily open in the early years.

In addition to similar conclusions reached by Dr. Bloom and Professor Kirk, Professor J. McV. Hunt of the University of Illinois has concluded that "the assumptions that intelligence is fixed and that development is predetermined by the genes are no longer tenable.

"It is no longer unreasonable to consider that it might be feasible to discover ways to govern the encounters that children have with their environments, especially during the early years of their development, to achieve a substantially faster rate of intellectual development and a substantially higher adult level of intellectual capacity."

The evidence indicates that not only educational achievement but also developed intelligence is dependent upon *successful* experience at each stage of development.

Across the entire spectrum of human abilities there exists an untapped potential of intellectual capacity waiting to be developed through the discovery of new methods of improving instruction on the one hand and of enriching the environment on the other, thereby creating new learning opportunities that significantly affect the child's progress and development. As a former educator, I know only too well the difficulties of creating new methodology and new stimuli for learning and the significance of the early impregnation of the motivation to learn.

A dramatic example of the importance of providing preschool children with an environment conducive to learning is the work done by Professor Omar Kahyam Moore of Yale University, who believes that the years from two to five are the most creative and intellectually active of our lives. My first introduction to the work of Professor Moore came via the March 12, 1965, issue of *The New York Times*.

Professor Moore has developed a method of teaching reading and writing to three-year-olds. He uses an electric typewriter, a tape recorder, a slide projector, and a computer.

To the people who say, "Life is hard enough as it is; let's leave the early period alone," Dr. Moore replies: "Of the 102 children we have seen so far, we have yet to run into one who'll come in, explore the place, and not want to come back." The child comes in for only half an hour a day. He is free to leave after a few minutes if he so desires.

The following information has been gathered from publicly printed matter concerning the Responsive Environments Foundation and Responsive Environments Corporation.

The "talking typewriter" that I saw was at the Responsive Environments Laboratory in Hamden, Connecticut. It is in a separate cubicle and consists of a standard-size typewriter keyboard with colored keys, a small speaker, an exhibitor (a frame on which printed matter can be displayed) with a red pointer, a projector that resembles a miniature TV screen, and dictation equipment. Blank paper in the typewriter stands ready to take anything the child types in jumbo type. Only the keyboard is accessible to the child: all the other gadgets are enclosed in plexiglass or in a wooden cabinet behind the typewriter.

In this fully automated, soundproof, air-conditioned booth there is nothing to distract the child's attention from the machine. While the child is in the laboratory he is free of all outside pressures. His parents never come in with him and are never told how he is doing. Even his regular teachers, to whom he may be emotionally attached, stay out of the picture.

When the child arrives, the teacher at the laboratory paints the child's fingernails different colors, to match the color code on the typewriter keys. The game begins when the child presses a key and at once a large number or punctuation mark appears on the paper, and a soft voice names it through the loudspeaker. The same thing happens no matter what part of the keyboard he strikes, as rapidly and as often as he desires. (To test his newfound powers, one two-year-old gleefully struck the asterisk key 72 times in succession.)

When the teacher who has been watching through a one-way mirror sees that the child's interest is waning, she switches a control dial. A curtain lifts over the exhibitor and a red arrow points to a single letter. At the same time the machine's voice names it. Puzzled, the child may try to depress a key, but to his surprise, it doesn't work. He tries more and more keys, until he finds the right one. Then the key goes down and prints the letter while the voice names it again. As a new letter pops up on the exhibitor, the child faces an exciting puzzle, a game of "try and find me."

As the child advances he finds that the exhibitor suddenly shows him a series of letters, such as "CAT." By now he may be able to pick out a "T" right away, but when he tries this the key is blocked. "A" is blocked, too. When he strikes "C" however, the machine responds by typing it and saying, "C." The exhibitor's red arrow, which had been pointing to "C," then moves to the right over "A." As he strikes all three keys in the proper sequence, the machine prints them, names them one by one, and then says, "Cat." From now on, letters appear only in series but to the child they are still letters, not words. Then one day, although no one has been teaching him, the child suddenly realizes that the letters he knows so well determine words.

Dr. Moore hopes that the less gifted children will benefit even more than the brighter ones from their sessions with a "responsive environment." Because they are alone with the machine, those who don't understand quickly need not be embarrassed or suffer from constant comparison with the faster learners.

A "talking typewriter" has infinite patience. It plays no favorites. It does not hold out bribes or threats, nor need the child feel anxious about losing its love. For this reason it seems ideally suited to teaching retarded children and others with severe handicaps.

Last year, five retarded boys and girls who had been rejected by public school kindergartens because of their low IQ's and behavior problems came to the laboratory, tried out the gadgets, and liked them. After seven weeks of work their attitude improved enough for their schools to agree to take them back conditionally. After a year of work in the laboratory, all had learned to read simple material. Their IQ's ranged from 59 to 72, classifying them as "educable" or mildly retarded. With the best of standard methods and three to four years of painstaking drills, they might be expected to read around the age of nine. Yet here was one of them, a six-year-old boy (IQ 64), typing away: "The goose laid a golden egg." Although it might take the retarded children five or six times as long to reach the same stage as a normal child, they made steady progress at their own pace.

Had these five children been institutionalized or simply deprived of further education, they would probably have become wards of the state for the rest of their lives.

The machines are costly ($35,000) but they need not be bought. They can be rented for as little as $760 a month, which, considering the number of children one machine can service, makes the cost for helping the individual child a reasonable consideration.

A third machine was purchased in 1965 by the New York City Board of Education. The machine was built by the Thomas Edison Research Laboratory of West Orange, New Jersey. It is being distributed by the Responsive Environments Corporation of 200 Sylvan Avenue, Englewood Cliffs, New Jersey.

26

Conclusion:
What Problems
Do We Face?

The United States is becoming oriented to the urgency of providing adequate care and rehabilitation resources for the mentally retarded despite the competitive clamor for further intensive and extensive opportunities for the gifted child. The thesis of the latter argument is that in this nuclear age our efforts and budget would better be spent developing the future genius mathematician and scientist. Some among these bolster their priority with such statements as "the mentally retarded are already too much of an expense to the state" . . . "a drag on the healthy population" . . . "useless" . . . "incapable of getting anything out of life or making any contribution."

In a learned article, "The Hurt Mind," published by the Ministry of Health in England in 1955, Dr. Margaret Nelson Jackson had this to say about retarded children with whom she had worked for years:

> They are full of personality and character: and more astonishing still, excepting the few difficult ones, their personalities and character are exceptionally nice. They are friendly, cheerful, affectionate, helpful, delighted to join in whatever is going on and do their best, are never bored and are enormously pleased with small pleasures. In fact, if you stopped thinking of intellect as the most important thing, and gave first place to other qualities and to the virtues, these mentally defective children are well ahead of the rest of us.
>
> In addition, the mentally retarded can turn out all manner of well-made articles, from brushes and mats to electrical equipment and upholstery. They can learn to do all kinds of

maintenance work, repair and decorate buildings: they can be found tailoring, shoemaking, printing and embroidering, and undertaking the manufacture of goods for outside firms. Many of them earn good wages, and some are contributing to the support of old parents or helping a younger brother or sister.

Even if our inhumane objective was to create a sterilized society of high IQ's, we cannot close our eyes to the facts. We already have 5,400,000 mentally retarded whose existence directly impinges on 15 to 20 million people.

How is the future going to affect these families?

The standard of living is rising and, steadily surpassing it, the cost. Parents have, therefore, less resources to devote to a retarded child, particularly as in many instances the child has brothers and sisters.

More families move, more live in metropolitan areas. Relatives are no longer readily available to help. More of the burden of young children is being placed on the mother. More mothers are in the labor force. While facilities for substitute care through regional planning, foster care plans, nursery school programs, and homemaking services are increasing, they are not anywhere nearly enough to fill the need. Twenty-four-hour help is becoming increasingly difficult to obtain.

In addition to the physical causes of retardation, there are unfavorable influences that interfere with normal emotional and intellectual development. Poverty and culturally deprived environments breed abuse, neglect, and inadequate intellectual stimulation, all or any of which may result in retardation.

A large percentage of the severely mentally retarded have additional handicaps such as being smaller than normal, having impaired hearing, impaired vision, difficulty in interpreting what is seen, poor muscular coordination, and other physical deformities.

There have been some surgical and biochemical breakthroughs. In addition to the VJ shunt to relieve the pressure of the accumulated water on the brain of the hydrocephalics, there is a recognized operative procedure to relieve the condition known as craniostenosis, the premature closing of bones in the head, which causes the liquid to press down on the brain. The skull is opened to relieve that pressure.

Researchers must be supplied with enough resources to go forward. The chemistry, the physics, the physiology of retardation need much clarification.

What have we now in this country to identify and provide for our retarded population?

We have some major means by which the mentally retarded can be identified. One is medical diagnosis but unfortunately only the most marked retardation can be definitively diagnosed in early childhood. Mental retardation often does not reveal itself until the child enters school, and mild and moderate retardation can be overlooked even then.

Failure to walk and talk at appropriate times are manifestations, but even that is not absolute. My own son could say only a single word until he was twenty-seven months old. He started to talk in a rush of sentences and is enormously verbal today.

School tests and academic underachievement begin to identify the child in kindergarten and first grade. It is important that the school be fully cognizant of the need to test and recognize mental impairment, and the emphasis should be on as early a diagnosis as possible. This is difficult to do and places a large responsibility on the school. The provision of a sufficient number of diagnostic clinics would increase the chances of successful early recognition. We must also find means of recognizing social inadequacy, for it is often not observed until adolescence when too much valuable time has lapsed.

Education for the mentally retarded has made progress, but as of the President's panel report of 1961, it reaches only two out of ten children. As of 1966, some states do not provide any classes for the trainable or moderately retarded child, and few states have enough classes for the educable or mildly retarded. Research in special curricula, teaching machines, and other suitable methods of pedagogy for this group has lagged.

At the Responsive Environments Foundation I learned that some teachers have been resisting the prospect of working with the "talking typewriter" on the mistaken premise that the machine would eventually do away with teaching services. There is no substitute for learning through personal relationships. The Foundation is not alone in the be-

lief that successful communication between one human being and another is the key to civilization. However, any means that helps the
teacher perform that function should be conscientiously considered,
particularly since the present trained teaching staff for the mentally
retarded is only 20,000 strong as against an immediate need of 55,000,
which will rise to 90,000 by 1970.

The state vocational agencies' rehabilitation programs are reaching
only 3 percent of all mentally retarded.

In 1961 there were 200 workshops for retardates in 42 states of the
Union. The other 8 had none. Holland, approximately one-quarter the
size of New York State, had 180.* While it is true that the number in
the United States has since doubled, it is still woefully inadequate.

Over 25 percent of the mentally retarded in workshops cannot be
placed in the outside community, and must remain in a long-term, or
terminal, work situation. This does not mean they are unproductive.
They are being constructive with their time and energy and contributing within a more limited sphere. There is a desperate need for long-
term workshops for those who can never leave.

After a study of the late President Kennedy's Panel Report on Mental Retardation, coupled with my own observations in this country and
abroad, I suggest the implementation of the following measures.

A justifiable reason for attempting to amass this compendium on
mental retardation was the fact that there was *no one place* in the
United States where this information could be found. Time can be a
determining factor in a retarded child's future. We desperately need a
national clearinghouse on every aspect of mental retardation where
parents can receive immediate and intelligent direction.

(1) *More diagnostic and clinical services.* Varying figures are offered
as to the number of diagnostic clinics because some children's general
clinics do test for retardation. According to the information released
by the Department of Health, Education, and Welfare, there are in the
50 states of the Union about 110 government-supported clinics devoted

---

* Some of the workshops include the physically as well as the mentally
handicapped.

to specializing in testing the mentally retarded. (There are several others privately sponsored.) For each there are two to three hundred people on the waiting list. The family's suffering on the discovery of the damage to the child is further compounded by the agony of their having to wait six months to three years for a diagnosis in order to ascertain the extent of the damage.

(2) *Improved and more individual care in residential institutions.* The President's Panel recommends smaller and more accessible centers providing day-care parent counseling and treatment of the retarded closer to their homes. If Seaside at New London, Connecticut, is an example of this, the suggestion is of inestimable value. Whenever community facilities are coordinated and utilized to help the child function constructively at home and in his community, the situation is sound.

Thirty such regional centers have been proposed for New York State to the Joint Legislative Committee of Mental Retardation. The project has been approved, but the state as of this writing has made no budgetary provision or time schedule.

On the other hand, if the intent is to build smaller institutions in more accessible regions for lifetime residence, I would qualify that recommendation, for this would still plan for impersonal, non-family-type living. Denmark is building individual homes for no more than 8 to 10 residents in each plus parent figures. They operate under the supervision of a central administration housed in a building nearby. The number of persons rehabilitated is ample verification of the validity of its program.

(3) *Research of biological and behavioral complications.* In books devoted to emotional disorders of childhood, some doctors present the premise that many emotional disorders are chemical in base. Perhaps one day we may find this to be true of mental retardation. Certainly the research efforts in phenylketonuria (inability to tolerate certain proteins) and galactosemia (carbohydrate abnormality, improper metabolism of fats) have been more than justified.

Aphasia, that is, loss of speech, can be a cruel concomitant of mental retardation. The Central Institute for the Deaf in St. Louis, Missouri, the Institute of Logopedics and the Special Education and Clinical Psychology Departments of the University of Kansas, both in

Wichita, the Cove School for retarded in Wisconsin, Dr. Kasteins of Columbia Presbyterian, and Dr. Semmel of the University of Michigan are all moving doggedly ahead in their study and treatment of aphasics, confident that one day the breakthrough must come.

A challenging project has been undertaken by the New York State Department of Mental Hygiene, subsidized by their Facilities Improvement Fund. Research in the functions of the nervous system in mentally retarded persons is being conducted at the New Institute for Basic Research on Staten Island under the direction of Dr. George Jervis, one of the most outstanding physicians in the country associated with mental retardation.

Studies such as these are the foundation of our hope for the future.

(4) *Special education and vocational rehabilitation.* Mothers are desperately in need of preschool nursery training for their retarded children. Massachusetts has an outstanding preschool program for the young retardates. Rhode Island, Missouri, and Washington are among 22 states with public support for day-care centers. Twenty-three states have made some provision for preschool services, but they are insufficient, and 3 states have none.

We are in need of more vocational training and workshops for retardates over eighteen years of age. The establishment of more workshops quickly would provide a learning situation before it is too late for those retarded who were deprived of educational opportunities earlier in life.

Equally important are provisions for the establishment of hostels and halfway houses for retardates who are ready to undertake some degree of independent living.

By virtue of citizenship and the payment of taxes, they are entitled to it.

(5) *Home care and parental guidance.* Additional psychiatric social workers and public health nurses are needed to counsel parents and demonstrate proper procedures in caring for and training the mentally retarded child.

The United States Government and private agencies distribute pamphlets on such procedures. This is a help for those who can follow the impersonal printed page, but how many learn "intellectually"?

Furthermore, nonguided parents' anxiety can communicate itself quickly to all children, normal or retarded, and can be a great obstacle to the child's learning.

Trained personnel are free of parental tensions. They should be chosen with a view to their empathy with mentally handicapped children and their willingness to explore new ways of stimulating learning by appealing to all the senses.

The Kennedy Center at Bridgeport, Connecticut, in addition to parent counseling and group therapy, has instituted a parent-training program. Children are accepted in their out-patient department only if the parents promise to cooperate with the Center. They take notes on speech therapy given to the child and reinforce it at home. They get weekly demonstrations of techniques and goals. They are given picture sheets demonstrating therapy procedure. They are permitted to take music records home from the music library to help the child. Whatever resources the Center has are at their disposal.*

A psychologist at the Kennedy Center told me that some parents at either end of the economic scale are unable to help: those of low income cannot cope with an added burden; the wealthy ones have too much pride in their social standing; but in 3 out of 5 cases the parents are totally cooperative. And the difference between the child helped at home and the one who is not is amazing.

Retarded children are lonely children. Companionship for them is a pressing problem. After-school recreation centers slanted toward their physical, emotional, and social abilities would do much to alleviate that problem.

Many of our bright, energetic young people today long to give useful social service without expecting pay. A few trained key personnel could draw on this untapped army of volunteers to lead programs in such centers.

(6) *Emphasis on maternal and infant care.* Of the 1,300,000 babies born every year in the United States, 450,000 are born to indigent mothers; of these mothers 100,000 have complications in pregnancy and need special services. This includes unwed mothers under the age of

---

* The Kennedy Center was founded by Evelyn Kennedy.

twenty. The highest percentage of retarded children come from the lowest economic group.

To tell such mothers to take care of themselves is absurd, for obviously in many cases they cannot do so properly. Clinical programs such as the proposed project for expanded prenatal care at Metropolitan Hospital in New York City should be offered automatically. Economizing on the early care of mothers and children can become a woeful extravagance in later costs of institutional, hospital, and permanent care.

In Denmark there are 8 centralized Mothers' Aid Centers. They hold consultations in 86 cities, serving the "lonely mother." This includes the unwed, divorced, widowed, sick, or economically deprived. This service, under the Maternity Welfare Act, is in addition to preventive medicine, prenatal care, and mandatory medical examinations of infants.

(7) *Preparation for the recruitment of professional personnel.* For years, misinformation, bigotry, and deliberate mind-closing have formulated public attitudes toward retardation. People working with retarded classes have been held in contempt—sometimes set apart from the rest of the teaching staff.

The image of contempt for the retarded child and his teacher must be obliterated. This can be done by sending qualified speakers to enlighten opinion-making groups: PTA's, religious organizations, public and private schools, colleges and universities, women's clubs, youth organizations, health and welfare organizations, and service and fraternal organizations.

Another incentive is to provide liberal scholarships for training teachers of retardates.

Increased appropriations for improvement and extension of classes are imperative.

An example of initiative and individual exercise of the imagination has been offered by Dr. La Crosse who, under the aegis of the Child Study Center connected with Newark State Teachers College,* conceived of an additional source of trained manpower for child care and for work in day centers.

---

* See the latter part of Chapter 18 for a full description of this center.

A one-year course is offered at the Child Study Center for qualified persons between the ages of eighteen and fifty-five. The course, which includes 500 clinic hours spent in day-care and cerebral palsy centers, has attracted those who could not go on to college: women whose children are now in school and can fit in these work hours, older people who wish to become active, and those who are dissatisfied with the work they are doing and want to give service.

Thirty-seven people enrolled in the first-year course. The college expects to place all 37 who were graduated in June, 1965. The salary starts at approximately $3,900 a year.

One worker summed it up effectively. It's bringing two people together who need each other.

In 1963 the late President Kennedy proposed in a report that later became included in the famous bill named for him, that the Federal Government provide funds for up to three-fourths of the cost of the construction of great centers for research in mental retardation.

Research would be aimed at all aspects of mental retardation—the causes, the prevention, the treatment—and would involve biological, medical, social, and behavioral sciences.

This would be a five-year, $30-million program leading to the establishment of 10 research centers in universities and research institutions throughout the country.

"From these new research centers may come, someday, the knowledge that will help us greatly reduce, if not eliminate, mental retardation—as in the past, through research, we have conquered other killers and cripplers. For this we must wait and hope."

Friends of mine who are fine physicians nodded Amen. The most important thing is to concentrate on the etiology—the cause. Everything else is secondary.

But they do not have a retarded child!

It is little consolation to a parent to consider that, perhaps one day, long after she and her child are gone from this earth, a retarded child may swallow a series of pills and be restored to adequate functioning.

Research and mobilization of immediate resources must accompany each other.

Sweden has demonstrated that with present resources she has been able to rehabilitate half of her mentally handicapped. To which I add my husband's favorite philosophical observation: "One must consider whether the glass is half empty or half full." Should we commiserate because 1.8 percent of Sweden's 3.7 percent retarded population remains unable to live independently, or rejoice that through proper diagnosis, education, workshops, halfway houses and hostels, 1.9 percent have been rehabilitated so that they are absorbed into economic and social activity?

Retarded children's parents are first-class citizens. They pay full taxes and of necessity must assume all the burden the allegiance to one's country demands. As first-class citizens, they also have the right to full care of their children: planned services, education, and rehabilitation opportunities. The teaching must be real and oriented to future social placement. Retardates are capable of insight about themselves and can make changes. If they are told the kind of life they are going to have, they can prepare themselves to meet the challenge. But they need your help.

The date is today and the time is now.

In this country, as in many others, we have a National Association for Retarded Children at 420 Lexington Avenue, New York City. The members work unceasingly for the retarded and need many hands. Support your local chapter with whatever you can spare of either time or money.

Check your local area. Is there a chapter of the NARC? If not, perhaps you can be the first to form one. It is not necessary to have a retarded child in order to help.

Call your local Board of Education. Are there any nursery classes, special classes for the severely, moderately, or mildly retarded?

How effective are these classes? For example, handicapped children up to seven or eight years need a flexible nursery-school type of training where the emphasis is on learning by doing through self-help, domestic play, and active outdoor play; through creative experience with sand, clay, water, and paint; through music movement and simple dramatic work, not stereotyped handwork. The children must be given freedom and opportunity to experiment for themselves and find meaning in the world around them through physical activity and experimental play.

Are there any day centers, recreation centers, training centers, workshops for retardates? If not, why not? Investigate your institutional facilities by calling the Department of Institutions. "Adopt" a child or patient in an institution. A little loving attention can generate a tremendous response. Perhaps you and your friends can help establish a Short Stay Home or Creche where children can be cared for, and harassed parents given some relief.

Do not allow yourself to be discouraged by the suggestion that community rehabilitation opportunities will cost more tax dollars, for in reality they will cost less. Lifetime institutional care of retarded children has placed a far greater tax burden on us than reeducation to prepare for a place in the community ever can or will.

The League of Women Voters or the Town Clerk's office will supply the name of the Congressman of your district. Tell him of your findings or lack of them. Ask him what residential and nonresidential facilities are available in your town, county, or state.

We must be wary of workshops being used as repositories where a mother can dispose of the retardate to keep him out of the house.

Each trainee should learn to work at a job whether it is in a long-term or transitional workshop in preparation for a community situatiton. This necessitates a staff of professional workers who know how to train the slow learner.

We need to canvass the community for job opportunities for marginal workers. There is a provision in the federal law which states that a physically or mentally handicapped person can work for less than the minimum wage where he is less productive. Union cooperation should be sought to help make it possible for retardates to work in businesses where, because of their slow output, they will not necessarily be entitled to receive the legal minimum wage. Employers should be reoriented in their attitudes toward the less personable retardates, recognizing that there are specific jobs that they can not only cope with but do well. This has been proven by many private industries both at home and abroad. It has been found that many mentally retarded are almost as productive as the nonhandicapped individual and sometimes more so, and show a much lower absentee and tardiness rate.

Who is there to say that an academic IQ summarizes an individual's ability in all areas? Should we not try to evolve other means of evaluating the whole person?

Many so-called normal people need assistance throughout the years. Why not help safeguard the handicapped by fighting for a similar extended counseling service for them as, for example, when they want to get married and have children.

We have a tremendous reservoir of manpower—of young and older people who want to give without getting any compensation other than the greatest joy of all—the pleasure of giving.

We have sent a Peace Corps to help people in other lands who are in need. Let us create a Service Corps to help people give of themselves to those who need it so urgently here. Assuming responsibility gives people dignity and, with it, courage.

"And there has always been an American dream of a land in which life would be better and richer and fuller for every man, with opportunity for each according to his ability or achievement."

We can make that dream come true by drawing the less fortunate from the darkness of the past to the light of living in the future.

We can make that dream come true by admitting the inability to achieve the ultimate in ourselves unless we learn to love and help achieve the ultimate in others.

Bibliography

ADAMS, MARGARET. "Social Services for the Mentally Subnormal in Britain," National Association for Mental Health, January, 1964.

BARNES, HENRY, and LYONS, NATHAN. "Education as an Art." New York: The Rudolf Steiner School, 1967.

BECK, HELEN L. (St. Christopher's Hospital for Children, Philadelphia), "Advantages of a Multi-Purpose Clinic for the Mentally Retarded," *American Journal of Mental Deficiency*, LXVI, No. 5, March, 1962.

———. "Casework with Parents of Mentally Retarded Children," *American Journal of Orthopsychiatry*, XXXII, No. 5, October, 1962.

———. "Counselling Parents of Retarded Children," Pennsylvania Association for Retarded Children.

BOGGS, ELIZABETH. "New Hope for the Retarded," *Rotarian Magazine*, July, 1963.

BOYD, DAN. "The Three Stages," National Association for Retarded Children.

BRECHER, RUTH, and BRECHER, EDWARD. "Saving Children from Mental Retardation," *The Saturday Evening Post*, November 21, 1959.

BUCK, PEARL. *The Child Who Never Grew*. New York: John Day Company, 1950.

———, and ZARFOSS, GWENETH T. *The Gifts They Bring and Our Debt to the Retarded*. New York: John Day Company, 1965.

Bureau for Children with Retarded Mental Development, *Administrative Proceedings and Programs*. New York: New York City Board of Education.

CAPA, CORNELL, and PINES, MAYA. "Retarded Children Can Be Helped." Great Neck, N. Y.: Channel Press, 1957.

CARLSON, BERNICE WELLS, and GINGLAND, DAVID R. *Play Activities for the Retarded Child.* Nashville, Tenn.: Abingdon Press, 1961.

CHAMBERLAIN, NAOMI N., and MOSS, DOROTHY H. "The Three R's for the Retarded (Repetition, Relaxation, and Routine)," National Association for Retarded Children.

CHARNEY, LEON, and LACROSS, EDWARD. *The Teacher of the Mentally Retarded.* New York: John Day Company, 1965.

CHESS, STELLA. "Psychiatric Treatment of the Mentally Retarded with Behavior Problems," *American Journal of Orthopsychiatry,* XXXII, No. 5, October, 1962.

"The Community Is Our Neighbor," National Society for Mentally Handicapped Children, 125 Holborn, London, WC 1.

Conference of Mental Retardation. Proceedings published in *Journal of the American Medical Association,* Vol. 191, No. 3, pp. 183–232.

CORVIN, GERDA, and MITZBERGER, JEROME. "The Shop: A Working Community for the Training and Treatment of Mentally Retarded Adolescents and Adults." New York: The Training Center and Workshop.

Directory of Sheltered Workshops Serving the Mentally Retarded. New York: National Association for Retarded Children.

DITTMAN, LAURA L. "The Mentally Retarded Child at Home." Washington: U.S. Department of Health, Education, and Welfare, Social Security Administration, Children's Bureau.

DOMAN, ROBERT; SPITZ, EUGENE; ZUCINAN, ELIZABETH; DELACATO, CARL H., and DOMAN, P. T. S. "Children with Severe Brain Injuries," *Journal of the American Medical Association,* CLXXIV, September 17, 1960.

DYBWAD, GUNNAR. "Group Approaches in Working with the Retarded and Their Parents (an Overview)," presented at the 86th Annual Meeting of the American Medical Association, May 4, 1962.

———. "Rehabilitation for the Adult Retarded," *American Journal of Public Health,* July, 1961.

———. "Trends and Issues in Mental Retardation," White House Conference on Children and Youth, 1960.

DYBWAD, ROSEMARY. "The Widening Role of Parent Organizations Around the World," presented at the 41st Annual Convention of the

Council for Exceptional Children, National Education Association, Philadelphia, April 19, 1963.

EDMUNDO, L. FRANCIS. "Rudolf Steiner Education," Rudolf Steiner Educational Association, Michael House, Ilkeston, Derbyshire, England.

"Education of the Handicapped Pupil, 1945-1955." London: Ministry of Education, H.M. Stationery Office.

EGG-BENES, MARIA. *When a Child Is Different.* New York: John Day Company, 1964.

"England's Mental Health Act of 1959." London: H.M. Stationery Office.

ERNST, PAUL. "Miracle in Pennsylvania (The Story of David Posnett)," *Good Housekeeping,* September, 1962.

"European Congress on Education, Training, and Employment," Symposium held at County Hall, London, and The Hague, European League of Societies for the Mentally Handicapped, London.

"An Experimental Demonstration Project for the Training of Child Care Workers in the Field of Mental Retardation," Union State Teachers College, Union, N.J.

FARBER, BERNARD. *Effects of a Severely Retarded Child on a Family Integration.* Society for Research in Child Development Monographs, 24, No. 2, Serial No. 71, Child Development Publications, 1959, Purdue University, Lafayette, Ind., 1959.

———. *Family Organization and Crisis: Maintenance of Integration in Families with a Severely Mentally Retarded Child.* Society for Research in Child Development Monographs, 25, No. 2, Serial No. 75, Child Development Publications, University of Chicago, 1960.

———. "Interaction with Retarded Siblings and Life Goals of Children," *Marriage and Family Living,* February, 1963.

FRAENKEL, WILLIAM A. "The Mentally Retarded and Their Vocational Rehabilitation: A Resource Book," National Association for Retarded Children.

———. "Understanding the Rehabilitation Potential of the Mentally Retarded," address at the Evaluation Training Institute, Elwyn School, Elwyn, Penn., Association for Help to Retarded Children.

FRENCH, EDWARD L., and SCOTT, CLIFFORD. *Child in the Shadows.* New York and Philadelphia: J. B. Lippincott, 1960.

GIANNINI, MARGARET, and GOODMAN, LAWRENCE M. S. W. "Counselling Families During Crisis Reaction to Mongolism," *American Journal of Mental Deficiency,* LXVII, No. 5, March, 1963.

GIANNINI, MARGARET; SNYDER, ELKIN; MICHAL-SMITH, HAROLD, and SLOBODY, LAURENCE B. "A Home Training Program for Retarded Children," *Pediatrics,* XIII, No. 3, March, 1954.

GOLDSTON, IAGO. "Heuristic Hypotheses About the Variant Child in Our Culture," Child Study Treatment and Research Center of the Woods School, Langhorne, Penn.

GOODMAN, LAWRENCE M. S. W. "Continuing Treatment of Parents with Congenitally Defective Infants," *Social Work,* IX, No. 1, January, 1964.

———. "Homemaker Services to Families with Retarded Children." Washington: U.S. Department of Health, Education and Welfare, July–August, 1966.

———. "The Social Worker's Role in Clinics for the Retarded," *Child Welfare,* April, 1965.

———. "A Treatment Program for Young Adult Retarded Blind," *Blindness '67,* Association of Workers with the Blind, Washington, D.C.

———, and ARNOLD, I. "Training and Utilization of Non-Professional Personnel," *Mental Retardation,* December, 1967.

GRANACHER, ALBERT. "Rehabilitation in Switzerland." Berne: Federal Office for Social Insurance.

HARGROVE, APHRA. *Serving the Mentally Subnormal.* London: National Association for Mental Health, 1966.

HART, EVELYN. "How Retarded Children Can Be Helped," Public Affairs Pamphlets, 22 East 38th Street, New York.

"Health Services for Mentally Retarded Children, a Progress Report," Washington: U.S. Department of Health, Education and Welfare, Social Security Bureau, 1961.

"Home Training for Retarded Children," *Children,* May–June, 1957, National Association for Retarded Children.

HORMUTH, RUDOLF P. (compiler). "Clinical Programs for Mentally Retarded Children," Washington: U.S. Department of Health, Education and Welfare.

HUTCHINSON, ALEXANDER, "Special Care Units for the Severely Retarded," International League of Societies for the Mentally Handicapped, Brussels, Belgium, 1967.

JACOBS, ABRAHAM. "Rehabilitation of the Mentally Retarded in Israel,"

United Nations Commissioner for Technical Assistance, Department of Economics and Social Affairs.

JORDAN, THOMAS E. *The Mentally Retarded*. Columbus, Ohio: Charles E. Merrill Books, Inc., 1961.

KANNER, LEO. *The History and Care and Study of the Mentally Retarded*. Springfield, Ill.: Charles C. Thomas, Publisher, 1964.

"Lapeer." Lapeer, Mich.: Lapeer State Home and Training School.

LEVINSON, ABRAHAM. *The Mentally Retarded Child*. New York: John Day Company, 1965.

"A Manual on Program Development in Mental Retardation," supplement to *American Journal of Mental Deficiency*. Austin, Tex.: American Association on Mental Deficiency, Mustin State School, Box 1152.

MARTIN, F. M. "Mental Subnormality and Community Care." P.E.P. 16, Queen Anne's Gate, London, SW 1.

MARY THEODORE, SISTER. *Challenge of the Retarded Child*. Milwaukee: The Bruce Publishing Co., 1963.

"Mental Retardation." Washington: U.S. Department of Health, Education and Welfare.

MICHAL-SMITH, HAROLD. *Management of the Handicapped Child*. New York: Grune & Stratton, Inc., 1958.

MONTESSORI, MARIA. *Discovery of the Child*. Notre Dame, Ind.: Fides, 1967.

MOORE, OMAR KAHYAM. "Autotelic Responsive Environments and Exceptional Children." Hamden, Conn.: Responsive Environments Foundation, 20 Augar Street.

MORRISON, MARCIA. "How They Are Grown," National Association for Retarded Children (originally published by the State of Minnesota, Department of Public Welfare).

MURRAY, MRS. MAX A., "Needs of Parents of Mentally Retarded Children," *American Journal of Mental Deficiency,* May, 1959.

"The Needs of Mentally Retarded Children," Report of a working party set up by the Pædiatric Society of the South-East Metropolitan Region. London: National Society for Mentally Handicapped Children, 125 High Holborn, WC 1.

"The Organization of the Employment Exchange Service in Great Britain," Ministry of Labour, revised December, 1962.

"Parents Voice," *Journal of the National Society for Mentally Handicapped Children,* XIII, No. 1, March, 1963.

PEARSON, GERALD HAMILTON JEFFREY. *Emotional Disorders of Child-hood*. New York: W. W. Norton & Company, Inc., 1949.

"Plymouth State Home and Training School Budget Request, 1964–1965," Northville, Mich.

"A Proposed Program for National Action to Combat Mental Retardation," President's Panel on Mental Retardation, October, 1962.

"The Psychotic Child." London: National Society for Mentally Handicapped, papers at Victoria Hall, Bloomsbury Square.

"The Regional Approach," Office of Mental Retardation, Connecticut State Department of Health, 79 Elm St., Hartford, Conn.

"Rehabilitation and Care of the Handicapped in Denmark." Copenhagen: International Relations Division, Ministries of Labor.

"Report of the Task Force on Education and Rehabilitation." Washington: U.S. Department of Health, Education and Welfare, President's Panel on Mental Retardation, August, 1962.

"The Retarded Can Be Helped." New York: National Association for Retarded Children, 420 Lexington Avenue.

ROGERS, DALE EVANS. *Angel Unaware*. Westwood, N.J.: Fleming H. Revell Co., 1953.

ROSENZWEIG, LOUIS E., and LANG, J. *Understanding and Teaching the Dependent Retarded Child*. Darien, Conn.: Educational Publishing Corp., 1960.

ROTHSTEIN, JEROME H. *Mental Retardation*. New York: Holt, Rinehart & Winston, Inc., 1961.

SAENGER, GERHART. "Factors Influencing the Institutionalization of Mentally Retarded Individuals in New York City." Albany: New York State Interdepartmental Health Resources Board, 84 Holland Avenue, January, 1960.

SANSONE, ROBERT. "Annual School Report, Brookville School, 1962–1963." Association for the Help of Retarded Children, Nassau County (N.Y.) Chapter.

SCHOENBLIN, HANS R. *Botton: An English System for the Rehabilitation of the Mentally Retarded*. New York: reprinted by Camphill Village U.S.A., 64 East 86th Street, New York City.

"School Facilities for Mentally Handicapped Children in Sweden." Stockholm: Board of Education, Kungl. Skoloverstyrelsen.

SHOSTAK, JOSEPH V., and HUNTER, MARVIN H. "Community Services for the Trainable Retarded Child." New York: Institute for Retarded Children, Shield of David, 1800 Andrews Avenue, Bronx.

Spock, Benjamin, and Lerrigo, Marion. *Caring for Your Disabled Child*. New York: The Macmillan Company, 1965.

Standing, E. M. *Maria Montessori, Her Life and Work*. Fresno, Calif.: Academy Library Guild, 1957.

Stern, Eva Michaelis, "Care of Retarded in Israel," Canadian Association for Retarded Children, July, 1961.

Tobias, Jack. "Promoting the Employment of Mentally Retarded Workers." New York: Association for Help to Retarded Children, Draft Proposal, Title II Project.

————. "Training for Independent Living (A Community Program for Severely Retarded Adults)." New York: Association for Help to Retarded Children.

————, and Fraenkel, William A. "A Vestibule School Program for Low IQ Children Below Age Seven." New York: Association for Help to Retarded Children, August, 1963.

Wakin, Edward, "The Return of Montessori," *Saturday Review*, November, 1964.

Waskowitz, Charlotte H., "The Parents of Retarded Children Speak for Them," *Journal of Pediatrics*, LIV, No. 3.

Weigl, Vally, "About Rhythm and Its Effects on Kinetic Impulses," *Bulletin of the National Association for Music Therapy*, May, 1961.

"What Is the Camphill Movement?" New York: The Secretary, Camphill Village, 64 East 86th Street; or London: The Secretary, 122 Harley Street.

"White House Conference on Mental Retardation, Proceedings." Washington: Department of Health, Education and Welfare, 1963.

Yannet, Herman. "When to Institutionalize the Retarded Child," *Consultant*, November–December, 1962.

"Youth Employment Service in Great Britain." London: Biography Service, Reference Division, Central Office of Information, April, 1963.

Programs for Trainable Children

AHRC EDUCATIONAL CENTER
WEEKLY PROGRAM FOR PRESCHOOL TRAINABLE CHILDREN
AGES 4–6 OR 7 YEARS

Teacher _____

Room _____

Robert Sansone, *Principal,* Associate Program Analyst for Mental Retardation Services, New York State Department of Mental Hygiene.

TIME	MONDAY	WEDNESDAY	FRIDAY

9:30–9:50   SOCIALIZATION
Arrival: Children assemble in Rotunda. Stress social behavior. Encourage children to sit. Elicit verbal responses, i.e., "good morning," etc. Control hyperactivity. Stress management and control of personal possessions: clothing, lunch boxes, etc. Stress appropriate social relationships. Seek social responsiveness and cooperation. Seek adaptability to transitions: stair climbing, carrying lunch boxes, etc.

9:50–10:00   SELF-HELP
Arrival in classrooms: Removal of wraps. Stress unclothing, manipulation of fasteners, zippers, buttons, etc. Store lunch boxes. Toileting routine, washing, followed by short free play period.

10:00–10:30   LANGUAGE ARTS
Opening exercises: Encouragement to sit. Roll call. Self-identification. Identification of others. Encourage verbalization, language development. Discuss days of week, coming holidays, breakfast, weather, appropriate clothing, experiences, appropriate behavior on bus, etc.

10:30–11:30   SENSORY CONCEPT TRAINING
Table activities leading to prevocational skills and fine motor coordination: pegs, puzzles, coloring, pasting, cutting (scissors). *Concept development:* sensory stimulation—visual, auditory, tactual, olfactory, taste, etc. Picture concepts geared around family, immediate community. Colors, circle, square, triangle, etc. Stress sharing and corporate attitude throughout.

TIME	MONDAY	WEDNESDAY	FRIDAY

11:30–11:45   SELF-HELP
Preparation for lunch: Replacement of materials, cleanup area. Toileting routine, washing, etc.

11:45–12:15   SELF-HELP
Lunch: Find and identify lunch boxes, table setting. Emphasis on eating skills: pouring, unwrapping, manners, etc. Cleanup area, wash thermos, dispose of garbage. Stress appropriate behavior throughout.

12:15–12:45   SOCIALIZATION
Rest period: Children assist in setting up cots. Emphasis on cooperation and relaxation.

12:45–1:15   CULTURAL APPRECIATION
Storytelling, singing, rhythm band, dancing, marching. Stress group participation and individual responses.

1:15–1:30   SOCIALIZATION
Dismissal: Find hats, coats, lunch boxes. Assemble in Rotunda. Emphasis is the same as 9:30–9:50 A.M.

AHRC EDUCATIONAL CENTER
WEEKLY PROGRAM FOR DAY CARE CHILDREN
AGES 7–12 YEARS

Teacher _____   Robert Sansone
Room _____   *Principal*

TIME	TUESDAY	THURSDAY

9:30–9:50   SOCIALIZATION
Arrival: Children assemble in Rotunda. Stress social behavior. Heavy emphasis on sitting and control of hyperactivity. Stress management of personal possessions within limits. Work for the elimination or modificaton of bizarre and offensive mannerisms. Heavy emphasis in gross motor area: walking, stair climbing, carryng of lunch boxes, etc.

9:50–10:00   SELF-HELP
Arrival in classrooms: Take off hat and coat. Attempt to hang up coats. Assistance is given, but each child is encouraged to perform for himself. All unclothing and clothing activities are set within reasonable limits.

10:00–10:30   SELF-HELP–SOCIALIZATION
Preopening activities: Take a chair, put it in circle. Heavy emphasis on sitting. Children leave circle in turns. Toilet routine. Wash hands then back to circle of chairs.

TIME	TUESDAY	THURSDAY

10:30–11:30   SOCIALIZATION—BASIC CONCEPT TRAINING
Opening exercises: Good morning. Try to get each child to respond to his own name (children still in circle format). Identify (touch) nose, eyes, mouth, etc. Follow simple verbal directions: "stand up," "point to shoes," etc. Pass ball around circle, from one child to another. Music, simple games: rolling ball in circle, etc.

11:30–11:45   SELF-HELP
Preparation for lunch: Put things back on shelf. Toilet routine.

11:45–12:15   SELF-HELP
Lunch: Heavy stress on very basic eating skills: keep food on table, do not touch food of others, holding sandwich, proper chewing, drinking from cup, etc. Emphasize appropriate behavior throughout.

12:15–12:45   SOCIALIZATION
Rest period: Emphasis on behavior, controlled hyperactivity, cooperation, and relaxation.

12:45–1:15   SOCIALIZATION—ORGANIZED PLAY
Out-of-doors (weather permitting): Stress structured activities involving gross motor challenge: playground equipment, sand boxes. Try to keep children moving as much as possible.
Indoors: Circle games, hold hands, etc. Large cardboard blocks. Activities designed to encourage movement and the stimulation of action systems.

1:15–1:30   Dismissal: Emphasis on adaptive behavior in Rotunda as 9:30–9:50 A.M.

AHRC EDUCATIONAL CENTER
WEEKLY PROGRAM FOR OLDER DAY CARE CHILDREN
AGES 12–19 YEARS

Teacher _____   Robert Sansone
Room _____   Principal

TIME

9:30–9:50   SOCIAL ADJUSTMENT
Arrival: Children assemble in Rotunda. Emphasis is placed upon adaptive behavior, social competence, and appropriate relationships. Strive for elimination of bizarre and offensive mannerisms. Attention is given to personal neatness upon arrival: zippers secured, buttons buttoned, etc. Emphasis on stair climbing. Encouragement to carry lunch boxes, make way to classrooms unassisted.

9:50–10:00   SELF-HELP
              Arrival in classrooms: Encouragement to take off wraps, hang them up,
              store lunch boxes. Toileting. Stress clothing and unclothing. Encourage-
              ment to take seats.

10:00–10:30   LANGUAGE STIMULATION
              Opening exercises: Teacher addresses children individually regarding bus
              trip, weather, weekend activities, etc., in hope of stimulating some mean-
              ingful reaction (verbal or nonverbal). Where children possess speech,
              teacher tries to elicit appropriate replies and responses.

10:30–11:25   PREVOCATIONAL DEVELOPMENT
              Table activities: Collating by size. Collating by color. Group collating
              activities. Assorting activities: shoe taps, buttons, etc. Envelope inserting.
              Assorting coins: pennies, nickels, etc. Simple nut-bolt disassembly. Thread-
              ing aluminum hardware: elbows, tee fittings, etc.

11:25–11:30   SELF-HELP
              Replacement and storage of materials.

11:30–12:15   SOCIAL ADJUSTMENT
              Lunch: Children are supervised in table manners, neatness, good eating
              habits, appropriate behavior, etc.

12:15–1:15   PREVOCATIONAL DEVELOPMENT
              Table activities: Resume activities of morning: collating, assorting, nut-bolt
              disassembly, etc.

1:15–1:30   SOCIAL ADJUSTMENT
              Dismissal: Emphasis in Rotunda is same as A.M.

Index of
New York
State Schools

Rome State, Rome, New York. Capacity: Male, 1,794; female, 1,537. Special approval for children under five.

Craig Colony and Hospital, Sonyea, New York. Capacity: Male, 1,102; female, 1,128.

Willowbrook, Staten Island, New York. Capacity: Male, 2,369; female, 1,904. Actual number of inmates 6,100. Heretofore no restrictions but now attempting screening.

Syracuse State School, Syracuse, New York. Capacity: Male, 457; female, 398. For mildly retarded from 50 to 70 IQ, ages seven to fourteen.

Letchworth Village, Thiells, New York. Capacity: Male, 2,296; female, 2,039. From five years of age. Actual occupancy over 6,000. Children under five need special permission.

Wassaic State School, Wassaic, New York. Capacity: Male, 1,777; female, 1,775. Children under five admitted only by approval of Department of Mental Hygiene.

Sampson State School—Division of Willard State Hospital, Willard, New York. Capacity: Male, 300; female, 209. For sixteen years of age and over. Of these, 379 are severely or profoundly retarded. No new admissions—only transfers from other state hospitals.

Newark State Training School, Newark, New York. Capacity: Male, 1,708; female, 1,475. No restrictions. Waiting list for children under five.

West Seneca State School, Perrysburg, New York. Capacity: Male, 170; female, 170.

Suffolk State School, Melville, Long Island, New York. Capacity: 2,000. Waiting list for certain of the services. Population fairly evenly divided. In 1968, children under five will be admitted.

General Index